NOT TO PERISH:
ARTICLES BY AN AMERICAN PROFESSOR OF RUSSIAN

By:

Lee B. Croft

Andrew W. Abbott   Alicia C. Baehr
Jeremy Ecton   Jon Harris
Patrick J. Heuer   Vadim S. Kagan
Kyle M. Kucharski   Jaime R. Nielsen
Megan Plachecki   Shane C. Sarlo
Eric D. Strachan   Shamella Tribble

CAPSTONE PUBLICATIONS
Phoenix, Arizona, USA
MMIX

Copyright © 2009 by the authors, whose collective agent is Lee B. Croft

All Rights Reserved Worldwide.

Capstone Publications is located at 11622 S. Tusayan Ct., Phoenix, Arizona 85044, USA. Telephone is 480-496-0229, Fax at 480-496-8274, and email at lbcroft@cox.net. Communications regarding this publication should be addressed to Editor-in-Chief Lee B. Croft, who serves as an agent for the other authors.

Editorial Board:

Lee B. Croft, Ph.D.   Rolfs Ekmanis, Ph.D.
George Gutsche, Ph.D.   Peter Horwath, Ph.D.
Donald K. Jarvis, Ph.D.   Delbert D. Phillips, Ph.D.
Danko Šipka, Ph.D.   Richard A. Watson, J.D.
Leo Columbus Wilcox, BSEE

The cover includes art by Ivan K. Aivazovsky (1817-1900)

Croft, Lee B. (1946--), Andrew W. Abbott, Alicia C. Baehr, Jeremy Ecton, Jon Harris, Patrick J. Heuer, Vadim S. Kagan, Kyle M. Kucharski, Jaime R. Nielsen, Megan Plachecki, Shane C. Sarlo, Eric D. Strachan, and Shamella Tribble. **NOT TO PERISH: Articles by an American Professor of Russian.** Capstone Publications, Phoenix, AZ 85044 USA, 2009, 299 pp. il. ISBN is 978-0-578-00468-6 and the book is available at www.lulu.com/content/5400071.

Table of Contents

Foreword by **Prof. Lee B. Croft**……………………………...p. 5

1. "A Radical New Method of Language Learning"
   by: **Eric D. Strachan**……………………………..p. 12

2. "Deciphering a Russian Poem by Igor Chinnov"
   by: **Megan Plachecki**...……………………….p. 30

3. "Russian-to-English Homographs"
   by: **Andrew W. Abbott**…………………………p. 51

4. "Reality and Truth in Russian Grammar"
   by: **Kyle M. Kucharski**……………………….....p. 59

5. "An Early International Example of Cinema's Influence on Literature"
   by: **Shamella Tribble**…………………………..p. 91

6. " Linguistics, Memory, and Teaching"
   by: **Shane C. Sarlo**………………………………p. 111

7. "Translating the Form as Well as the Content"
   by: **Jaime R. Nielsen**…………………………...p. 132

8. "Why Memorize?"
   by: **Jeremy Ecton** ……………………………….p. 138

9. "The Professor and the Pushkin Pornographer"
   by: **Vadim S. Kagan**……………………………....p. 157

10. "A Russian Biography of an American Scientist"
    by: **Patrick J. Heuer** …………………………...p. 169

11. "Putting Meaning into the Memory"
    by: **Alicia C. Baehr** ....p. 184

12. "Why so Many Threes?"
    by: **Jon Harris**..p. 203

13. "The Magic of Alphamagic Squares"
    by: **Lee B. Croft**.......................................p. 238

14. Appendix: "A Javascript Computer Program to
    Generate Third-order Russian Alphamagic Squares"
    by: **Samuel Comi**......................................p. 288

15. PROLOGUE: "What Have We Learned"..............p. 296

<u>Photographs</u>
   1. <u>Russian in Arizona</u> cover........................... p.7
   2. <u>Russia: The Missionaries' Tales</u> cover…………...p. 9
   3. Photo and letter from Martin Gardner................p. 26
   4. Igor Chinnov, Russian émigré poet..................p. 34
   5. Megan Plachecki at Dostoevsky's grave...........p. 39
   6. Megan Plachecki at Pushkin's duel site............p. 58
   7. Hayden L. Croft at TU-154 controls..................p. 90
   8. Alicia C. Baehr at Lenin's Mausoleum...............p. 110
   9. Hayden L. Croft with Borodino generals.............p. 131
  10. Patrick J. Heuer at Boris Yeltsin's grave............p. 156
  11. **Тайные Записки**/<u>Secret Notes</u> cover.............p. 162
  12. Irving Langmuir-Nobel laureate......................p. 173
  13. Patrick J. Heuer at "**Спас на крови**" Church.....p. 183
  14. Lee and Hayden Croft at Tchaikovsky's grave....p. 240
  15. Albrecht Dürer's *Melencolia I*............ ... ...p. 245
  16. Alphamagic runes............................pp. 248, 295
  17. Shamella Tribble at the Kremlin Gate..............p. 299.

Foreword

By:
Lee B. Croft

For its students subject to the 2005-and-newer catalogues, Arizona State University's Bachelor's Degree program in Russian has adopted a policy requiring its graduating seniors to complete a "capstone project" in their final year of study. The capstone project is supposed to pair these advanced students with a senior professor in their field of major and require that they, under the professor's direction, engage in some project of value to them that utilizes the knowledge, attitudes, and skills they have gained in the course of their undergraduate work. Many others of our nation's leading universities have also adopted such a capstone requirement in the past five years, so that university professors all over the land are now grappling with the task of deciding "what to do" with their students as a worthy capstone project. This foreword describes what I have done, being now, after thirty-five years here, the Senior Professor of Russian at ASU and Head of its Faculty of German, Romanian, and Slavic Letters and Cultures.

As my first crop of Russian BA-program seniors encountered this new requirement in the fall of 2006, I decided that, utilizing our hard-earned research, writing, and polylingual, polyalphabetic word processing skills, we should conceive, write, edit, and publish a book together. That way the students would finish their undergraduate academic careers having a co-authored book to their credit in seeking future career opportunities. And, of course, I thought that they would learn much about the entire process of publishing…something that I had learned as a consequence of being a major university professor and having to "publish or perish" in order to stay one.

The first capstone project in our ASU Russian BA program involved four seniors, Barry Boosman, Kathryn Lutz, James C. Nielsen, and Aimee M. Raymer, in a project to publish a comprehensive history of our program itself—a pioneering "programography" as it were, entitled <u>RUSSIAN IN ARIZONA: A History of Its Teaching</u>. It was a very ambitious project, attempting to feature EVERY person who had EVER taught Russian ANYWHERE in the State of Arizona, as well as a large share of the students who took it as a subject from the birth of Russian instruction in the state at ASU in 1946 to the present day. Published by the tri-organizational collaborative *Institute for Issues in the History of Science* of Tempe, Arizona and Perm, Russian Federation, in 2007 (ISBN 978-1-4303-2355-6), it includes mention of over 1600 people, with sixty photos, charts, graphs, and other illustrations in its 260 pages...see Andrew John Conovaloff's website, www.Russianaz.org, under "sponsors" for THREE ways to order it. The book's award-nominated cover shows the iconic St. Basil's Cathedral on Moscow's Red Square transplanted precariously onto a cliff of Arizona's iconic Grand Canyon...a precariousness of perch that is, in my view, entirely iconic itself to the situation of the state's Russian programs in its educational apparatus. My four student co-authors and I took two semesters to produce it, even though the students were only registered in the capstone project as a one-semester course. We worked our behinds off, interviewing people, photographing people, writing, editing and producing this book. We are proud of it and feel that we've done something novel and important. Our Prof. Emeritus S. C. Couch, featured in the book as a "large figure" in the history of the teaching of Russian in the State of Arizona, commented to me that he found the book "Monumental." That's just the right word for it, in my opinion. Certainly it affirms my own legacy here and may constitute my own career "capstone project."

In the fall of 2007 I had another crop of seniors register into the RUS-498 capstone project, and this crop was almost DOUBLE the size of the former. Six students—Andrew T.

Gunn, Electronica Kolasa, Scott C. Legler, Heather Nyhart, S. Zachary Tanner, and Travis Webb, joined former student Christopher D. Johnson with me in a project to publish a book entitled <u>RUSSIA: The Missionaries' Tales.</u> This book, to which Prof. Emeritus of Russian at Brigham Young University Donald K. Jarvis contributed a wonderful foreword, is an anthology of stories of the missionaries of the Church of Jesus Christ of Latter Day Saints' (LDS, or "Mormons") personal and linguistic adaptation to the Russian culture while on their two-year missions there. The authorial team, five of whom (but not I) are returned LDS Russian missionaries themselves (as are more than one-third of my graduating seniors in Russian for the past decade) contacted over 200 former LDS Russian missionaries, urging them to submit the constituent "tales." Forty tales were eventually published in the book in summer of 2008. We decided as a group (in the spirit of entrepreneurship that I always try to encourage in my students) to publish it ourselves under the imprimature of a new company we formed together called CAPSTONE Publications (11622 S. Tusayan Court, Phoenix, AZ. 85044…my home address). This book, ISBN 978-1-4357-1264-5, can also be ordered in THREE ways (color-photo "Presentation" edition, black-and-white-photo "Market" edition, or color-photo edition download in pdf. without the cover for only $5.00…again see Andrew John Conovaloff's website www.Russianaz.org under "sponsors" for a nice feature about the book, including the Table of Contents and hyperlinks to the online digital printer www.lulu.com to place an order most economically).

Given the effort involved in producing two books in two years while doing everything else long required in this position, you can understand my trepidation at having TWELVE Russian BA seniors (see the title page, of course) register for the RUS-498 Capstone course this Fall of 2008 semester. As I have explained, the precedent of publishing a book together had been set by the two former efforts…and was indeed a big part of the reason why so many sought registration in the course (some could have escaped the requirement by writing an undergraduate honors thesis...a two-semester project credited under RUS-492 and RUS-493)...but they preferred to participate in this capstone project. But what kind of book could positively involve thirteen co-authors (me included) in the learning process as they produced a book together? We discussed several possibilities—writing an anthology of anecdotes from former students under the title "Where are they now?" with each co-author being responsible for contacting an agreed-upon number of alumni (perhaps a future project, eh?); putting together a photo album of pictures of Russia taken by those students who had been in Russia during the course of their study (another future book?); and several others. But at last I found consensus in the publication of this anthology of thirteen (I hope it isn't an unlucky number for us) of my previously published scholarly articles, with each of the co-authors presenting the articles' publicational circumstances, scholarly impact in subsequent citations, etc. The title, <u>Not to Perish: Articles by an American Professor of Russian</u>, makes reference to the dictum "publish or perish" mentioned earlier. In this way each student becomes, as a result of this process, not only a co-author of the whole book itself, but a sole author of the included article of presentation under a separate title (as well as a share-holder in any publication revenues from their publisher CAPSTONE Publications...may we all get rich!). My hope is that the reader finds these articles and their presentations interesting. They are, I think, strikingly diverse in topic and approach and will give the reader "something completely different" (as the Monty Python absurdist comedy group used to say) to think about. I admit to choosing works of a certain quirky appeal: "Synthetically Induced and Electrically Maintained Trance Glossolalia as a Method of Language Learning," (Now just WHAT is that, eh?); "Russian-to-English Homographs in Ozhegov's Dictionary" (newly significant in the internet age); and "Thrice to Tell the Tale: People in Threes Going Up in Smoke and Other Triplicities in Russian Literature and Culture" (Spontaneous Human Combustion yet…and tripled in the telling to boot). All are presented ("translated," as it were, actually or virtually) by the individual co-authors so that the lay reader (particularly those without knowledge of Russian) can understand and, hopefully, enjoy them.

If you read my curriculum vitae you will see that I have always tried to involve my students into my own publication ventures. More than fifty are mentioned as co-authors or published contributors to my works—books, articles, or talks and scholarly presentations. This is, to me, an integral part of what being a "professor" is about. Teaching and mentorship is what is paramount in this profession, in my view. But that is not all. Research, writing, and publication are the avenues by which we "profess" what we learn, what we know. And professors have to teach this too. That is what this book …our capstone project…is about. Here we are all "professors," only some for the first time.

--Lee B. Croft
  Phoenix, AZ
  October 12, 2008

A RADICAL NEW METHOD OF LANGUAGE LEARNING

By:

Eric D. Strachan

Eric Strachan was born in Quincy, Massachusetts, and raised in Phoenix, Arizona. He graduated from Washington High School in May of 1989. He attended Arizona State University in Tempe, Arizona, and graduated with a B.S. in Psychology and a B.A. in English in May of 1994. Eric returned to Arizona State University as a graduate student in 1999 after completing a ten-week course of study at Moscow State Linguistics University, and received a

Masters degree in Political Science in December of 2001. As a National Security Education Program graduate fellow, Eric studied Tatar and Russian at Kazan State University in Tatarstan (Russia) during the 2001-2002 academic year. Eric is currently working as a high school English instructor and has recently returned to Arizona State University to pursue a B.A. degree in Russian.

THE ARTICLE:

Reprinted from The Journal of Biological Psychology/The Worm Runner's Digest, Vol. XIV, #2, 1972.

TITLE: SYNTHETICALLY INDUCED AND ELECTRICALLY MAINTAINED TRANCE- GLOSSOLALIA AS A METHOD OF LANGUAGE LEARNING

AUTHOR: Vyacheslav A. Obmanov
Director of Research
Moscow Psycholinguistics Institute

TRANSLATOR: Lee B. Croft
157 Bundy Road
Ithaca, New York 14850

The following is a report of experiments performed on 800 subjects between July and November, 1972. Much of the previous research in this area of scientific development has taken place in the United States, and this research is accordingly cited here. It must be pointed out, however, that Western scientists have been unable to utilize their own research to the extent presented in this report due to the lack of cooperation of governmental agencies. Only in an environment of scientific encouragement such as that found in the Soviet Union could such advancements be made.

It is well known that learned behavior is molecularly stored in the cell structure as well as in the fluids of the human brain. The particular molecules involved, 15-residue peptides of amino acids found in RNA, have been specified by a series of experiments carried out by Western scientists since 1960. In these experiments, planaria (flatworms) conditioned to seek a spot of light in which to feed were chopped up and fed to unconditioned planaria. These unconditioned planaria then manifested this learned trait. This experiment, pioneered by Professor James V. McConnell of the Mental Health Research Institute at the University of Michigan,[1] has now been carried out at several U.S. universities and the results well verified. Scientists at Cornell and Baylor have carried this type of experiment one step further in examining the behavior of rats. One sample of rats was conditioned to fear the dark, a behavior contrary to the norm for rats. An RNA-fraction, extracted from the brain fluid (ventricular cerebro-spinal fluid) of the rats of this sample by the 'hot phenol' method was injected into the

---

[1] McConnell, James V. "Memory transfer through cannibalism in planarians." <u>Journal of Neuropsychiatry, 3</u>, supp. 1, 42.

brains of rats, which were not so conditioned. Subsequently, the time of conditioning of the previously unconditioned rats was significantly reduced with regard to the trait in question, fear of the dark.[2] Research into finding the optimum concentrations of the involved RNA-fractions has been carried out for memory transfer in goldfish by Professor N. Longo of Colgate University and two associates, Professor R. Bisping and Professor O.H. Zahl-Begnum, of the Psychological Institute of the University of Duesseldorf in West Germany. This research indicates that small concentrations of the RNA-fraction may produce effective memory-transfer results in the goldfish.[3] In 1969, Biochemist Wolfgang Parr succeeded in synthesizing an RNA-fraction. The resultant drug, called scotophobin, has been shown to have positive effects in increasing recall in the memories of both rabbits and chimpanzees.

Both the United Nations' International Brain Research Organization and the United States' National Institute of Mental Health have refused financial grants to researchers whose intentions included the investigation of biochemical memory transfer in humans. This refusal seems even more reactionary when it is common knowledge that the injection of human brain fluid into other humans is harmless in regulated amounts. Indeed, early medical

---

[2] See: Ungar, Georges. <u>Molecular Mechanisms in Learning and Memory.</u> New York: Plenum, 1970. And also: Rosenblatt, Frank. Induction of discriminatory behavior by means of brain extracts. In W. L. Byrne (Ed.), <u>Molecular Approaches to Learning and Memory</u>. New York: Academic Press, 1970.

[3] The report of this research is reviewed by U. Niemoller and H. Reinauer in <u>Journal of Biological Psychology</u>, 1971, 13(2), 32-35.

treatments of phenylketonuria (PKU), a hormone imbalance in the brain fluids of infants, included such injections to remedial effect.

In May of 1972, brain-fluid extract from 34 native speakers of Cheremis, a Finno-Ugric language spoken in Asiatic regions of the U.S.S.R., was injected into a similar number of volunteers belonging to a Molokan religious sect in Sverdlovsk. These volunteers were then enrolled in Cheremis language courses along with university linguistics students in the Philological faculty of Moscow State University. These volunteers, of course, were largely uneducated. The object of the experiment was to discover whether these volunteers could develop with facility the learned trait in question, the speaking of Cheremis. The other students in the classes were to be taken as a control.

Within 15 days of the injection, it appeared that our experiment had failed. The Molokan volunteers appeared unable to master even the most elementary linguistic concepts and were shortly far behind the other students in every measurable respect. The volunteers were sent home to Sverdlovsk.

It was shortly thereafter that a remarkable observation was reported to us by a colleague in Sverdlovsk, Professor E. A. Shutkina. Professor Shutkina has been observing the Molokan religious ritual to complete a study being done by the Sverdlovsk Institute of Social Sciences. In observing the phenomenon of glossolalia, Comrade Shutkina noticed a marked change in the behavior of those volunteers who had returned to the sect after the experiment in Moscow. Enlisting the aid of linguist V.Z. Naprasov, Comrade Shutkina was able to identify the glossolalic behavior as Cheremis. The fluency level of Cheremis being spoken during such behavior was far greater than that previously thought possible in only 15 days of instruction. The trait, however, was only manifested during glossolalic behavior.

In investigating the reasons why the trait was only manifested during glossolalic behavior, we were once again forced to rely upon Western scholarship being published by several linguists and psychologists in the United States and Canada. Professor James R. Jacquith of Washington University[4] and Professor William J. Samarin of the University of Toronto[5] agree that glossolalia is not necessarily a "trance" behavior only associated with religious ritual. They point out that glossolalia is, like other communicative behavior, socially conditioned. Professor Jacquith, utilizing a seminal work in the field (Lombard, Emile. De la glossolalie chez les premiers chretiens et des phenomenes similaires, Lausann, Bridel, 1910), mentions "Xenoglossie" as that type of glossolalic behavior in which people speak in foreign tongues, but notes that, "In most cases the subject has had previous contact with the languages even though he may be unable to speak them when he is fully rational and conscious."[6] Although not necessarily so, the phenomenon of glossolalia may be linked with altered states of consciousness in the subject. In fact, this is often the case.

---

[4] Jacquith, James R. "Towards a typology of formal communicative behaviors: Glossolalia." Anthropological Linguistics, 9 (8), 1-8.

[5] Samarin, William J. "Variation and variables in religious glossolalia." Language in Society, 1(1), 121-130. Professor Samarin mentions that there are also Molokans in the United States who practice glossolalia.

[6] Jacquith, James R. Op. cit., 1.

Professor Felicitas D. Goodman of Denison University has published several works on glossolalia as linked to the "trance" state of consciousness.[7] Professor Goodman cites another very interesting study done on the human memory during altered states of consciousness by Professor Donald W. Goodwin and several associates of the Psychiatry Department of the Washington University School of Medicine.[8] These works suggest that, indeed, the human memory may recall learned behavior during altered states of consciousness that cannot be recalled in the normal state. This holds true, evidently, for linguistic behavior as well, as in the case of "trance-glossolalia." Ironically, Professor Goodman's research into trance-glossolalia was supported by the same government agency which has refused to underwrite memory transfer experiments in humans. Professor Goodman was supported by Public Health Service Research Grant MH 07463-03 of the United States National Institute of Mental Health. It is again testimony to the disorganized state of affairs in United States scholarship that connections between different research projects, even those considered by the same governmental agency, are not recognized and pursued.

Already by July, 1972, an experiment had been arranged with 800 volunteer subjects from the Potma rehabilitation facility in the Mordvinian Republic of the U.S.S.R. All the subjects were male monolingual speakers

---

[7] Goodman, Felicitas D. "The acquisition of glossolalia behavior." <u>Semiotica</u>, 1971, 77-82. See also Professor Goodman's recent book, <u>Speaking in tongues: A cross-cultural study of glossolalia</u>. Chicago: University of Chicago, 1972.

[8] Goodwin, Donald W. et al. "Alcohol and recall: State-dependent effects in man." <u>Science</u>, 1969, 163, 1358-1360.

of Russian between 25-40 years of age. Non-specific, RNA-fractional brain-fluid extract from speakers of four different languages (French, Chinese, Finnish, and Hindi) was suspended in a saline solution and injected into these volunteers in a proportion of 200 subjects to each language. The amount of each injection was 40 ml. of 0.25% brain-fluid extract. The injections were given under local anaesthetic with the aid of a surgical drill into the brain cavity just behind the left temple. This location is just above the third convolution of the left frontal lobe, known as Broca's area, in which the speech function of the brain is located. The depth of the injections was sufficient to enter the cerebral cortex. No further action was taken for a period of one week.

Beginning in the first week of August, 1972, a team of psychiatrists under the direction of Academician Ya. P. Utkonosov was engaged to place the subjects into the trance state by means of hypnosis. This method was used because of the unreliability of inducing such a state by the exact duplication or simulation of the conditions leading to the manifestations of glossolalic behavior in the context of religious fanaticism. Approximately one-third of the subjects were found to be unacceptable hypnotic subjects, leaving the following proportions of subjects with which the experiment would continue: French (152), Chinese (170), Finnish (110), and Hindi (121). This left a total sample of 553 subjects.

While in a hypnotically induced state of suggestibility, each subject was brought to a condition of trauma, an altered state of consciousness judged on the basis of electroencephalogram readings to be similar to that exhibited by persons manifesting glossolalic behavior. Specifically, each subject was told that a person "dear to them" was to be executed by mistake by the

French/Chinese/Finnish/Hindi students present during the session. This execution, it was suggested, could be averted if only the subject could explain the mistake to the student observer. The student observers were, of course, instructed to answer only in the language desired in the behavior of the subject. It was hoped that the subjects would be able, using the students' answers as a catalyst, to quickly gain the fluency needed to make the explanation. The results were startling.

The following table represents the outcome of session #1 of the experiment.

	Hypnotically acceptable subjects involved	Subjects able to make necessary explanation in 10 minutes	Subjects unable to make necessary explanation in 10 minutes	Percentage of subjects showing desired behavior in 10 minutes
French	152	123	29	81%
Chinese	170	132	38	78%
Finnish	110	79	31	72%
Hindi	121	105	16	86%
Total	**553**	**449**	**104**	**81%**

Each subject spent three such sessions with Academician Utkonosov's psychiatric team and the student observers. At the completion of the three sessions for all the subjects under investigation, an additional 10 (5%) subjects exhibited the desired French, 11 (6.5%) subjects exhibited the desired Chinese, 6 (5.5%) subjects exhibited the desired Finnish, and 7 (6%) subjects exhibited the desired Hindi. In all, 473 of 550 subjects completing the experiment (3 subjects died during the two month period of August 1, 1972 to October 1, 1972 of unrelated causes) exhibited the desired behavior in some degree. Those subjects who were able to make the necessary explanation on the first try were, by the end of the three sessions, remarkably fluent in the languages in question. Notice also that the success percentage is higher in those languages more closely "related" in a linguistic sense to Russian (i.e. French and Hindi as opposed to Finnish and Chinese) although negligibly so. The total success percentage was a phenomenal 86% over the course of all three sessions. Of course, the behavior was only present during the hypnotically induced traumatic state.

During the course of the experiment so far related, methods were explored for the maintenance of traits learned in altered states of consciousness. What was desired was a means to preserve this behavior in the normal state of consciousness. It was theorized that the relation of trauma to specific behavior manifestation was due to the different levels of electrical activity in the brain during the trauma state as opposed to the normal state. The measurable levels of electrical energy in the brain during trauma are higher than the levels measured during the normal state. It is this principle, of course, which contributes to the accuracy of such instruments as the polygraph. At the present state of scientific knowledge, it is impossible to ascertain with exactitude the physiological correlate in the brain which allows this behavior during trauma when the electrical energy level is high but not during the normal state. Nevertheless, our present state of knowledge about memory storage and recall does allow us to propose and test a method for the preservation of the desired behavior in the normal states of consciousness.

Basic to the preservation of this behavior is the notion of repetition. Repetition, the old Russian saying tells us, is the mother of learning. It is, on a more scientific level, repetition, which enables an experience which is impressed on our 'short term' memory to transfer to the permanent storage of our 'long term' memory.[9] This notion is, of course, basic to the experience of language learning as well. How then, do we simulate repetition in the minds of the subjects in order to transfer the desired behavior to permanent storage? This was the problem we addressed ourselves to in the months of August and September 1972.

It was concluded that the repetition of hypnotic trauma inducement would be awkward and unmanageable for the number of repetitions needed for the transfer of the language behavior. Perhaps though, we theorized, the behavior could be repeated synthetically merely by raising the electrical energy level in the brain the required number of times once the hypnosis had psychologically 'set' the specific behavior into the transfer process.

The 473 subjects who had exhibited the desired language behavior during the first phase of the experiment were, during October, 1972, subjected without further hypnosis to repetitive increases of electrical brain energy. This was done by the application of 0.125 volt of electricity in increments of 1 second for 1000 repetitions. The electrical charge was transmitted through the brain cavity by the use of needles stuck into acupuncture points in the center forehead near the point of the trigeminal nerve and in the upper neck above the vagus and hypoglossal nerves. By the end of October, the month that celebrates our great revolution, it had become apparent that our efforts were

---

[9] See: Halacy, D.S. <u>Man and Memory</u>. New York: Harper & Row, 1970, 55-58. Also see: Fjerdingstad, Ejnar. <u>Chemical transfer of learned information</u>. Amsterdam: North Holland, 1971 (distributed in the U.S. by American Elsevier Publ. Co. as <u>Frontiers in biology</u>. Neuberger and Tatum (Eds.), Monograph No. 22).

successful. Of the 473 subjects, 430 (91%) were able to converse fluently in their respective languages. Each successful subject appears to have a complete command of vocabulary and morphological and syntactic processes. This behavior is readily elicitable from the normal state of the subjects' consciousness and has, at the time of this writing (December 28, 1972), every indication of being permanent.

The consequences of this line of research to language learning and, indeed, to Mankind in general stand as obvious. Refinement and implementation are all that remain. My colleagues and I at the Moscow Psycholinguistics Institute are presently recruiting volunteers for new experiments along these lines of development. The Soviet Academy of Science has announced that similar efforts will be made to see what other specific behaviors may be transferred in this manner. Once again, I would like to emphasize that it is the inherent superiority of a system of scholarship encouraged by government that has enabled us to make such significant advances where other scholars under other systems, even with the preliminary work completed and at hand, have been unable to accomplish.

PRESENTATION:

In 1972, Prof. Croft was working on his doctoral dissertation in Slavic Linguistics as a graduate student in Cornell University's Division of Modern Languages and Linguistics (DMLL). In Cornell's historic Morrill Hall where the DMLL was housed, there was a lounge on the second floor where faculty and graduate students would "hang out" and interact with each other in ways both personal and scholarly. A table in this lounge was covered by piles of pre-publication drafts of scholarly papers for commentary by whomever might be interested enough to read them. Prof. Croft reports that in only an hour of inspired silliness he wrote and prepared mimeographed copies of a scholarly ***HOAX***...the previously reprinted article...and placed these copies on the table in the DMLL Faculty Lounge. The name of the translator in this first version was "Nick & Tony Znayette" (a rough transliteration of the Russian "**Никто не знает**," meaning "No one knows"). Soon many faculty members and graduate students were discussing the possibilities of molecularly transferring language behavior "like the Soviets had done." When it was subsequently revealed to be a hoax, Croft received general congratulation for his cleverness at "pulling it off." Some colleagues jokingly suggested that he should "apply for a federal grant" to replicate this "important scientific discovery." But Dr. Gerald Kelley, the prominent sociolinguist who then headed the Cornell University DMLL, called Croft in and told him seriously *not* to carry the hoax further by applying for federal grant money. "I'm afraid you'll get it," he said.

At first, in January of 1973, Croft sent the hoax to <u>Slavic and East European Journal</u> (<u>SEEJ</u>), a leading scholarly publication in language, linguistics, and language pedagogy as well as literature studies, but he received a letter from Editor Frank Y. Gladney that <u>SEEJ</u> policy was not to publish "translations" (cf. a copy of that letter in Megan Plachecki's article following). Since the basis of the hoax involved molecular memory transfer, a theory then current because of the research on the conditioning of planaria by

Prof. James V. McConnell of the Mental Health Research Institute at the University of Michigan, Croft decided to send a copy of the hoax, with his own name and address listed as the translator, to McConnell to be considered for publication in Worm Runner's Digest, an upside-down compendium of satire and spoofery attached to the quarterly issues of the serious research organ, The Journal of Biological Psychology. McConnell's reaction was positive and he assented to publish the hoax, even writing to Croft in his acceptance letter from 26 March, 1973, that "Oddly enough, I rather imagine the 'technique' that you spoof *would really work* (italics mine…EDS). I suppose some day someone (perhaps in Russia) will actually try it." And, after the hoax was published in McConnell's journal (the 1972 date reflects the journal's editorial backlog), Croft unexpectedly received a letter of compliment on the personal stationery of Scientific American's renowned mathematical games columnist, the now legendary Martin Gardner, a leading authority on pseudoscience to be sure. The text of the letter, dated 6 June 1975 is as follows:

"Dear Mr. Croft:

I very much enjoyed reading your hoax paper, which I had not previously seen (although for a time I was a subscriber to Worm Runner's Digest). I particularly enjoyed it because, as (a) former fundamentalist (in my early youth in Oklahoma), I am quite familiar with glossolalia. (It plays a role in one of the wilder scenes in my religious novel, The Flight of Peter Fromm.)

I've never written about glossolalia (except in my novel), but if I ever do, I will be glad to have your marvelous paper on file.

With many thanks,

M. Gardner"

Here is a copy of the letter and the envelope it came in, with its 10¢ stamp (and a more recent photo of Martin Gardner):

MARTIN GARDNER

10 EUCLID AVENUE
HASTINGS-ON-HUDSON
NEW YORK 10706

Dear Mr. Croft: 6 June 75

I very much enjoyed reading your hoax paper, which
I had not previously seen (although for a time I
was a subscriber to Worm Runner's Digest).
I particularly enjoyed it because, as a former
fundamentalist (in my early youth in Oklahoma),
I am quite familiar with glossolalia. (It plays
a role in one of the wilder scenes in my religious
novel, The Flight of Peter Fromm.)

I've never written about glossolalia (except in
my novel), but if I ever do, I will be glad to
have your marvelous paper on file.

With many thanks,

M. Gardner

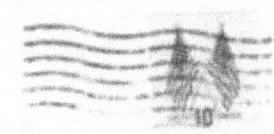

Lee B. Croft
Dept. of Foreign Languages
Ariz. State Univ
Tempe, Ariz 85281

This letter from Martin Gardner (cf. http://en.wikipedia.org/wiki/Martin_Gardner; and also the October 2006 interview with him by "Card Colm" (Colm Mulcahy) for the Mathematical Association of America at http://www.maa.org/columns/colm/cardclm200610.html, from where the relatively recent photograph of Martin Gardner (1914--) was taken) is among Croft's most treasured possessions to this day.

Prof. and Editor James V. McConnell, once a major figure in American science, died in 1990, his research on molecular memory transfer largely discredited or "set aside." In 1985 he was one of the targets of the "Unabomber," Theodore Kaczynski, a disturbed former Professor of Mathematics who had resigned in disillusionment from his position at the University of California-Berkeley. McConnell suffered hearing loss when one of Kaczynski's bombs, disguised as a manuscript package, exploded when it was opened at his home by his research assistant, Niklaus Suino (cf. http://en.wikipedia.org/wiki/James_V_McConnell and http://en.wikipedia.org/wiki/Unabomber).

This might have been the end of the story of Croft's "Soviet Glossolalia Language Learning Hoax," but there is more. From ASU's Russian Section's first "capstone project," <u>Russian in Arizona: A History of Its Teaching</u> (IIHS, Tempe, AZ/Perm, Russian Federation, 2007, ISBN 978-1-4303-2355-6, pp. 36-7) comes Prof. Croft's account of his 1978 case for academic tenure:

"When I went up for tenure and promotion in 1978 I anticipated no trouble. But I got an unexpected call to appear before the college-level committee. With trepidation I appeared in Dean Guido Weigend's office, only to find Dr.

David William Foster of Spanish…, our departmental representative on the college council, sitting in the lobby. He soberly told me that he had decided to absent himself from the council's hearing of 'my case.' When I faced the council, I could feel a certain hostility. First, they wanted to address my 'rather modest' record of scholarly publication. I could only point out that I had, in fact, at that time, outpublished in their terms all the other professors of Russian language and literature (I exempted the prolific Dr. Ekmanis here as a Baltic specialist for obvious reasons) in the entire state combined. There was a long silence as they abandoned that direction of attack. Then a prominent scientist among them (now controversially embattled as the recently relieved head of ASU's Cancer Institute) got to the bottom line. 'Dr. Croft,' he said, 'this council takes a dim view of faculty members who claim to have authored the works of others.' I was stunned. He explained that they had looked up my article in The Journal of Biological Psychology/The Worm Runner's Digest from 1972 and discovered that I was only the translator of an article entitled 'Synthetically Induced and Electrically Maintained Trance Glossolalia as a Method of Language Learning,' which was written by 'Academician Viacheslav Obmanov of the Moscow Psycholinguistics Institute.' This was, in fact, a scientific hoax I had authored which used the precepts of molecular memory transfer to give the impression that the Soviets had found a method to transfer language fluency from one prison-camp inmate to another with injections of cerebral spinal fluid. The hoax had received considerable attention, even in the local press after I made an ASU Honors Lecture out of it. But none of the council members were aware of this, and they had obviously 'bought' the whole thing…and were angry at me for 'stealing' such significant research from Academician Obmanov (whose name, based on the Russian word for 'hoax' I had made up, along with other names like 'Naprasov' (Futile) and even 'Utkonosov' (Platypus)…which they, non-Russians, didn't pick up). As I listened to the college council lay out the case against me, I had the thought that, if I then explained the matter to them in the wrong way, the backlash of their embarrassment would bury me yet. So I tried to break it to them delicately, even pointing out to them that news clippings about my earlier presentation of this hoax had been submitted to them apart from my vita in the file. There was another silence and more grim faces. But then a respected Professor of English (Dr. O. M. "Skip" Brack, still teaching at ASU) broke out laughing, and other nervous laughter quickly spread. I was given tenure and promotion to Associate Professor."

Prof. Croft considers it ironic, but somehow appropriate, given his career here at ASU interacting with the many "Chichikovs" in academia and teaching about the great imposters (the "False Dmitrii," the "Felon of Tushino," the "False Peter," Fyodor Kuzmich, Nikolai Marr, Trofim Lysenko and others) in the Russian culture too, that his very first scholarly publication was a hoax.

Deciphering a Russian Poem by Igor Chinnov
By:
Megan Plachecki

Megan Plachecki was born in Chandler, Arizona in 1987 and has lived there ever since. She graduated from Hamilton High School in 2005 and began attending Arizona State University on the Provost Scholarship. Although originally majoring in physics, she was always interested in languages and began studying Russian in 2007 at the Critical Languages Institute. In the spring of 2008 she was inducted into ASU's Epsilon Epsilon chapter of **Добро Слово**, the

National Slavic Studies Honorary. Megan studied in St. Petersburg and Moscow during the summer of 2008 and plans to graduate from ASU in 2009 with a B.A. in Russian. She hopes to attend graduate school for Russian translation and someday have a career in government service.

PRESENTATION:

In 1970 Prof. Croft was a graduate student of Slavic Linguistics at Cornell University in Ithaca, New York. As part of his minor field of Russian Literature he took a seminar in Russian poetry from Prof. H. W. "Bill" Chalsma (sometimes spelled "Tjalsma"), who had once been a fellow graduate student at the University of Wisconsin-Madison with our ASU professors of Russian emeriti, Sandy Couch and Rolfs Ekmanis. Prof. Chalsma's seminar at Cornell was focused on Russian émigré poetry and included a number of other graduate students in Russian studies: Andrew Zigelis, later Professor of Russian at the University of Georgia, Mark Orton, later Massachusetts language teacher, Charles "Chuck" Winkler, later analyst for the U.S. government's Institute for the Analysis of Military Threat, and Thomas Marullo, later Professor of Russian Literature at the University of Notre Dame (notice that these people, along with Croft's USSR-1972 roommate Jack E. Evans of the College of Wooster in Ohio, are mentioned in the article's acknowledgments). Croft decided to write his term paper in the class on the poetry of "second wave" (i.e. after World War II) émigré Igor Chinnov (1909-1996), who was at that time a Professor of Russian Literature at Vanderbilt University in Tennessee. When he presented his term paper to the seminar, Prof. Chalsma and the other students reacted very positively to his attempt to explain the subtext of

Chinnov's strikingly atypical poem, "Horses Fall into the Caspian Sea." As a result, Prof. Chalsma, who later served on Croft's doctoral committee, suggested that he do further work on the poem with the intention of finding an avenue of publication for it. It was Prof. Chalsma who then put Croft in contact with George (Yurii) Ivask, prominent émigré poet himself and Professor of Russian Literature at the University of Washington (where he was a mentor of later ASU Prof. of Russian, Dora Burton). By mail and in personal conversation at a New York City professional conference, Prof. Ivask, who knew Chinnov and his work well, elucidated for Croft further aspects of the poem's subtlety.

As the poem's analysis progressed through Prof. Croft's graduate work at Cornell in 1970 and 1971, he decided that he would have to meet and talk to Igor Chinnov himself about the poem. So he wrote to Prof. Chinnov at Vanderbilt and arranged to meet with him while both were attending a national AATSEEL meeting in New York City during the Christmas Break of 1972. He remembers that Chinnov was "an eccentric individual," relating:

"He was a small man, wearing a gray suit and tie. He wore prominent eyeglasses that made him appear a bit 'owl-like.' When I approached him and reached out to shake his hand, he pulled his own hand back, pointing to a sore on the side of a finger that he did not want to aggravate. It was obviously bothering him, and he held his arm as if it were in a sling, although it wasn't. We walked out of the convention hotel and went into a small sidewalk café, sitting at the dining bar instead of in a booth. I ordered a soda and a sandwich, but all he wanted was a cup of tea. As we talked in both English and in Russian, I soon came to the conclusion that Chinnov's ability to analyze his own verse was surprisingly quite limited. He said he thought that the image of 'the gray wolf riding on Ivan Tsarevich' (instead of vice-versa) was a portrayal of the Soviet Union's 'riding on the backs of its people.' His mention of such political symbolism seemed quite antithetical to my own interpretation of the poem as a comment on the human condition that transcended politics, and I was puzzled by his comments being 'so far off the mark.' Perhaps, I thought, he created this poem he later (in a letter to me) called his '**бессмыслица**' ('little bit of senselessness') unconsciously and without a sense of what was in its subtext. So, then, was my analysis of the poem valid at all? Did he think I should proceed with the idea of publishing it? I didn't get an answer. He called to the waitress behind the dining bar for some more tea. But she ignored him. She was standing in a slump, leaning against the stove front, with her head slowly nodding. My perception was that she had lapsed into a drug-induced stupor and was entirely oblivious to the outside world. But Chinnov called out to her again, raising his empty teacup with his able arm. This time he shouted out to her in Russian, as if that would help. No answer. After another attempt or two, he became agitated and stood up, very indignant, and, pointing at her, began to shout: 'Cuckoo! Cuckoo! Cuckoo!' The crowd in the café unanimously turned attention to him, and to me. 'Cuckoo!' he kept shouting. So I, embarrassed, put some money on the bar and ushered him out onto the street. 'Back to the hotel and away from such madness!' he said, 'I've endured too much of this kind of thing'."

Igor Chinnov (1909-1996)

Prof. Croft sent his analysis of Chinnov's poem to <u>Russian Literature Triquarterly</u> at the University of Michigan. But, in her letter of Oct. 18, 1972, Editor Ellendea Proffer wrote: "Your essay is an excellent deciphering of the poem. It shows the kind of talent that we will look forward to seeing in RLT in the future—but unfortunately we don't think that we can devote this much space to this one short piece in the journal." So, Croft then sent, on Nov. 9, 1972, a long letter of submission to Editor Charles Schlacks, Jr. at <u>Canadian-American Slavic Studies</u> at the University of Pittsburgh's University Center for International Studies. But again the decision was negative, with Schlacks writing on 9 January, 1973, that "I regret to tell you that our editorial board has rejected your manuscript entitled "The 'Method to Madness': A Study in the Poetic Process" for publication in this journal. The consensus is that your contribution certainly contains valuable ideas, but is too weak for publication." Schlacks then suggested a rewrite with a "better structural framework" so that the article might appeal to a more "strictly literary journal." Prof. Croft relates that he was subsequently part of a group at ASU who hired Charles Schlacks, Jr. away from the University of Pittsburgh to produce several of the scholarly publications under his editorship here, but that in 1981 ASU's Russian and East European Publications board, on which Croft served, fired Schlacks. This story is told in Russian in Arizona: A History of Its Teaching (IIHS, Tempe, AZ/Perm, Russia, 2006, pp. 41-3). But, in early 1973, while he was still a graduate student at Cornell, Croft took Charles Schlacks' advice and rewrote the article, submitting it to Editor Kiril Taranovsky of Harvard University for consideration at Russian Literature. Taranovsky very quickly sent Croft his THIRD rejection, but made some helpful comments on the content and recommended that Croft send the article to Prof. Frank Y. Gladney of the University of Illinois at Urbana-Champaign, the editor of the Slavic and East European Journal (SEEJ). The problem with this from Croft's point of view was that he had already sent Editor Gladney at SEEJ a copy of his hoax article, "Synthetically Induced and Electrically Maintained Trance Glossolalia as a Method of Language Learning" (see Eric D. Strachan's article preceding this one) which he had written at Cornell in late 1972. But, imagining that the SEEJ editorial staff could well consider two articles instead of just one from the same author, Croft sent Editor Gladney the Chinnov article too on 6 February,

1973. In answer, Croft received the following letter (dated 7 March, 1973) from SEEJ Editor Gladney:

"Mr. Lee B. Croft
157 Bundy Road
Ithaca, New York 14850

Dear Mr. Croft,

Thank you for your prompt response to our request for the ribbon copy of your paper, "The 'Method to Madness':A Study in the Poetic Process." We will now proceed with the evaluation and hope to have an editorial decision for you sometime this spring.

Concerning Academician Obmanov's article, it is stated in the Editorial Policy that SEEJ does not publish translations. However, the implications of the research reported are so broad that we are writing to the Moscow Psycholinguistics Institute about the possibility of a report on this research addressed specifically to SEEJ readers.

Your cooperation with the work of the Journal is greatly appreciated.

       Sincerely,

       Frank Y. Gladney
slh   Editor"

  Croft did not know then, and he does not know now, whether Gladney's paragraph about the broad implications of Academician Obmanov's research being such as to compel him to write to the Moscow Psycholinguistics Insitute to request a report for the SEEJ readership was "tongue-in-cheek" or serious. The fact that no such report was ever published in SEEJ doesn't really resolve this question. But Croft did understand that his hoax was not going to be published in SEEJ, and that is why he found another, more appropriate as it turned out, avenue of publication for it at Prof. James V. McConnell's Journal of Biological Psychology/Worm Runner's Digest. As Eric D. Strachan points out in the preceding article, Professor and Editor McConnell wrote Croft an acceptance letter for the hoax on 26 March, 1973. It actually appeared in print in the fall of 1973, even though it was dated as a 1972 edition due to the editorial backlog.

Editor Gladney's referees on the Chinnov article included Prof. Victor Terras of Brown University, who recommended the article for publication and "broke editorial cover" to send Croft very helpful further suggestions for analysis that Croft then incorporated into yet another rewrite. When Croft received the final publication proofs in the summer of 1973 he was displeased about how Editor Gladney had changed his translation of Chinnov's line "**по-сибирски снежок серебрится**" from a morphologically analogous "Siberiously a light snow silvers" to "In the Siberian manner a light snow silvers." Croft wrote Gladney to argue for including the word "Siberiously" in the translation, but Gladney refused. During the epistolary 'dialogue' on this (and also the request by Kiril Taranovsky to have his name removed from a footnote that he saw when Croft fortunately sent him a set of the SEEJ proofs), Croft accepted the position as Assistant Professor of Russian at ASU and moved in August with his family from Ithaca, New York, to Tempe, Arizona. From his new job at ASU, Croft wrote Gladney a letter saying that if the poetically disruptive phrase "In the Siberian manner..." was to appear instead of the word "Siberiously" in the translation, then

Gladney was NOT to publish the article. Croft would, he said, send it somewhere else. But Editor Gladney *ignored Prof. Croft's letter* and published the article in the Winter 1973 Slavic and East European Journal ("SEEJ", Vol. 17, No. 4, pp. 408-413). He had removed the entire footnote mentioning Kiril Taranovsky, but left Taranovsky's name in the acknowledgments (likely with Taranovsky's approval). He had changed the title to "The Method to Madness in a Poem by Chinnov." And he added the affiliation "Arizona State University" to Prof. Croft's author's line.

Prof. Croft says that someday he should tell Frank Gladney, whose term as the editor of SEEJ is now a part of the distant past, that *he is grateful to Gladney* for ignoring his letter calling for withdrawal of the article (notice, however, that the article as published here uses the term "Siberiously"). The publication of this article in such a leading professional organ did much to give Prof. Croft esteem in his field and later to help assure Prof. Croft's case for tenure at ASU.

Prof. Croft stayed in intermittent touch with Igor Chinnov by mail until Chinnov's death in Florida retirement in 1996. A subsequent SEEJ (Vol. 20 (1976), No. 4, pp. 486) published Croft's review of Chinnov's 1976 collection, **Пасторали.** He has saved several of Chinnov's handwritten letters. In one, Chinnov told Croft that he was "grateful for having a reader" like him. And once, one of Chinnov's colleagues at Vanderbilt, Professor of Russian Literature and literary translator Antonina Filonova Gove, sent Prof. Croft a letter complimenting him on this article, calling it a "model explication" of poetry. Following her example, Croft has made it a practice to write letters of compliment to other scholars whose published work he has found valuable or enjoyable. This article was subsequently cited as exemplary scholarship on Chinnov by the eminent

Victor Terras in his **Handbook of Russian Literature**, Yale University Press, 1985, pp. 84. And, a description of this article as the only one about a "second wave" Russian émigré poet is included in David Bethea's article "Emigration and Heritage" in the thirtieth anniversary issue of **Slavic and East European Journal** (Vol. 31, 1987, pp. 153). It is available digitally online at www.jstor.org. A comprehensive and acute article on Chinnov with a long interview entitled "Игрушка—Записки об Игоре Чиннове" ("The Toy—Notes about Igor Chinnov") by Prof. Maxim Shrayer can be found at http://magazines.russ.ru/druzhba/1999/shraer.html.

Megan Plachecki at Fyodor Dostoevsky's Grave in St. Petersburg

The Method to Madness in a Poem by Chinnov

By:

Lee B. Croft

The early work of Igor Chinnov[10] expresses a doleful aimlessness which associates it with the "Parisian note" school of emigré poetry. A desire for a sense of belonging, an insecure wonder before nature and fate, the poignancy of melancholia, and reflections of the bitter ennui engendered by a seemingly futile search for new goals and directions are characteristic of this poetry. The prevailing worldview here

---

[10] Igor Chinnov (b. 1909) grew up in Estonia and left the Soviet Union during World War II. He has published poetry in the emigré journals **Возрождение, Граны, Мосты, Опыты**, and **Новый Журнал**, and there are now five collections of his verse: **Монолог** (Paris: Rifma, 1950), **Линии** (Paris: Rifma, 1960), **Метафоры** (New York: **Новый Журнал**, 1968), **Партитура** (New York: **Новый Журнал**, 1970), and **Композиция** (Paris: Rimfa, 1962). Translations of his poetry by Theodore Weiss and L.P. Izhorsky can be found in Tri-Quarterly, 28 (Fall 1973), 433-34, by R.H. Morrison in R.H. Morrison, ed., America's Russian Poets (Ann Arbor: Ardis, 1975), and in Vladimir Markov and Merrill Sparks, eds., Modern Russian Poetry (New York: Bobbs-Merrill Co., 1967), 486-87. For an introduction to Chinnov's poetry within the context of Russian emigré literature see Èmmanuil Rajs, "**Поэзия Игоря Чиннова**," **Возрождение**, 235 (Sept. 1971), 131-45.

and in his later work is pessimistic. In recent years, however, Chinnov's poetry has diverged from traditional emigré themes and methods of expression; its syncopated sound patterns (reflected in the musicological titles of his two recent collections) and especially its eccentric surrealistic effects have puzzled the older generation of emigré reviewers. Nevertheless, there is "method in the madness of these strange aggregates of impressions," to quote Victor Terras,[11] and this paper will endeavor to illustrate it through analysis of a poem from **Партитура**, "Horses Fall into the Caspian Sea" ("**Лошади впадают в Каспийское море**"). This poem seems to mark a turning point in Chinnov's poetry, and it demonstrates the power of poetry to convey specific meanings, which are virtually independent of literal statement.

Александру Гингеру

Лошади впадают в Каспийское море.
Более или менее впадают и, значит,
Овцы сыты, а волки- едят Волгу и сено.
О, гармония Логоса! И как же иначе?
Серый волк на Иване-царевиче скачет
(по-сибирски снежок серебрится)

---

[11] SEEJ, 15 (1971), 511. For a different point of view see Georgij Adamovič's review of **Партитура** in **Новый Журнал**, 102 (1971), 282. I am grateful to Professors George (Yurii) Ivask, Victor Terras and Kiril Taranovsky for their helpful comments and to Prof. Jack E. Evans, Prof. H.W. Chalsma, Andrew Zigelis, Mark Orton, Charles Winkler, and Thomas Marullo for their interest and suggestions; responsibility for errors and shortcomings is of course mine.

и море,
которому пьяный по колено,
зажигает большую синицу
в честь этой победы Человека.
Человек, это гордо!
Любит карась погреться в сметане,
Чтобы милая щука поела, дремала.
Перстень проглотил рыбу царского грека.
Дважды два семь, не много, не мало.
Солнце ясней, когда солнце в тумане.
Солнце слабеет. Как бледно и серо.
У Алжирского носа под самым Деем
Тридцать пять тысяч одних курьеров.

{Horses fall into the Caspian Sea. They fall more or less, and that means the sheep are full, and the wolves eat the Volga and hay. O, the harmony of Logos! And how else could it be? The gray wolf on Ivan-tsarevich is galloping (Siberiously a light snow silvers) and the sea, to whom the drunk is knee-high, sets fire to the great titmouse in honor of this victory of Man. Man- that is proud! The carp likes to warm himself in sour cream, so that the dear pike might eat, doze. The signet ring swallowed the fish of the royal Greek. Twice two is seven, not a lot, not a little. The sun is clearer when the sun is in fog. The sun is weakening. How pale and gray. The Algerian nose has under its very Dey thirty-five thousand couriers, and then some.}

At first reading, one wonders why this apparently nonsensical poem is seriously dedicated to another emigré poet (Alexander Ginger) and included in a volume with other, more obviously serious poems; its disjoint series of fantastic images reminds one of the nursery rhyme, "Hey diddle diddle, the cat and the fiddle..."¹² But, for the initiated, these images evoke certain vivid reminiscences, which are obscured or distorted here in various ways. In fact the entire poem is a filigree of Russian literature, folklore, and proverbs, with certain items left out and other, somehow associated items, substituted for them. In it Chinnov has utilized a device of Russian folk poetry, the switching of words and phrases within a syntactic unit to create an attention-arresting image (e.g., **Ехала деревня мимо мужика, /а из-под собаки лают ворота**... "Drove a village past a peasant, and from under the dog the gates were barking").¹³ Chinnov's substitutions are not capricious or arbitrary however. The associations of both sense and sound which link the reshuffled items within any given syntactic unit reveal much which is obscure at first glance. Further, the associations within any one syntactic unit are systematically related to those in other syntactic units, so that a coherent thematic development results.

To begin, consider Ippolit Ippolitovič, a character in Čexov's short story "The Grammar Teacher" ("**Учитель словесности**"), the title of which may be ironically significant considering the nature of this poem. Ippolit, we are told, only speaks to tell us "that which is already known

---

[12] Èmmanuil Rajs remarks in this connection, that "mockery for the sake of mockery becomes, as it were, 'purposeless' in the remarkable poem 'Horses Fall into the Caspian Sea' " (p.137). In a private letter to me Chinnov himself has referred to this poem as "bessmyslica" ("**бессмыслица**"... "a little bit of senselessness").

[13] This poetic precedence was suggested to me by Victor Terras.

to all."[14] When he is dying he repeats deliriously, "The Volga falls into the Caspian Sea. Horses eat oats and hay." (p. 398.) This utterance has since come to connote the trivial or inane.[15] Chinnov begins by replacing "Volga" with "horses" ("**лошади**"), and then using "Volga" to replace "oats" ("**овёс**"). Needing a new subject for the second sentence that is capable of eating, he chooses "wolves" ("**волки**"). The similarity in sound between Volga and **волки** is surely a factor in this substitution. But these wolves now find themselves eating the Volga and hay, and a fantastic effect is achieved. Wolves are, of course, well known in Russian folklore for their appetite for sheep. The Russian saying, "The wolves are full and the sheep are whole" ("**Волки сыты и овцы целы**"), was perhaps chosen by Chinnov as the basis for his next transformation, because it involves wolves and a similarity in sound exists between words for "oats" ("**овёс**")- the only word still left out of the transformed phrases above- and "sheep" ("**овцы**"). The transformation of this saying to "the sheep are full" ("**овцы сыты**") enhances its euphony and maintains the pattern of animal actors continued later in the poem. In its opening line, Chinnov has thus created images which are fresh and light from utterances strongly identified with the trite and banal. Yet nothing has been lost. The essential structure of the utterances is "more or less" ("**более или менее**") the same.

---

[14] **А. П. Чехов, <u>Собрание сочинений</u>** (12 vols.; M.: GIXL, 1960-64), VII, 388.

[15] **Н. С. Ашукин и М. Г. Ашукина, ред. <u>Крылатые слова</u>**, 2ᵒᵉ изд. (M.:GIXL, 1960), 107. This source gives the history of the phrase and cites its use by V.I. Lenin and A. Vixrev. **Волга впадает в Каспийское море** is also the title of Boris Pil'njak's 1930 novel.

The fourth line, which appears to be tongue-in-cheek, probably reflects the poet's thoughts on his poetic method; it can thus be understood as the key to the poem's interpretation. The phrase "O the harmony of Logos!" ("**О, гармония Логоса!**") extols the already demonstrated property of words. They can be related by associations of sense and sound, so that new harmonies may be found within the old familiar schemes. Would we want it any other way (the translation of "**И как же иначе**")? Endless combinations of this nature are possible, as Chinnov has begun to demonstrate.

In the fifth line, folklore characters, the gray wolf ("**серый волк**") and Ivan-tsarevich ("**Иван-царевич**"),[16] are reversed in their roles as to who rides whom, predicting two reversals soon to follow. Chinnov preserves here the animal-as-actor scheme while associating the gray wolf with the wolves in the third line. The parenthesized sixth line "Siberiously a light snow silvers" ("**по-сибирски снежок серебрится**") is a gem, an interpolated specification of scene, which gives a light, crystalline aura to the imagery (Snow is a frequent image in Chinnov's poetry). Alliteration and a kind of palindromic symmetry can be observed in the consonants (the sequence **б, р, с, к** is echoed from the other side of an axis through the middle of **снежок** by the reverse sequence **к, с, р, б**), while the dominance of front vowels is harmonious with the light imagery; the resultant synaesthetic effect impresses the line

---

[16] Insofar as a specific referent is possible for these two characters, it is probably Vasilii Žukovskij's **Сказка о Иване-царевиче и сером волке**, which is usually Russian children's first exposure to them. **Василии А. Жуковский**, **Собрание сочинений** (4 vols.; M., L.: GIXL, 1959-60), III, 204-33.

subtly on one's memory. What is more, the falling, silvery snow partially obscures a darker-colored world visually, just as the poem's whimsical transformations only partially conceal the pessimism at the heart of the poem…so that the poem's imagery is iconic to the underlying meaning.

There are two Russian sayings that share a reference to the sea and a concern with human pride and delusion. "The titmouse sets fire to the sea" ("**Синица зажигает море**") describes someone who thinks he can do anything, no matter how difficult. "To a drunk the sea is knee-high" ("**Пьяному море по колено**") is very similar in meaning. Through these sayings, Chinnov moves from the Caspian Sea to the sea in a more general sense; using "sea" as a pivot, these two sayings may be combined to yield: "The titmouse sets fire to the sea, which is knee-high to a drunk" ("**Синица зажигает море, которое пьяному по колено**"). Chinnov then reverses subject and object in the main clause, and the relation of the sea to the drunk in the subordinate clause: "The sea, to which the drunk is knee-high, sets fire to the titmouse" ("**Море, которому пьяный по колено, зажигает синицу**"). To the titmouse Chinnov adds the improbable adjective "great" ("**большую**"), heightening the surrealistic effect. The irony in all this becomes apparent in the next line; it is "in honor of this victory of Man" ("**в честь этой победы Человека**") that the sacrifice of the great titmouse is made by the sea. "This victory of Man" probably refers to the "harmony of Logos." After all, it is the ability to create this harmony which distinguishes man from the titmouse. But what does man gain by it? Isn't he also small, weak, and deluded, as the three consecutive reversals beginning with Ivan-tsarevich suggest? Thus, the last line of this section of the poem points to man's delusions and pride.

In act four of Maxim Gorkij's The Lower Depths (**На дне**) the character Satin exclaims in a resurgence of self-respect, "Man- that sounds proud!" ("**Человек- это звучит гордо!**")[17] This exclamation sounds ludicrous in the squalid and depraved atmosphere of his surroundings. In the next line Chinnov paraphrases this exclamation, "Man- that is proud!" ("**Человек-это гордо!**"), to re-emphasize the illusory quality to man's proud pretensions; they are stymied from the start by the inescapable, ignoble nature of things. This is implicit in the reference to Saltykov-Ščedrin's satiric tale, "The Carp-Idealist" ("**Карась-Идеалист**," 1884),[18] in the next two lines: "The carp likes to warm himself in sour cream, so that the dear pike might eat, doze" ("**Любит карась погреться в сметане,/ чтобы милая щука поела, дремала**"). In this tale the carp thinks that he can reason with a pike and persuade him to adhere to principles which would allow all fish to swim freely anywhere. His reasoning is logical enough and noble too, but it is futile; the pike is governed by a greater natural law which enables him to swallow the carp without the slightest remorse. This inescapable law is reflected in the Russian saying, "That's why the pike is in the sea, so that the carp doesn't doze" ("**На то и щука в море, чтоб карась не дремал**"). When the foolish carp confronts the pike, the pike is so puzzled that he would not have eaten him, except that, in his surprise, his mouth fell open, sucking in both water and the carp. The moral is that the carp's idealistic pretensions to a nobler nature were his

---

[17] See **Ашукин и Ашукина, стр.** 659-60, for citations of this phrase from **В. Ермилов и М. Мамусовский**.

[18] **Н. Щедрин (М. Е. Салтыков), Собрание сочинений** (12 vols.; M.: Pravda, 1951), X, 348-56. See also **Ашукин и Ашукина, стр.** 284-85, with regard to this story.

downfall. Of course in Chinnov's transformation of the saying we are told that the carp likes to serve himself up as a hot meal in sour cream for the "dear pike." These fish are elements in the poem's associated sea images and its use of animal actors, especially those omnivorous wolves.

The next line in the associative chain also refers to a fish and a meal, but its source is concerned with the inescapability of fate rather than with idealism and delusion. Herodotus, in his <u>Histories</u>, writes of the Greek king Polykrates of Samos, whose good fortune was extraordinary. Everything he attempted turned out well. Amasis, the Egyptian king, told Polykrates that fate begrudged its good fortune and that the more good fortune one enjoys, the more catastrophic will be its inevitable reversal. The legend of Polykrates' attempt to fend off this reversal by throwing his signet ring into the sea (the ring later being found in the stomach of a fish he was to eat) is transformed by Chinnov into, "The signet ring swallowed the fish of the royal Greek," ("**Перстень проглотил рыбу царского грека**") where the underlying subject "fish" ("**рыба**") and object "ring" ("**перстень**") are reversed.[19] Confronted by depressing inevitabilities, man's real triumph, or his sole refuge, resides in his capacity to choose the illogical, to produce new creations contrary to the nature of things. "Twice two is seven, not a lot, not a little," ("**Дважды два семь, не много, не мало**") if man but says it is. In Russian literature, appeals to the illogical through the phrase "twice two" are familiar (<u>Notes from the Underground</u> and <u>Rudin</u>, for example). Chinnov, however,

---

[19] This legend was popularized in Russia by Žukovskij in his poem "**Полыкратов перстень**," an 1831 translation of Schiller's "Der Ring des Polykrates"; **Жуковский**, II, 167-69.

has stretched the usual illogical product of twice two from three or five to seven. The phrase "Not a lot, not a little" ("**не много, не мало**") echoes the phrase "more or less" ("**более или менее**") from above in defining vaguely the limits to such inventive distortions of reality. Thus, logic dictates that the sun will be less clear in a fog, so Chinnov states, "The sun is clearer when the sun is in fog" ("**Солнце ясней, когда солнце в тумане**"). The word "clearer" ("**ясней**") is also associated with the expression "twice two" through the saying, "As clear as twice two makes four" ("**Ясно, как дважды два четыре**"), which further emphasizes the illogical nature of this sun image.

The brightness of the imagery is lessened in the final three lines. "The sun is weakening" and the atmosphere is "pale" ("**бледно**") and as "gray" ("**серо**") as the gray wolf above. The verb "to weaken" ("**слабеть**") alliterates significantly with both "sun" ("**солнце**") and "gray" ("**серо**"), and the darkening of the imagery parallels Chinnov's movement from praiseworthy illogicality to its extremity, madness and the grotesque. The source, appropriately enough, is Gogol's "Notes of a Madman", which concludes with the insane, deliriously trivial utterance of the madman, "And do you know that the Algerian Dey has a growth right under his nose?" ("**А знаете ли, что у алжирского дея под самым носом шишка?**").[20] Xlestakov, in Gogol's The Inspector-General, exaggerates phantasmagorically his own importance by mentioning his department employs "in couriers alone thirty-five thousand" ("**трицать пять тысяч одних курьеров**"), a phrase which has since been

---

[20] **Н. В. Гоголь**, <u>**Собрание сочинений**</u> (6 vols.; M.: GIXL, 1959), III, 193.

used to refer to any excessive exaggeration.[21] Chinnov produces surrealistic exaggeration of even more epic proportions by combining the statements and creating an independent Gogolian nose, the lump under whose Dey has been transformed into "thirty-five thousand couriers, and then some" ("**У алжирского носа, под самым деем, тридцать пять тысяч одних курьеров**").

The development in this poem of these familiar themes is clever and original. At the heart of the new harmony of words produced by their mechanical rearrangement and subtle sense and sound associations is the poem's whimsical, surrealistic imagery, which is not bound by reality but preserves enough of it for understanding. Within this madness we can perceive the coherent movement from insanity and delusion to illogicality and madness. Chinnov's basic pessimism is only partially masked by his art.

---

[21] **Гоголь**, IV, 50; see also **Ашукин и Ашукина**, 607, for later uses of this phrase by Leskov and Čexov.

RUSSIAN-TO-ENGLISH HOMOGRAPHS
BY:
ANDREW W. ABBOTT

Andrew W. Abbott was born and raised in Phoenix, Arizona, and graduated from Apollo High School in Glendale, Arizona, in May of 2004. He enrolled at Arizona State University the following semester and will graduate in May of 2009 with concurrent B.A. degrees in Anthropology and Russian. He is a proud member of both the Phi Beta Kappa Honorary Society and ASU's Epsilon Epsilon chapter of the **Добро Слово** National Slavic Studies Honorary. He is athletic and a fine table-tennis player, winning the Russian Language Club's doubles championship with Prof. Croft in Spring 2007. In the Fall semester of 2008 he studied in Moscow and St. Petersburg, Russia, as a participant of the University of Arizona's Russia Abroad program. After graduation he will continue his pursuit to understand the Russian language and culture in an effort to improve U.S.-Russian relations.

PRESENTATION:

This article was originally published by Editor A. Ross Eckler in <u>WORD WAYS: The Journal of Recreational Linguistics</u>, Vol. 8, No. 4 (Fall 1975). This was well before our days of polyalphabetic word-processing on the computer. In 1975 and before, Prof. Croft typed interlineal Russian Cyrillic and English Roman alphabet letters on two separate *Olympia* mechanical typewriters with a shared transferable platen. He mentions several aspects of Russian-to-English homographs' literary significance in the text. But the article has acquired important new significance in the current Internet era. Online scam artists are now able, using interlingually homographic letters like the ones shown here, to construct visually identical, but digitally invisible, 'false fronts' as integral elements of their financial "phishing" schemes. A person seeing on their computer a visibly exact replica of their online bank home page might be surprised to learn that it is not actually their bank's site at all, but differs only by having some of its labeling alphabet letters drawn from another language's (and another ASCI or UNI code) homographic letters...Russian Y (phonetic /u/) instead of English Roman Y, for example. Subsequent police investigators seeking the site by spelling the name of the bank's name entirely in English letters will not find it. They must rely upon a more comprehensive computerized compendium of letter correspondence possibilities, including the interlingual homographic ones.

RUSSIAN-TO-ENGLISH HOMOGRAPHS IN OZHEGOV'S DICTIONARY

BY:

Lee B. Croft
Tempe, Arizona

Most dictionaries define homographs in terms of words taken from the same language, saying nothing about words from two different languages involving partially overlapping alphabets (e.g., the English Latin alphabet and the Russian Cyrillic alphabet). For example, in their Dictionary of Linguistics (Littlefield and Adams, 1969), Mario Pei and Frank Gaynor define homograph as "a word identical in written form with another given word of the same language, but entirely different in origin, sound and meaning". In contrast, this paper, in considered conformance with the etymology of the word from the Greek, defines an interlingual homograph to be one of two or more words, which are identically written regardless of their meanings, derivation, pronunciation, language membership or alphabet constituency.

This non-discriminatory definition enables one to thwart any literary derogation of this kind of study in that it includes the following literary uses of Russian-to-English homographs. The first such usage may be found in the November 1973 Intellectual Digest (pp. 10) in an interview of the Russian poet, Andrei Voznesensky, by Herbert R. Lottman. This interview mentions that, in his collection of experimental visual poetry, **Мага**, Voznesensky presents the English words ECHO WHEN with the Russian words **ТЕСНО МНЕ** ("I feel cramped") lying flat below them as if reflected upward from a pool. The second usage involves the Russian letter '**Н**' (phonetic 'n') which Agatha Christie's detective hero, Hercule Poirot, found embroidered on the corner of a handkerchief in <u>Murder on the Orient Express</u>. At first, of course, this vital clue was disregarded since it was assumed that the letter was an English 'H'. A third, more critical, literary usage of Russian-to-English homography may be found in a scholarly article entitled " 'P' or 'R': Who wrote the <u>Mnemosyne</u> review?" (<u>Russian Literature TriQuarterly</u>, No. 10, pp. 274-278) in which Antonia Glasse mentions the fact that a letter 'Р' written in signature after the review in question could be either Latin 'P' (standing as an initial, perhaps, for 'Pushkin') or Cyrillic '**Р**' (phonetic 'r', standing as an initial for 'Ryleev' or more likely, an abbreviation of 'redaktor', the Russian word for 'editor').

With these literary usages in mind, **С. И. Ожегов**'s 53,000 word **Словарь русского языка** ("<u>Dictionary of the Russian Language</u>" by S. I. Ozhegov), published in Moscow in 1960, was scanned to see if any other Russian-to-English homographs could be found. The first problem was to decide which of the 33 letters of the Russian Cyrillic alphabet would be allowed as homographic. After some sampling, it was decided that **А, В, Е, К, М, Н, О, Р, С, Т, У** and **Х** would be allowed even though some of the lower-case variants differed slightly from those of English. Cursive variants were not considered at all, although there are some cursive variants of Russian letters, which are not allowed in printed form, which would be recognizable to an English reader. Perhaps another study could include cursive homographs as well as printed ones.

In scanning the Russian dictionary, one has to keep in mind not only the form cited, but also the many possible inflectional variations, which may occur. For example, Russian **РОК** (fate) has no English counterpart until one recalls the prepositional case ending **–Е** which then yields **РОКЕ**, and the Russian **СНОСКА** (footnote) has no counterpart unless one uses the genitive plural zero ending which yields **СНОСК**. Also, a word may have more than one counterpart as in the case of the English TOM, which, in Russian, is either prepositional (that) or nominative (volume). In addition, one-letter words are excluded as are Russian words which are homographic with English abbreviations: Russian **НУ** (well), past tense verb **РОС** (he grew), and inflected forms **РТА, РТЕ, РТУ**, of **РОТ** (mouth).

In the following lists, an English translation of each Russian word is given, sometimes with bits of grammatical information. The English meanings of the words are left to the reader who can easily look them up in Webster's. The lists follow the Russian alphabetical order.

АН 'but'　　　　**НА** 'on'　　　　**ОН** 'he'

АУ 'hello, hi'　　**НЕ** 'not'　　　　**ОХ** 'och!'

АХ 'ach!'　　　　**НО** 'but'　　　　**ТО** 'this'

　　　　АРТ 'art'　　　　　**ОНО** 'it'

ВАР 'pitch, wax'　　　　　**РАМ** gen. pl. 'frames'

ВАТ gen. pl. 'weddings'　　**РАН** gen. pl. 'wounds'

BOH 'over there'

BOP 'thief'

BOT 'here is..'

MAK 'poppy'

MAT 'check' (in chess)

MAX 'stroke, blow'

MEX 'fur'

MOP 'pestilence'

MOT 'squanderer'

HAP gen. pl. 'slat bed'

HEM short adj. 'dumb'

HET 'no'

HOC 'nose'

HOT gen. pl. 'notes'

PAC gen. pl. 'races'

POM 'rum'

POT 'mouth'

CAM 'himself'

CEP short adj. 'grey'

COB gen. pl. 'owls'

COM 'small fish'

COP 'litter, trash'

COX gen. pl. 'wooden plows'

TAM 'there'

TAP gen. pl. 'packings'

TOM prep. 'that', 'volume'

TOP gen. pl. 'Torahs (?)'

TOT 'that'

ATOM 'atom'

BATE prep. 'wadding'

BOCK 'wax'

MAKE prep. 'poppy'

MAMA 'mama'

MACK gen. pl. 'masks'

MATE prep. 'check' (in chess)

MOPE 'sea'

МОТЕ prep. 'squanderer'

НАТЕ 'to these'

НОВО short adj. neut. 'new'

РАМЕ prep. 'frame'

РАСА 'race, genotype'

РАСЕ prep. 'race, genotype'

РОКЕ prep. 'fate'

РОМЕ prep. 'rum'

СЕРЕ prep. 'sulphur'

СОКЕ prep. 'juice'

СОКУ dat. 'juice'

СОМА gen. 'small fish'

СОМЕ prep. 'small fish'

СОРЕ prep. 'litter, trash'

СОСК gen. pl. 'nipples'

ТОМЕ prep. 'volume, tome'

ТОСК gen. pl. 'sadnesses'

НАРАХ prep. pl. 'slat beds'

СНОСК gen. pl. 'footnotes'

СОСКУ acc. 'nipple'

ТОТЕМ 'totem'

As it turns out, no homographic Russian verb forms were found despite the likely inflectional endings −**ЕТ** (3rd singular), -**ЕМ** (1st plural), -**ЕТЕ** (2nd plural) and −**УТ** (3rd singular). (Note that the 3rd plural −**АТ** is precluded by the possible range of preceding Russian letters.) There are no legitimate homographs of more than five letters in the list. The English counterpart of the Russian **ТАРТАР** (Tartar) is hyphenated, and Webster's doesn't include the possible (?) English counterparts of **ВЕРЕСК** (heather) or **РЕАКТОР** (reactor). Analogously, there appears to be no Russian counterpart to the English word **PECTATE**, mentioned in the February 1973 Word Ways as the longest English word written entirely with Cyrillic characters. **ATOM**, **MAMA** and **TOTEM** are the only homographs which have the same meaning in both Russian and English.

Megan Plachecki at the Duel Site where Alexander S. Pushkin was mortally wounded, St. Petersburg, 2008.

Reality and Truth in Russian Grammar
By:
Kyle M. Kucharski

Kyle M. Kucharski is a native to Phoenix, Arizona, graduating in 2003 from Pinnacle High School. Kyle came to ASU as a student of Philosophy, adding Russian and East European Studies to his curriculum in 2005. He plans to graduate with B.A. degrees in Philosophy and Russian in addition to the Melikian Center for Russian, Eurasian, and East European Studies' Baccalaureate Interdisciplinary Certificate in Russian and East European Studies. Kyle plans to enter the academic sector at home and abroad, exploring literary translation and critique, philosophy, and linguistics.

PRESENTATION:

A university professor's doctoral dissertation is often reworked into that professor's first important scholarly publication to be considered by colleagues in the evaluation of his or her case for promotion and tenure. This article, derived from Prof. Croft's 1973 Cornell University doctoral dissertation entitled <u>The Semantics of Modality in Russian Syntax</u>," was prepared to be read at a very significant international conference, the *Soviet-American Conference on the Russian Language* (SACRL) that was held in Amherst and Cambridge, Massachusetts, in October of 1974. This conference was the first conference on the Russian Language to unite language, linguistic, and language-pedagogy scholars from both the United States and the Soviet Union…this at a time when the "cold war" between the U.S. and the U.S.S.R. caused deep anxiety in both countries' populations. Being selected to make a scholarly presentation at such an important international conference was a distinct honor for Prof. Croft, who was a twenty-eight-year-old Assistant Professor at still "upstart" Arizona State University. It was, in fact, the first international scholarly conference he had ever attended or witnessed. When he related to his own father, a Montana oilman, how he had addressed several hundred of the world's leading Russian linguists and language experts in Kresge Auditorium at Massachusetts Institute of Technology on his father and mother's anniversary, October 12th (1974), his father said, "Son, look how far you've gotten away from your roots. But you're grazing in the tall grass."

The Russians' scholarly reaction to the SACRL conference papers was published in the main organ of linguistic interest of the Soviet Academy of Science, **Вопросы языкознания** ("Questions of Linguistics," 1975, No. 3, **стр.** 147-152 (**см.** 149)) by the eminent Russian linguists from Moscow's Pushkin Institute of the Russian Language, **П. Н. Денисов** and **В. Г. Костомаров.** Croft remembers talking at the conference with one of these men, Prof. Vitalii G. Kostomarov, one of the authors of the world's most widely used Russian-language text for foreign-language speakers, **Русский язык для всех.** The assessment of Prof. Croft's article was as follows (translation mine…KMK):

"In the report by L. Croft (University of the State of Arizona (*sic*)) the category of modality was analyzed in a contrastive scheme. The author did not use the term 'functional-semantic category' introduced by A. V. Bondarko. L. Croft examines the grammatical category of mood, of modal words (words like **безусловно, небось, мол, дескать, явно,** and others), modal helping elements (modal auxiliaries: **мочь, следовать, нужно, надо,** можно, нельзя, and others) in a single system of functional-semantic (in essence) coordinates."

After the conference, Professor Munir Sendich of Michigan State University, the Editor of <u>Russian Language Journal</u> (<u>RLJ</u>), agreed to publish the entire texts of selected papers from the SACRL conference (others were published in a separate volume, Vol. 19 (1975), Nos. 1 and 2, of <u>Slavic and East European Journal</u> (<u>SEEJ</u>) and subsequently in a separate book entitled <u>Soviet American Russian Language Contributions</u>, Richard D. Brecht and Dan E. Davidson (eds.) AATSEEL by G & G Press, Urbana, IL, 1977). So Prof. Croft worked to prepare a publishable text of his presentation, and this article, published in <u>RLJ</u>, Vol.XXIX (1979), No. 104, pp. 5-24, is the result. It is reprinted here with the permission of the staff of <u>RLJ</u>. The reader here will desirably be able to understand both the English and the Russian in order to understand what Prof. Croft is trying to show: that speakers of both languages add attitudinal content to the basic core of what they say by the use of a wide (and differing) range of grammatical forms that express modality—concern for the basic core content's realizational status (*fictivity*) and its truth value (*factivity*).

THE EXPRESSION OF MODALITY IN ENGLISH AND RUSSIAN: A CONTRASTIVE ANALYSIS

By:

Lee B. Croft
Arizona State University

The concept of modality in grammar has been troublesome both for linguistics and for second-language teachers. Previous works on the subject by both American and Soviet scholars have attested to the frustrating nature of the problem. Arndt, for example, has termed modality "…a grammatical no-man's land…"[22] and Zolotova begins her work on modality emphasizing that "The importance for syntax of the problem of modality is as evident as is evident its insolubility."[23] Calbert, in a case-grammar approach to the problem of modality, writes that what is needed is a "…better understanding of the underlying logical relationships of modality."[24] This "better understanding" is the primary aim of this paper.

---

[22] Walter Arndt, "Modal Particles in Russian and in German," Word, XVI (1960), No. 3, pp. 323. In the interests of compactness, the Russian modal particles (**же, вот, ведь, уж, да, то**...) are not treated here.

[23] **Г. А. Золотова**, "О модальности предложения в русском языке," Научные доклады высшей школы, **Филилогические науки, 4 (1962), стр. 65.** This quote serves as an epigraph to both Crockett (1971—see note 35) and Croft (1973—see note 25).

[24] Joseph P. Calbert, "Modality and Case Grammar," Working Papers in Linguistics, No. 10, (Charles Fillmore, Ed.), Ohio State University, Columbus, 1971, pp. 85.

In order to begin, let it be understood that modality can best be defined as "an attitude toward the content of what is said."[25] This attitude is a qualification on the part of the speaker that expresses either the degree to which he wishes to be held accountable for the truth-value of what he says or the manner in which what he says relates to his conception of reality.

Modality takes in a wide grammatical territory in that it may be expressed by any of several syntactic means. In Russian, for example, one may preface the sentence **"Он пошёл домой"** with a verbal qualification to obtain the less factually reliable **"Я думаю, что он пошёл домой."** Similarly, **"Он пошёл домой"** differs from **"Он наверно пошёл домой"** in that the speaker does not want to be held strictly accountable for its truth. He therefore adds the word **"наверно"** which, although it expresses likelihood, subtracts from the absolute truth-value of what is said. In addition, the speaker can attribute the accountability for the truth-value of what is said to some unspecified other, as in **"Он дескать пошёл домой."**

Truth-value, although a basic consideration, is not the only kind of attitude that can be expressed toward the content of what is said. **"Иди домой!"** and **"Пусть он идёт домой!"** both mean that the speaker views the as-yet unrealized content of what he says as being necessary for some reason, as does **"Он должен пойти домой." "Он**

Calbert's treatment centers on the German modal auxiliaries.

[25] Lee B. Croft, "The Semantics of Modality in Russian Syntax," an unpublished Ph.D. dissertation, Cornell University, Ithaca, New York, 1973. In Part I, I examine the philosophical bases of this definition and reconcile it to those of others.

бы пошёл домой," in any of its interpretations, means that the action expressed in the content is unrealized with respect to some context-specified temporal reference point.

We see then that modality, as it is here defined, may be expressed by many different syntactic means, including certain verbs, verbal auxiliaries, adverbs, and the forms (primarily, in Russian the **"бы"** and the imperative form symbolized here by **"-ай"**) associated with verbal mood.

This paper seeks to establish as basic to the concept of modality the spectral considerations of *Factivity* (concern, either positively or negatively expressed, with truth value) and *Fictivity* (concern, either positively or negatively expressed, with realizational status). With these basic considerations in mind, a more lucid picture of modality may be presented which unites much grammatical phenomena that have previously been regarded as disparate. Specifically, it will be shown that these considerations allow the inclusion into the concept of modality of the recently treated "factive" and "implicative" verbs.[26] Further, these considerations, backed by considerable syntactic evidence, make clear many of the semantic differences between the Russian and English modal auxiliary systems. This

---

[26] These terms are derived largely from Carol and Paul Kiparsky, "Fact," in Semantics: An Interdisciplinary Reader in Philosophy, Linguistics and Psychology, (Danny Steinberg and Leon Jakobovitz, Eds.), Cambridge at the University Press, 1971, pp. 345-70, and from Lauri Karttunen, "Implicative Verbs," Language, 47 (1971), No. 2, pp. 340-58. Also important are the works of Talmy Givon, Lauri Karttunen, and John P. Kimball to be found in John P. Kimball, Ed. Syntax and Semantics, Vol. I (1972) and Vol. II (1973), Seminar Press, New York. The term "implicative" corresponds to my term "Neg-fictive."

clarification, of course, could have desirable pedagogical consequences.

Several previous works have appropriately observed that modality is a deictic phenomenon.[27] This means that the expression of modality refers or points to its expressor, usually at some level other than that upon which the expression takes place. For the most part, these levels refer to the "speech event" and the "narrated event," and the deixis of the modality expressed consists of an obligatory reference from the narrated event to the speech event. Brecht, however, distinguishes two types of deixis. He terms the type of deixis that has referents in the speech event *Exophoric deixis*. The type of deixis that has referents still within the narrated event (largely in hypotactic structures such as embedded sentences) is termed *Endophoric deixis*.[28]

---

[27] Notably Roman Jakobson, <u>Shifters, Verbal Categories and the Russian Verb</u>, Department of Slavic Languages and Literatures, Harvard University, Cambridge, Massachusetts, 1957 (also in <u>Selected Writings</u>, Vol. 2). See also Richard D. Brecht, "Problems of Deixis and Hypotaxis in Russian: Towards a Theory of Complementation," an unpublished Ph.D. dissertation at Harvard University, 1972, and Richard D. Brecht, "Deixis in Embedded Structures," <u>Foundations of Language,</u> 11 (1974), pp. 489-518.

[28] In his dissertation, Brecht (see note 27) uses the term "Anaphoric," but he has since come to use "Endophoric," regarding it as more accurately descriptive. I should mention here that Brecht (by his 1974 article, see note 27), has abandoned the distinction between "speech event" and "narrated event" as formulated here.

A clear example of the difference between these two types of deixis may be shown by considering the tense of the verbs in the embedded sentences:

1. (a) **Милиционер видел, как воры убегают.**

    (Present tense)

    (b) **Милиционер видел, как воры убегали.**

    (Past tense)

Both of these sentences may be rendered into English as "The policeman saw the thieves running away." It is important to notice that the deixis exhibited by the embedded present tense verb of sentence (a) has its point of reference still within the narrated event. That is, the present tense is used because it expresses simultaneity with respect to the event (albeit in the past) expressed by the matrix verb **"видел."** In sentence (b), on the other hand, the tense of the embedded verb is defined with respect to the speech event itself (when the sentence is actually uttered by the speaker), as is the matrix verb. The tense of the embedded verb in sentence (a), then, exhibits endophoric deixis, while the tense of the embedded verb in sentence (b) exhibits exophoric deixis.[29]

One may apply this distinction to modality in a similar manner. Traditionally, mood, as represented in the following examples by the form **"бы,"** is treated as expressing the modality of the speaker (a component of the

---

[29] It is not always the case that endophoric deixis is expressed from hypotactic structures. The "historical present" in independent sentences may be considered endophoric as well since the reference point for the tense is still within the narrated event, as in: "**В 1812 году Наполеон** *пишет* **о своём детстве.**"

speech event). In the following sentence, then, the **"бы"** is said to express "doubt" on the part of the speaker.

2. **Какие собрания, чтобы они не устроили, были отложены.**

Here we see that it is the speaker himself who has doubts about whether any "meetings" were actually "arranged" or not. This sentence, however, is rare in that there is no other participant available except the speaker who is eligible to serve as a referent of the expressed modality. More typical is:

3. (a) **Мать настаивала, что мы украли деньги.**

   (b) **Мать настаивала, чтобы мы украли деньги.**

In this case, the modality expressed in the embedded sentence of (b) is certainly not showing the attitude of the speaker, but of the "mother," a participant of the narrated event. A good test to prove that the modality of an embedded sentence does not have to express the attitude of the speaker is to utilize a clause with a first-person subject, which blatantly contradicts the attitude expressed as:

4. **Николай не думал, чтобы Пётр так хорошо спел арию, но я всё время знал, что он мог петь как соловей.**

Obviously, any "doubt" which is expressed by the **"бы"** in the embedded sentence of (4) must be attributed to a participant other than the speaker (**"я"**) who contradicts that doubt in the same sentence. Thus we see that modality, like tense, may exhibit endophoric as well as exophoric deixis. This is a fact which will become useful in the survey of modality-expressing forms which follows.

It will be shown how the considerations of *Factivity* and *Fictivity* capsulize common semantic strains running through various syntactic ways to express modality. We will begin with a semantic classification of verbs in terms of what they imply with respect to the content of their complements. The first four categories of verbs array themselves along what we might call the "Axis of factivity."

A. "Factive" verbs imply the truth of what is said in their complements relative to the speech event itself. This means that factive verbs exhibit exophoric deixis such as: **знать, помнить, понимать, удивляться, жалеть, забывать, узнавать, сознавать, признавать, радоваться, обижаться,** and others.[30] Consider:

5. **Высокий парень всегда обижался на то, что его прозвали маяком.**

Note that this sentence assumes that, relative to the real world of the person who utters it, the "tall lad" was, in fact, nicknamed "lighthouse."

---

[30] Notice that I use the word "imply" consistently throughout, as opposed to "presuppose." Talmy Givon, in the article "The Time-Axis Phenomenon," Language, 49 (1973), No. 4, pp. 890-925, insightfully distinguishes an "implication" from a "presupposition" by setting up what he calls a "Time-Axis" of verbs. I view the inclusion of these verbs into the concept of modality and the deictic distinction drawn by Brecht (see note 27) as sufficient to explain these phenomena. Also, I include the verb **знать** ("to know") because I don't agree with the Kiparskys (see note 26) that one cannot say "I know the fact that..." Furthermore, this verb meets the other syntactic criteria here examined with respect to **чтобы** complementation.

But these classifications are not merely intuitive in nature. Ideally at least, any semantic trait should have a corresponding syntactic consequence, and, accordingly, each group of these verbs has its own peculiar syntactic characteristics as well. For example, the factive verbs' implications are unaltered by negation. Furthermore, the factive verbs cannot be complemented with **"чтобы"** either in the positive or in the negative, such as:

6.   (a)   **Пётр удивился, что она ему об этом ничего не говорила.**

    (b)   **Пётр не удивился, что она ему об этом ничего не говорила.**

Both sentences (positive a) and (negated b) imply the truth of the statement that "She didn't tell him anything about it." Thus negation does not affect the factivity of the complement. In addition, neither of the following sentences are acceptable [indicated by an asterisk]:

    c)   *****Пётр удивился, чтобы она ему об этом ничего не говорила.**

    d)   *****Пётр не удивился, чтобы она ему об этом ничего не говорила.**

We see that factive verbs are unable to take a complement introduced by **"чтобы."**[31]

---

[31] This type of testing, type of verb, negation and **"чтобы"** complementation is to be credited to Brecht (see note 27). Notice here that the fact that these verbs cannot take a **"чтобы"** complementizer does not mean that **"бы"** is excluded from their complements. This is because, when not attached to the **"что,"** the fictivity that is signalled by the **"бы"** stands in no relation to the matrix verb which, in this case, merely implies the truth of that fictivity, as in: **"Они знают, что я бы написал роман."** This sentence

B. "Factively committal" verbs modify the commitment of the subject of the matrix sentence to the truth-value of the complement. This means that the modality expressed by these verbs exhibits endophoric deixis,[32] as in these verbs: **думать, верить, казаться, чувствовать, подозревать, предполагать, утверждать,** and others. These factively committal verbs are also syntactically homogenous in that they can take a **"чтобы"** complementizer only in the negative as in the following:

7. (a) **Кто думает, что мы заблудились?**

   (b) **Кто не думает, что мы заблудились?**

   (c) **Кто не думает, чтобы мы заблудились?**

   (d) *****Кто думает, чтобы мы заблудились?**

C. "Inverse factively committal" verbs express inverse commitments of the matrix subject to the factivity of their complements. In some sense, they are inherently negative, or at least antonymal to the above group as "to doubt" is the opposite of "to believe." The modality expressed by these verbs exhibits endophoric deixis. They include **сомневаться, бояться,** and **отрицать.** As one might expect, these verbs behave in a fashion opposite to those above syntactically. That is, these inverse factively committal verbs can take a **чтобы** complementizer only when in the positive. Compare the following set of sentences with set 7 above:

---

simply implies the truth of the statement "I would write a novel."

[32] This statement is true unless, of course, the matrix subject is the first-person "I," specifying the identity of the endophoric referent and the exophoric referent. First-person subjects are always tricky when examining questions of deixis.

8.
   (a) **Солдат сомневался, что я мог плавать.**

   (b) **Солдат не сомневался, что я мог плавать.**

   (c) **Солдат сомневался, чтобы я мог плавать.**

   (d) ***Солдат не сомневался, чтобы я мог плавать.**

Also, it is after these inverse factively committal verbs that one is likely to find the "pleonastic '**не**'" in Russian, as in:

9. **Я боялся, чтобы *не* простудиться.**

Because of the discord of the embedded negation with the inverse commitment of the matrix verb, this sentence may be accurately translated into English with a positive embedded verb as "I was afraid that I might catch a cold."

D. "Neg-factive" verbs imply that the content of what is said in their complements is false with respect to the world of the speaker; this means that the modality expressed by these verbs exhibits exophoric deixis. These verbs are: **лгать, врать, сниться, мечтать, вображать, притворяться,** and others. One can, for example see that the following sentence implies the falsity of its complement:

10. **Иван притворяется, что он спит.**

Thus we know that "Ivan" is not really "sleeping." A good syntactic test to make this clearer is the addending of a contradictory clause. The addended clause, contradicting the implication of the matrix neg-factive verb toward its complement, results in unacceptable sentences. Compare:

11.
   (a) **Князь вам солжет, что он был ранен во время войны, но я знаю, что он не был ранен.**

(b) *Князь вам солжет, что он был ранен во время войны, и я знаю, что он был ранен.

"Neg-factive" verbs, like the "factive" verbs described earlier, cannot take a **"чтобы"** complementizer either in the positive or in the negative.

Let us now turn to the verbs, which array themselves along the "Axis of Fictivity." Analogous to the above, four categories follow:

E. "Fictive" verbs imply that the content of what is said in their complements is unrealized with respect to the narrated event of the matrix verb, i.e., that the modality expressed by these verbs exhibits endophoric deixis. These verbs include: **хотеть, желать, намереваться, собираться, стараться, стремиться, предотвращать, советовать, требовать, просить, приказывать, велеть,** and others. They are said to be fictive because in sentences like:

12. (a) **Мы намеревались, чтобы вы стали офицером**

    (b) **Мы намереваемся, чтобы вы стали офицером,**

We know that the action of "you" becoming an "officer" is unrealized with respect to the time (whenever it is, matrix verb tense has no effect) when "we" are doing the intending.

The distinguishing syntactic characteristic of these verbs is that they must, in this meaning, take a **"чтобы"** complementizer whether positive or negative:

13. (a) **Учитель хочет, чтобы ты закончил работу.**

    (b) **Учитель не хочет, чтобы ты закончил работу.**

Other complementizers are not possible, as we see by the clear unacceptability of the following:

14. (a) *Он попросил, что мы с ним путешествовали.

    (b) *Он попросил, как мы с ним путешествовали.

An infinitive complement is, of course, often possible, but we can, without unsettling difficulty, regard these as reduced **"чтобы"** clauses, as in:

15. (a) **Он приказывает, чтобы мы убрали целое здание.**

    (b) **Он приказывает нам убрать целое здание.**

The most important point is to affirm that in each of the acceptable sentences above the content of the complement is unrealized from the point of view of the narrated event specified in the matrix structure.

F. "Fictively committal" verbs modify the commitment of the matrix subject toward the realization of the action expressed in the complement. Specifically, these verbs commit the matrix subject to the non-realization (fictivity) of the content of the complement, as in these verbs: **воспрещать, отговаривать, обескураживать** and others.

G. Inverse fictively committal" verbs modify the commitment of the matrix subject toward the realization of the action expressed in the complement in a manner opposite to that of the above "fictively committal" verbs. That is, these verbs express the commitment of the matrix subject to the realization (neg-fictivity) of the content of the complement, as in: **разрешать, позволять, ободрять,** and others.

H.   "Neg-fictive" verbs are verbs which, when expressing realized actions themselves, imply that the action expressed in their complements is already realized with respect to the speech event. In this syntactic environment, then, these verbs express modality of exophoric deixis. These verbs are: **заставлять, успевать, удаваться,** and others.

To make the implied realization of the complement expressed by these verbs more clear, we can compare the acceptability of contradictory clauses after these verbs which only express a commitment toward the fictivity of the complement. Thus, while it is possible to say:

16.   (a)   **Я ей воспретил курить, но она всё-таки курила,**

   (b)   **Да, они разрешают мне курить, но я не хочу,**

One cannot say:

   (c)   ***Я заставил её не курить, но она всё-таки курила.**

This is because the verb **заставлять** ("to force") implies that the action of "her" not "smoking" is already realized with respect to the speech event. One cannot acceptably contradict this implication by saying that "she" smoked anyway.

When, however, these verbs express an action which is itself unrealized or "fictive" with respect to the speech event (as would be the case when they are found in the future tense or are themselves marked with "**бы**"), then the implication of realization with respect to the speech event no longer holds. Consider:

17.   (a)   **Он бы заставил меня дать ему деньги.**

   (b)   **Он заставит меня ему деньги.**

Neither of these sentences implies the realization of the action of "me" giving "him" any "money."[33]

II

Another way in which modality may be expressed in a sentence is the "modal words." The verb classification must, however, be kept in mind since the verb classes are involved in the syntactic characterization of these modal words to come.

"Modal words" comprise a semantic subset of the "sentence adverbs" and are here divided into two groups:

1. "Factive" modal words express degrees of commitment as to the truth-value of the sentence or clause in which they are found. Factive modal words include: "**безусловно, небось, наверно(е), возможно, несомненно, может быть, должно быть, вряд ли, мол, конечно, пожалуй, видимо, очевидно, дескать, естественно, по-видимому, явно,** and others."[34]

---

[33] One speculates here that futurity itself may be just a subclass of fictivity. We see, for example, that the future tense can be used to express such fictivity projected into complements after such problematic verbs as **надеяться** ("to hope") and we note that some scholars include futurity as a "modal operator." (see Ray Jackendoff, <u>Semantic Interpretation in Generative Grammar,</u> M.I.T. Press, Cambridge, Massachusetts, 1972, pp. 295).

[34] The word "word" is, perhaps, loosely used here, since some of these "modal words" consist of more than one "word." They do, however, as "**вводные слова**" ("interjected words") function as one syntactic unit.

2. "Fictive" modal words express degrees of commitment as to the realization of the action expressed in the sentence or clause in which they are found. They are: **обязательно, необходимо, непременно, действительно, разве, на самом деле, неужели,** and others.

Crockett argues on syntactic grounds that the modal words must be regarded as a separate part of speech. She differentiates them from manner adverbs and from short-form adjectives which they resemble. The resemblance is such, in fact, that ambiguities occur as:[35]

18.   **Они безусловно сдадутся китайцам.**

This sentence can either be translated as "They will surrender unconditionally to the Chinese," in which case **"безусловно"** is interpreted as a manner adverb, or it may be translated as "They will certainly surrender to the Chinese," in which case is **"безусловно"** interpreted as a modal word. Crockett's argument that modal words should be considered a separate part of speech includes the following characteristics of modal words as opposed to manner adverbs:

1. Verb phrases containing a manner adverb cannot be expanded by an additional manner adverb except by conjunction.

19.   (a)   **Вера говорила громко.**

---

[35] Dina B. Crockett, "Modal Words in Russian," <u>International Journal of Slavic Linguistics and Poetics</u>, XIV (1971), 53-62. This article is the real key to my thinking through this part of the paper. Even though I repeat many of Crockett's syntactic characterizations here (the examples, of course, are mine), I don't necessarily believe that modal words must be considered a separate part of speech.

(b) **Вера говорила громко и быстро.**

(c) ***Вера говорила громко быстро.**

However, verb phrases containing a manner adverb can be expanded by a modal word without conjunction.

(d) **Вера говорила несомненно громко.**

And, further, modal words cannot be conjoined.

(e) ***Очевидно и несомненно Вера говорила громко.**

2. Verb phrases with a manner adverb may be expanded by another "attributive" adverb, whereas modal words may not be:

20. (a) **Вера говорила слишком громко.**

(b) ***Вера слишком несомненно говорила громко.**

3. A manner adverb may be part of a nominalization, whereas a modal word may not be. Consider the nominalization of the ambiguous sentence (18) above:

21. **Их безусловная сдача китайцам...**

This nominalization can *not* be translated as "*Their certain surrender to the Chinese...." The interpretation of sentence 18 in which "**безусловно**" is considered a modal word cannot be properly nominalized.

It is also important to clarify how "factive" modal words are differentiated from "fictive" modal words and how the modal words relate to the verb classifications given earlier. Here also we will see that modal words may express modality of either exophoric or endophoris deixis.

Brecht has shown that the question of deixis stemming from the modal words is an important one.[36] In independent sentences, the deixis is always exophoric, for it

---

[36] See Brecht (above note 27), pp. 509-511.

is the speaker himself whose attitude is expressed. In hypotactic structures, however, the situation is more complex. First, in a sentence embedded after a fictive verb, only modal words that express fictivity can occur. This, of course, is what one would expect. Therefore, while one can say:

22. (a) **Он хотел, чтобы вы обязательно прочитали эту книгу,**

one cannot grammatically say:

(b) ***Он хотел, чтобы вы безусловно, наверно,... явно...очевидно...прочитали эту книгу.**

This is good evidence to support the semantic classification of the verbs involved. Notice, however, that the deixis of the modality expressed in the complement of sentence (22 (a)) is endophoric because it is the attitude of the subject of the matrix sentence which is expressed. After a factive verb, which implies the truth of its complement relative to the speaker, the deixis of modality expressed by a modal word is always exophoric, as in:

23. (a) **Борис понимает, что она вероятно выйдет замуж за моряка.**

(b) **Не помнишь ли, что он по-видимому умер от голода?**

This again is what one would expect, that the deixis of the modality expressed by the modal words which are admitted to an embedded sentence would be the same as the deixis of the modality already projected into the complement by the matrix verb. It is only after those verbs which only express a degree of commitment to the factivity of their complements (see sentences 7-10) that deictic ambiguities arise. Consider:

24. **Андрей верит, что Елена несомненно удавит блондинку.**

The modal word in the complement of this sentence ("**несомненно**," meaning "undoubtedly") can mean either that "I" (the speaker) regard the strangulation of the blonde as being "undoubted" and that "**Андрей**" believes that what I think is true, OR it can mean that "**Андрей**" himself regards the strangulation of the blonde as being undoubted whether "I" think so or not. This latter interpretation is verified by the grammatical acceptability of:

25. **Андрей верит, что Елена несомненно удавит блондинку, но я не так думаю.**

III

And in this section we shall examine the "modal auxiliaries." There are few problems in language learning that have given English-speaking students of Russian more trouble than that of translating the English modal auxiliaries into Russian. And, judging by **Зверева, и др.**, the problem is equally as thorny for Russian-speaking students of English.[37] We seek here to explain the reason for this

---

[37] **Е. А. Зверева, О. Н. Труевцева, и Н. С. Шукарева, Модальные глаголы в английском языке, Издательство "Наука" Ленинград, 1967.** This work includes a long list of tables giving the alleged correlation between the English and Russian modal auxiliaries and their meanings. The authors include as modal auxiliaries some of what I refer to here as modal words and include so many forms in each category of meaning that no precise correlation can be deduced.

difficulty. Also, of course, we want to kow just where these modal auxiliaries in Russian (contextual variants of: **должен, мочь, нужно, надо, можно,** and **нельзя**) fit into the picture of modality and how it is grammatically expressed.

Twaddell writes about the English "Modal Auxiliary System" that:

"There are four paired modals and four unpaired ones:

can   may   shall   will
                                  dare   must   need   ought
could might should would

The pairing consists in the relationship of *non-reality* and sequences-of-tenses with /*could/might/should/would*.... Thus modals fall formally into a major class *can-could, may-might, shall-should, will-would,* and a minor class *dare, must, need,* and *ought.*"[38]

We will be concerned here with the "non-past" forms of Twaddell's "major class" plus the word "must" as a representative of the "minor class." Generalizations drawn on these forms can easily be applied to others, even though the relationships between the pairs and even the elements of each pair are more complicated than they might at first appear (e.g. "should" is, in many contexts, not really a semantic pair with "shall" and the pair "can-could" appears to be annexing a major context of usage from "may-might").

Several scholars have observed that these English modal auxiliaries fall into two distinct semantic categories termed

---

[38] William Freeman Twaddell, <u>The English Verb Auxiliaries</u>, Brown University Press, Providence, Rhode Island, 1960, pp. 10.

the *root* as opposed to the *epistemic* modal auxiliaries.[39] There is a systematic ambiguity built into the English system along the lines of this distinction. This ambiguity may be represented by the following table:

Root	*Epistemic*
Must (necessity)	*Must* (logical entailment)
Can (ability)	*Can* (possibility)
May (permission)	*May* (possibility)
Shall (intention)	*Shall* (future prediction)
Will (volition)	*Will* (future prediction)

Sentences, then, such as the following, are ambiguous:

26. (a) Harry *must* jump from the airplane.

    1) necessity (*Root*)—he has to.

    2) logical entailment (*Epistemic*)—it appears so.

  (b) Harriet *may* be a prostitute.

    1) permission (*Root*)—is allowed to.

    2) possibility (*Epistemic*)—it is possibly the case.

---

[39] This distinction in these terms can be traced back to T. R. Hofman, "Past Tense Replacement and the Modal System," <u>Mathematical Linguistics and Automatic Translation Report</u>, No. NSF-17, Harvard Computation Laboratory, Cambridge, Massachusetts, 1966. See also F. Newmayer, "The 'Root' Modal: Can it be Transitive?" in <u>Studies Presented to Robert B. Lees by his Students</u>, (Jerry Sadock and Anthony L. Vanek, Eds.), Linguistic Research Inc., Edmonton, Alberta, 1970, pp. 189-97.

(c) Junior *won't* go to bed on time.

    1) volition (*Root*)—refuses to.

    2) future prediction (*Epistemic*)—I don't think he will.

Jenkins differentiates the two categories syntactically by the following properties:[40]

1. The epistemic modal (but not the root modal) may co-occur with progressive and perfective verbs:

27. (a) He *may* be reading now.

    *1) permission (Root)

    2) possibility (Epistemic)

(b) The butler *must* have done it.

    *1) necessity (Root)

    2) logical entailment (Epistemic)

2. The epistemic modals (but not the root modals) are excluded from conditional clauses. This is similar, of course, to the factive words being excluded from the complements of fictive verbs (see sentences 22 (a) and (b) above). Consider:

28. If you *must* get away, I'll buy you a ticket to Ouagadougou.

    1) necessity (Root)

    *2) logical entailment (Epistemic)

---

[40] Lyle Jenkins, "Modality in English Syntax," Ph.D. dissertation, Massachusetts Institute of Technology, Cambridge, Massachusetts, 1972, published by the Indiana University Linguistics Club in mimeo, see pp. 26.

By now it *should* be obvious that the epistemic modals are expressing degrees of factivity, and the root modals are expressing degrees of fictivity. In essence, the argument runs like this: what one must/can/may/shall/will do (interpreted as root modals—see table above), one has necessarily not done yet. This is fictivity. All the interpretations in the epistemic column in the table above infer something about the truth-value of the statement in which they are found. This, of course, is factivity.

In Russian, the "Modal auxiliaries" (**должен, мочь, нужно, надо, можно, нельзя**) correspond semantically only to the root or "fictive" modals in English.[41] This fact is the very core of great pedagogical difficulty in teaching these Russian modal auxiliaries to English-speaking students. The syntactic correlation between the English and Russian modal auxiliary systems should not be construed as implying a corresponding semantic correlation as well. The English epistemic or "factive" modals must be rendered into Russian by other grammatical means entirely, specifically by the modal words treated earlier. Consider:

29. (a) Vera *must* swim the river.

    1) necessity (Root-Fictive)—or else she'll drown.

---

[41] First of all, it should be noted that there may be no syntactic correlation between the English and Russian modal auxiliaries, (see Catherine V. Chvany, "Deep Structures with Dolžen and Moč'," an unpublished Harvard University Ph.D. dissertation, Cambridge, Massachusetts, 1970). Secondly, it may be the case that "**должен**" does have an epistemic usage, though one must be very careful in differentiating "**должен был**" from "**должен был бы**" that one does not become confused by the fact that English does not lexically (with "should") differentiate between a past obligation and past obligation that implies fictivity.

2) logical entailment (Epistemic-Factive)—at least we see her all wet on this side every day.

(b) Natasha *can* be a good teacher.

1) ability (Root-Fictive)—she is able to be.

2) possibility (Epistemic-Factive)—is likely to be.

As mentioned by Crockett, when these sentences are translated into Russian by means of the syntactically corresponding modal auxiliaries, only the root or fictive interpretation is possible:[42]

30. (a) **Вера** *должна* **переплыть через реку.**

1) necessity (Root-Fictive)

*2) logical entailment (Epistemic-Factive)

(b) **Наташа** *может* **быть хорошей учительницей.**

1) ability (Root-Fictive)

*2) possibility (Epistemic-Factive)

If one wants to get the epistemic or factive interpretation, one must resort to the modal words, as in:

31. (a) **Вера,** *должно быть,* **перепывает через реку.**

*1) necessity (Root-Fictive)

2) logical entailment (Epistemic-Factive)

(b) **Наташа,** *может быть,* **хорошая учительница.**

*1) ability (Root-Fictive)

2) possibility (Epistemic-Factive)

---

[42] See Crockett (note 35 above), pp. 55.

In sentence (31 (b)) above, the intonation and the only marginal possibility of getting an instrumental case form in the predicate indicate that "может быть" is, in this instance, a modal word to be taken as a unit and not a modal auxiliary plus the verb "быть" as in sentence (30 (b)) above.

IV

We turn now to look briefly at "Mood" in Russian. In the scholarship on modality there have been many previous attempts to subcategorize extensively the semantics of mood.[43] In this paper we shall examine only what seems to

---

[43] For example, Jakobson (see note 27 above) and Zbigniew Gołab, "The Problem of Verbal Moods in Slavic Languages," <u>International Journal of Slavic Linguistics and Poetics</u>, VIII (1964), pp. 322-361 and Oldřich Leška, "Formální a Funkčně Obsahová Struktura Ruského Imperativu (Injunktivu)," <u>Kapitoly ze Srovnávací Mluvnica Ruske a České,</u> (A. V. Isačenko, red.), III, Akademia Praha, 1968, str. 7-50. I discuss these subcategorizations in Part I of my dissertation (see note 25 above). A key work here is L. Durovič, <u>Modálnost: Lexikálno-syntaktické jadrovanie modálnych a hodnotiacich vztahov v slovenčine a ruštine</u>, Bratislava, 1956. This work has touched off some interesting debates led by Knut-Olof Falk in <u>Sprakliga Bidrag</u>, Lund, Vol. 6 (1971) and Vol. 7 (1972). See also P. Adamec, "Identifikace sémantiky modálnich sloves a jejich ekvivalentu v současné ruštině," in <u>Československé přednašky pro VII mezinárodní sjezd slavistů,</u> 1973, str.

be the primary opposition in the semantics of mood, and that, of course, is the one of factivity versus fictivity.

The indicative, or unmarked mood in Russian (as well as English), has an underlying assumption of factivity. This means that you are to regard what one says to you, unless specifically marked otherwise, as the truth. The marked or non-indicative moods both have a basic meaning (*"Gesamtbedeutung"*) of fictivity. These moods in Russian involve primarily the form "**бы,**" associated traditionally with "Conditional" (or "Subjunctive") meanings, and the imperative form of the verb (here symbolized by "**-ай**") associated with "Injunctive" meanings.[44] An examination of the uses of these forms will show that each may be used in contexts traditionally reserved for the other. That is, "**бы**" may be used to express injunctive meanings and "**-ай**"

103-115 and the review thereof by A. V. Isačenko in <u>Russian Linguistics</u>, I (1974), No. 1, pp. 83-4.

[44] The term "Injunctive mood" is meant to be a translation (first used by Roman Jakobson, I understand) of the Russian "**Повелительное наклонение**." The term "Imperative" refers here only to the form and not the meaning. There has been a troublesome terminological problem in the previous scholarship here in that "sentence types" have been listed as: declarative, interrogative, exclamative, and *imperative*; and "moods" have been listed as: indicative, subjunctive, *imperative*, and etc. Indeed, scholars have not even been in agreement as to what is what ("sentence type" or "mood" and are they both "modality?"). I discuss this problem further in my dissertation also (see note 25 above), pp. 7-9 and 47-59. See also: Kazimierz Polánski, "Sentence Modality and Verbal Modality in Generative Grammar," <u>Biuletyn Fonograficzny</u>, Poznan, X (1969), 91-100.

may be used to express subjunctive meanings, as in the following:

32. "**бы**" in injunctive meanings:

>   (a) **Заночевал бы, завтра пообедал бы!**
>   **(Мельников)**
>
>   (b) **Вы бы, доктор, шли спать. (Чехов)**

"**-ай**" in subjunctive meanings:

>   (c) *Явись* **перед ними умерший в прошлом году экзекутор...и** *дыхни* **он на них холодом могилы, оне не побледнели бы так, как побледнели, узнав Пересолина. (Чехов)**
>
>   (d) **Да** *накупи* **я всех этих, которые умерли...**
>   *Приобрети* **их, положим, тысячу...**
>   **Вот уже двести тысяч капиталу. (Гоголь)**

Furthermore, the "**бы**" is always used to signal the fictivity of marked mood in Russian (even *all* the injunctive meanings) when found in hypotactic structures. This means that when one embeds an imperative (as in reported speech) a "**бы**" is obtained, as in:

33. (a) **Делайте как вам велено!**

>   (b) **Я сказал, чтобы вы делали как вам велено.**

The fact that each form may, and in certain contexts must, be used to express meanings strongly identified with the other indicates that these forms do indeed share a basic element of meaning. That basic element is that which is here termed fictivity.[45]

---

[45] All the uses of both of these forms can easily be viewed as expressing "fictivity" except for the "Dramatic imperative"

Since there are no separate specific forms to express injunctive meanings in English, the modal auxiliaries are the primary forms that we associate with marked mood. As we have seen, because of the systematic ambiguity expressed by these auxiliaries, English marked mood embodies both the considerations of factivity and fictivity. The Russian modal auxiliaries, on the other hand, express only fictivity, but have little to do with what we regard as mood in any case. Marked mood is expressed in Russian by different forms entirely ("**бы**" and "**-ай**") but, even so, only fictivity is involved. Thus, there is no exact semantic or syntactic correlation between what is regarded as mood in English and what is regarded as mood in Russian. And yet, with the Russian modal words and the verbs of both languages considered, the same semantic axes of factivity and fictivity can be shown to underlie an equally varied total expression of modality in both languages.[46]

(see **А. В. Исаченко**, "К вопросу об императиве в русском языке," <u>Русский язык в школе</u>, 6 (1957), стр. 7-14), as in "**Мы с ним давно распрощались, а он и** *вернись*!" In this case, the "**-ай**" form expresses a past, real action of no present relevance and "fictivity" is hard to see. It is possible, however, that this form is really either an aorist remnant or a modern form analogous to it.

[46] I would like to give credit to Richard D. Brecht of Harvard for his scholarship and aid concerning deixis and factive verbs, Dina Crockett of Stanford for her previous article on "Modal Words," and to Lyle Jenkins for his M.I.T. dissertation on the English "Modal Auxiliaries." All shortcomings are, of course, my own. This paper was supported by Arizona State University Faculty Research Grant No. 980254 (1974).

Hayden L. Croft at the controls of a Russian TU-154 Airliner in Moscow's Aircraft Museum, 2002

An Early International Example of Cinema's Influence on Literature
By:
Shamella Tribble

Interviewed at work, Shamella Tribble gave the following first-person statement: "I am originally from Queens, New York. I used to dream about traveling around the world and learning all I can from different countries. I joined the U. S. Air Force in an effort to see that world I dreamed about as a child. I lived in Japan and Saudi Arabia. I have visited the United Kingdom, France, Mexico, and other countries. When I came back to the United States, I decided to go to the university. I decided to study Russian because I wanted to challenge myself. I loved the language and culture so much that I decided to make Russian my major. For a Fall 2005 ASU Sun Angel Undergraduate

Research proposal, Prof. Croft and I did research on the role of Russian scholars in the decipherment of "Rapa Nui Hieroglyphics" (Easter Island…see www.rongorongo.org), partnering to create a presentation of this work at the Arizona State AATSEEL convention in Tucson in April of 2006. After this, I applied for and won Gilman scholarship support to study for two semesters with the University of Arizona Russian Abroad program at the GRINT academic center in Moscow. I loved my time spent in Russia. I got a chance to see a culture almost completely opposite from my own. There were of course some great times and definitely some that made me aware that the world around me is not so welcoming. I am taking my experiences from Russia and using it to obtain a job that will allow me to work internationally. I hope eventually to help build relationships between the United States and the world that surrounds us. I hope to finish my education in December. I am very excited to see what the world has in store for me."

PRESENTATION:

Prof. Croft says that he first heard of Yurii Karlovich Olesha (**Юрий Карлович Олеша** (1899-1960)) and his 1927 novel Envy (Russian **Зависть**) and its derivative 1929 play Conspiracy of Feelings (Russian **Заговор чувств**) from Prof. Nicholas "Nick" Vontsolos while Croft was a graduate teaching assistant in the Russian M.A. program at the University of Arizona in 1969. Like many others, Croft admired the novel's striking imagery and its ornamental literary art while being intrigued by its symbolic treatment of a sensitive human being caught up in the "new requirements" of Soviet reality. When he took a course in

Soviet literature later from Prof. George Gibian at Cornell University in 1971, he decided to write his term paper on "Cinematic Aspects of Olesha's Envy" and, in discussion with classmates like Elaine Cohen Libit (who later wrote a Master's thesis on "circus themes" in Olesha's writing) focused his attention on the influence of Charlie Chaplin's early silent movies. In the summer of 1972, Croft went to the Soviet Union with the American Institute for Foreign Study (AIFS) under the deanship of Col. James Wilmeth of the University of Texas at Arlington. Wilmeth introduced him to Prof. Liudmila Koehler from the University of Pittsburgh, and it was through Prof. Koehler that Croft met O. Yakubovich, a vice-director of the Moscow central office of Gosfilmofond, the primary repository of Soviet films. Yakubovich later showed Prof. Croft unprecedented cooperation in giving him a list of Charlie Chaplin's films and the dates of their release in Russia. This list is given in the article's footnote 49. Just this data from such an authoritative Soviet source represented valuable information for other western scholars at the time.

Prof. Croft led groups of ASU students to Russia under the auspices of the AIFS in 1976 and, as overall program Dean, in 1977. He attended classes of the Intourist Summer Program of the Russian Language and Soviet Culture and made a presentation on Charlie Chaplin's influence on Yuri Olesha's Envy to a senior group studying with Emin Byul-Byulevich Mamedov, a talented and charismatic instructor. It was Mamedov who encouraged Prof. Croft to "write it up and submit it for publication." So, upon his fall 1977 return to ASU, he did this, adding the Gosfilmofond data to the text of his 1971 Cornell University term paper. Prof. Croft submitted the paper to Prof. Thurman B. O'Daniel of Morgan State University, Editor of the CLA Journal (The Official Quarterly Publication of the College Language

Association), a place where he had published earlier a review of a work on the "language of the oilfields." Editor O'Daniel quickly informed Prof. Croft that the article would be published without amendation, and it was, in Vol. XXI, No. 4, from June 1978. Later, Prof. Croft published another article in this journal, an article on "Spontaneous Human Combustion" in literature (see the later article on this from yet another place by Jon Harris), and another review, on a collection of "Émigré Russian Poetry." For years, ASU Prof. Rolfs Ekmanis, who taught the RUS-323 Survey of Soviet Literature course, would distribute copies of Croft's <u>CLA Journal</u> article on "Charlie Chaplin and Olesha's <u>Envy</u>" as the students' introduction to literary scholarship on a work (<u>Envy</u>) they were required to read.

Since its publication in 1978, Prof. Croft's article has often been cited by others. The E-notes have even devised an "E-anthology" of Croft's article and 18 other articles by 17 other prominent scholars on Olesha and/or <u>Envy</u> that is available online at: www.enotes.com/twentieth-century-criticism/olesha-yuri/lee-b-croft-essay-date-1978. There is further information online about Yurii Karlovich Olesha at http://en.wikipedia.org/wiki/yury_olesha and at www.kirjasto.sci.fi/olesha.htm. And, Prof. Croft provides an abstract of <u>Envy</u> at www.shvoong.com/books/classic-literature/1728626-envy/ The article is republished here with the permission of Editor Cason Hill and staff of the <u>CLA Journal</u>:

CHARLIE CHAPLIN AND OLESHA'S ENVY[47]
By:
Lee B. Croft

In the history of literature and cinema it may easily be said that the usual course of influence proceeded from the former to the latter. That is, literary texts rapidly provided a source of material for the burgeoning cinema industry. But finding early instances where cinematic productions had a noticeable influence on literature is more difficult. In the Soviet Union, however, where cinema was taken very seriously as an artistic medium even in the embryonic stages of its development, such an instance does exist. A clearly demonstrable example of this influence is to be found in Yuri Olesha's Envy, one of the most significantly artistic novels of the 'twenties.[48] In theme, plot, and especially in characterization, this novel was influenced by the cinematic portrayals of Charlie Chaplin.

The external evidence for such an influence is all there. We know, for example, that Olesha had ample opportunity to view the films of Chaplin during the period in Moscow

---

[47] The author would like to acknowledge the aid and inspiration of Prof. George Gibian of Cornell University, Elaine Cohen Libit (for her M.A. thesis, The Circus Theme in the Writings of Yurii Olesha, Cornell University, 1971), and Mona Deutsch.

[48] There have been several English translations of Envy (Зависть): Anthony Wolfe (London: Hogarth, 1936), P. Ross (London: John Westhouse, 1947), Andrew R. MacAndrew (Garden City: Doubleday, 1967), and T. S. Berczynski (Ann Arbor: Ardis, 1975) which is the translation used here.

when he was writing his novel. These films, of course, were silent and thus transcend the language barrier solely by their profound visual impact. Gosfilmofond, the Soviet government's organization for cinematography, lists 34 Chaplin films which were shown in Moscow from 1917 until the 1927 publication of <u>Envy</u>.[49] These films were very popular not only with the masses, but with the literary intelligentsia and even with the governmental cultural authorities. Victor Shklovsky, the prominent formalist literary critic, frequently praised Chaplin's films in the press. He wrote a critical work on Chaplin, which was published in Berlin in 1923 and maintained a correspondence with Chaplin himself.[50] The very influential Soviet minister of

---

[49] A personal communication from O. Yakubovich (**О. Якубович**), vice director of Gosfilmofond (October 1973), lists these Chaplin films by the date of their first showing in the Soviet Union: (1917) <u>The Champ</u>; (1918) <u>Between Showers</u>; (1920) <u>The Bank</u>; (1923) <u>Woman</u>, <u>Mabel at the Wheel</u>, and <u>The Tramp</u>; (1924) <u>Making a Living</u>, <u>His Favorite Pastime</u>, <u>The New Janitor</u>, <u>The Fatal Mallet</u>, <u>His New Profession</u>, <u>Her Friend the Bandit</u>, <u>His Trysting Place</u>, <u>Tango Tangles</u>, <u>Knockout</u>, <u>Dough and Dynamite</u>, <u>Property Man</u>, <u>Those Love Pangs</u>, <u>His Prehistoric Past</u>, <u>Triple Trouble</u>, <u>The Masquerader</u>, <u>Caught in the Rain</u>, <u>Face on the Bar-room Floor</u>, <u>The Kid</u>, <u>Carmen</u>, <u>Mabel's Busy Day</u>, <u>Cruel, Cruel Love</u>, and <u>Twenty Minutes of Love</u>; (1925) <u>Laughing Gas</u>, <u>The Rounders</u>, <u>Mabel's Predicament</u>, <u>A Woman of Paris</u>, and <u>Tillie's Punctured Romance</u>; (1926) <u>Sunnyside</u>. The dates in the article proper, however, refer to the initial production dates of the films mentioned.

[50] **Виктор Шкловский, <u>Чаплин</u>, Берлин: Издательство журнала <u>Кино</u>, 1923.** This correspondence, as one might guess, caused Chaplin some trouble later when his politics

culture, Anatoly Lunacharsky, in a 1927 Evening Moscow article termed Chaplin, "one of the greatest artists of world cinema" in the course of upbraiding American women for their support of a campaign to anathematize Chaplin during a scandalous lawsuit brought by his mother-in-law.[51] Thus it was both intellectually and politically permissable for Olesha to draw upon Chaplin's comedy as a source of influence.

Olesha's fascination with Chaplin's comedy is also subsequently evident in his autobiographical work, Not a Day Without a Line (**Ни дня без строчки,** 1965), in which he terms the "theme of the solitary man's fate" the "theme of Chaplin."[52] In the one version of Olesha's play, A List of Assets (**Список благодеяний,** 1931), there is a character described in the *dramatis personae* as "a little man looking like Charlie Chaplin."[53] And in 1936 Olesha wrote an article entitled "Thoughts about Chaplin" ("**Мысли о Чаплине**"), in which he stated that the appeal of Chaplin's films is due to the "fascinating qualities of the soul of Chaplin himself."[54]

The name of Charlie Chaplin has appeared with significant frequency in the previous scholarship on

---

came under suspicion in the anti-communist-conscious United States in the 'fifties.

[51] **Луначарский о кино,** Москва: Издательство Искусство, 1965, стр. 73-4.

[52] **Лев Левин,** Знакомые темы, Ленинград:Гослитиздат, 1936, стр. 78.

[53] **Юрий Олеша, Избранные произведения,** Москва: Государственное издательство художественной литературы, 1956.

[54] **Там же** (ibid)**, стр. 436.**

Olesha's work. Critics, both Soviet and Western, have long perceived that Chaplin was a source of Olesha's inspiration and a catalyst to his already fertile imagination. The Soviet constructivist critic, Kornelii Zelinsky (**Корнелий Зелинский**), in his <u>Critical Writings</u> (1932), wrote that "the main and, in fact, solitary theme of Olesha is the Chaplinesque."[55] Lev Levin, in his critical work, *On Familiar Themes* (1936), stated that "for Olesha the theme of the unemployed worker is tantamount to the theme of Chaplin."[56] Gleb Struve, in <u>Soviet Russian Literature</u> (1951), mentioned Olesha's interest in Chaplin, and Vyacheslav Zavalishin, in <u>Early Soviet Writers</u> (1958), wrote: "The hero of <u>Envy</u>, Nikolai Kavalerov, is an odd mixture of the Chekhovian intellectual and the sad tramp of American movies. No wonder that Igor Ilinsky, the Russian counterpart of Chaplin, wanted to act the part of Kavalerov on the screen."[57] Marc Slonim, in <u>Soviet Russian Literature: Writers and Problems</u> (1964), noted Olesha's "evocation of Hamlet and Charlie Chaplin, symbols of inner dispute and of the common man's plight."[58] In his book, <u>The Russian Novel</u> (1966), F. D. Reeve wrote: " Olesha admired Chaplin's films for the contrast they dramatized between the

---

[55]**Корнелий Зелинский,** <u>**Критические письма,**</u> **Москва, 1932, стр. 88.**

[56] **Лев Левин, там же** (op. cit.), **стр. 82**

[57] Vyacheslav Zavalishin, <u>Early Soviet Writers</u>, (New York: Frederick Praeger and Co., 1958), pp. 299. See also Gleb Struve, <u>Soviet Russian Literature</u>, (Norman: University of Oklahoma Press, 1951), p. 106.

[58] Marc Slonim, <u>Soviet Russian Literature: Writers and Problems</u>, (New York: Oxford University Press, 1964), p. 275

old values and the new requirements."⁵⁹ William E. Harkins, in his insightful article, "The Theme of Sterility in Olesha's Envy" (1966), mentioned the obvious similarities of appearance between Chaplin's little tramp and Olesha's character, Ivan Babichev.⁶⁰ Robert Payne (also the author of a critical study of Chaplin), in his "Foreword" to "Love" and Other Stories by Olesha (1967), wrote that Olesha "had a special reverence, amounting almost to adoration, for Charlie Chaplin."⁶¹ These critics, however, have always mentioned Chaplin's influence as a matter peripheral to some other scholarly focus. The specific nature of this influence has never been examined.

A brief plot summary shows Kavalerov, the hero of Olesha's Envy, caught up in the rivalry of two brothers. Andrei Babichev, a Soviet bureaucrat prominent for this founding of the "two-bit" food institution, beneficently takes Kavalerov into his apartment after finding him lying in the street, but only as a temporary affection surrogate for Andrei's absent ward, the soccer player Volodya Makarov. Ivan Babichev is a dreamer who claims to have invented an

---

[59] F. D. Reeve, The Russian Novel, (New York: McGraw Hill Co., 1966), p. 347.

[60] William E. Harkins, "The Theme of Sterility in Olesha's Envy," Slavic Review, XXV, No. 3 (1966), pp. 443-57, and reprinted in Edward J. Brown (ed.) Major Soviet Writers: Essays in Criticism, (New York: Oxford University Press, 1973), see p. 290.

[61] Yuri Olesha, "Love" and Other Stories, (translated and with foreword by Robert Payne), (New York: Washington Square Press, 1967), p. xx. See also Robert Payne, The Great God Pan: A Biography of the Tramp Played by Charles Chaplin, (New York: Hermitage House, 1964), which includes plot summaries of Chaplin's films.

anti-machine machine named "Ophelia" with which he will try to kindle in the world a "conspiracy of human feelings" against the impersonal technocracy represented by his brother. Andrei lays claim to the beautiful Valya, Ivan's daughter, through her involvement with Volodya. Ivan, in turn, enlists Kavalerov, who also falls in love with Valya, into his effort to win his daughter back to the personal values of a former world. The effort fails, however, as "Ophelia" turns on Ivan and both he and Kavalerov wind up sharing a bed with the gross widowed landlady, Annechka Prokopovich. The complex personal interrelationships in the plot suggest a variety of interpretational possibilities involving, as T.S. Berczynski points out, "both the psychology of Freud and the philosophy of Dostoevsky's Notes from the Underground."[62]

The plot of the novel, however, is all but subjugated in the reader's attention by the rich verbal texture and the stunning imagery which Olesha employs. This imagery is overwhelmingly visual and involves both rapid shfts of perspective and distortions of perception. In this sense, one might easily term the imagery "cinematic," in that it isn't limited to the reader's actual "eye" and his particular esthetic distance, but instead captures his attention in its own right by forcing him to see things in ways he may not have been entirely prepared to see them. The most arresting shift of perspective is that of the narrative voice, which begins in the first person (Kavalerov saying "I am a jester...a comic"[63]), but switches to the third person in Part Two ("Kavalerov turned around...Kavalerov recognizes the head...Kavalerov

---

[62] Yuri Olesha, Envy, (translated and with foreword by T. S. Berczynski), (Ann Arbor: Ardis, 1975), p. ix.

[63] Ibid, pp. 6 and 51.

sees..."⁶⁴). Nils Ake Nilsson, in discussing what he calls Olesha's "fantastic photography," explains the distortion of perception thus: "[Olesha] seldom gives us a direct and straight-forward description, a simple full-face view of an object or a person. Instead, we usually see his world of objects and people reflected in buttons, mirrors, and metallic surfaces; we catch distorted glimpses of them through glass windows and bars; they appear enlarged or diminished through binoculars, telescopes, or microscopes."⁶⁵ In his article, "Objective in Yuri Olesha's Envy," Wayne P. Wilson demonstrates the interdependency of this shift in perspective and the distortions of perception. Wilson may be paraphrased to state that the "shift in point of view is accompanied by altered perception as well, a change from two-dimensional to three-dimensional vision, from stereotype to stereoscopy. Stereoscopy requires not one but two related perceptions of an object. When Kavalerov's voice recedes into the background, Ivan and Andrei Babichev emerge as the defining limits of his potential. At the same time Andrei Babichev's image as the model Soviet man fades as attention is focused on the representatives of the future society, Volodya Makarov and Valya.⁶⁶ The mention here of "fantastic photography" and "stereoscopy"

---

[64] Ibid, pp. 98-9.

[65] Nils Ake Nilsson, "Through the Wrong End of the Binoculars: An Introduction to Yuri Olesha," Scando-Slavica, XI (1965), pp. 40-68 and reprinted in Edward J. Brown, Major Soviet Writers, op. cit., see p 254. In citing these other scholarly works there is sometimes necessitated a change in the transliteration of the Russian.

[66] Wayne P. Wilson, "Objective in Yuri Olesha's Envy," Slavic and East European Journal, Vol. 18, No. 1 (Spring 1974), p. 35

in relation to Olesha's imagery and narrative structure may be regarded as evidence of a general cinematic influence on Olesha's writing, especially in light of his avowed enthusiasm for the cinema. But if this discussion of inherent cinematic effects does not suffice to show this influence, then resort may be made to Olesha's description in <u>Envy</u> of the action at a soccer game wherein "Suddenly the ball, thrown out by someone's powerful and uncalculated kick, flew up high and sideways beyond the field, out of the game, in the direction of Kavalerov, whistled over the ducked heads of the lower rows, stopped for an instant and, all its laminae twirling, crashed down into the boards, towards Kavalerov's feet. The game stopped. The players froze, overcome by surprise. The picture of the field, green and variegated, moving all the time, now all of a sudden turned to stone. Thus *a motion picture* (italics mine...ST) stops all of a sudden at the moment of a break in the film, when they are already turning the light on in the theater but the projectionist has not yet managed to turn out the light, and the audience sees the strangely whitening still and the contours of the hero, absolutely motionless in that pose, which speaks of vast rapid movement."[67]

As we have seen above, Olesha's hero, Kavalerov, characterizes himself as a "jester'" and a "comic," and yet we see him also as a man who, at twenty-seven, realizes that he "...won't ever be either handsome or famous...won't come walking from the small town to the capital...won't be either a military leader or a people's commissar, or a scholar, or an adventurer." He dreams his "whole life of an extraordinary love," but returns instead to his "old apartment, to the room with the frightful bed," where there

---

[67] Yuri Olesha, <u>Envy</u>, (T. S. Berczynski translation), p. 106.

are "dismal surroundings" and the widow Prokopovich waits.[68] We laugh at his inadequacies, and yet we feel distinctly the pathos of his situation. We sympathize with his plight. This is comedy in the "laughter through tears" tradition which could be traced back in Russian literature to the works of Nikolai Gogol. The similarity of this form of comedy, however, to the particular cinematic comedy of Chaplin is too obvious to miss...he also was a clown who could make his audience cry.[69] It would seem then that Chaplin, the creator of the tragic clown, the "little tramp," and Olesha, the creator of Kavalerov's pathetic comedy, shared a certain aspect of their world-view. For this reason we are not surprised to find that Olesha's general interest in the cinema as a source of inspiration focused itself on the comedy of Charlie Chaplin.

One of the primary themes of Chaplin's early films is that of the representative of old-order sensibilities stranded in a new world. This is the dramatization of old values and new requirements of which F. D. Reeve wrote (above). Chaplin often evoked an empathetic reaction from his audience by exhibiting maudlin sentimentality in contrast to the indifferent, mechanized, hustle-bustle environment of the big city. In City Lights (1931), for example, Charlie discovers that his tenement-dwelling sweetheart is blind by holding a flower up to her eyes. "There are," wrote Olesha

---

[68] Ibid, p. 119.

[69] See Serge Eisenstein, Charlie Chaplin, (Zurich: Sanssouci Verlag, 1961) for a Soviet film director's view of Chaplin's comedy. Also, **А. Кукаркин, Чарли Чаплин, Москва,** 1961, which has a catalogue of the films in Russian with plots, actors, and a collection of photographic stills from the films.

in his 1936 article, "few such scenes in the art of cinema."[70] Furthermore, Charlie often sought and found companions of similar plight. Thus, he exhibits sympathy for the lot of a homeless dog in A Dog's Life (1918). The dog is depicted as Charlie's equal, and, needing each other, they form a sort of camaraderie of poverty. One still sees pictures of Charlie, cast out by his human counterparts for his inability to cope with their world, sitting arm and paw with a kindred soul, the dog. In Envy, Kavalerov imagines that he'll get Valya "--as a prize--for everything: for the humiliations, for the youth which I didn't have time to see, for my *dog's life*."[71]

Another companion in alienation is The Kid (1921), played by young Jackie Coogan. What a pathetic pair they make, little orphan Coogan in his shabby out-sized clothes and Charlie, the dejected glazier, each needing the other for consolation and support. Unable to survive, or, at least, unable to succeed separately in a milieu of contemporary social mores, they resort to extra-societal and picaresque means of mutual survival. Thus they devise a glass-breaking and repair scheme for livelihood.

Olesha's characters, too, represent a polarization of old values and new requirements. Nikolai Kavalerov and Ivan Babichev find themselves alienated in an impersonal culture. Helpless Kavalerov clings like the orphaned kid to Ivan Babichev, who hopes to lead a resurgence of personal feelings. Ivan Babichev confides in Kavalerov, telling him that their "fates are similar," because he sees Kavalerov as another last vestige of past values. Andrei Babichev and

---

[70] Юрий Олеша, Избранные произведения, from "Мысли о Чаплине," стр. 437.

[71] Yuri Olesha, Envy, (T. S. Berczynski translation), p. 40. Italics are the author's.

Volodya Makarov, on the other hand, represent the new values. This is clearly shown when Ivan Babichev, after calling Volodya Makarov the "new man" and blaming his brother Andrei for the alienation of his daughter's affections, says: "We are dying, Kavalerov...Milleniums stand like a sewer hole. In the hole wallow machines, pieces of cast iron, of tin, screws, springs...a dark gloomy hole. And in the hole shine pieces of rotten wood, phosphorescent fungi-mold. There are our feelings! This is all that is left of our feelings, of the flowering of our souls. The new man comes to the hole, rummages, climbs into it, chooses what he needs--some part of machine proves useful, a little nut--and the pieces of rotten wood he tramples, extinguishes...And so, the last dreamer on earth, I wander along the edge of the hole like a wounded bat..."[72] Thereafter, Ivan implicates Kavalerov in his plot to ridicule his respected and authoritarian brother. Squalidly attired, Kavalerov follows the buffoon and dreamer, Ivan Babichev, down the street. Ivan closely resembles Charlie Chaplin's little tramp in appearance. He is a "little man in a derby" and has a "hurried walk with the heaving of the whole torso"[73] just like Charlie's. Kavalerov, as does Jackie Coogan, walks a step behind his mentor, who frequently turns around to talk to him.[74] The similarity here to Chaplin's film, <u>The Kid</u>, is too close to be entirely coincidental. Even the warning of Ivan Babichev by the police bears, in its ominous tone and implications despite only passing plot significance, a resmblance to Charlie's occasional warnings by his mustachioed policeman foil.

One key scene in <u>Envy</u> finds Kavalerov trying to

---

[72] Ibid, pp. 74-5.

[73] Ibid, p. 22.

[74] Ibid, p. 73.

"rescue" a woman in a bar from some of her rowdy companions. This woman, of course, doesn't wish to be rescued and Kavalerov is made a fool of and then thrown out of the bar into the gutter. This scene is similar to a scene from Chaplin's The Face on the Bar-room Floor (1914), in which Charlie winds up studying the bar-room floor at nose length, just as Kavalerov lies in the gutter looking down the drain grate. Charlie had troubles with all manner of mechanical contrivances. He couldn't manage a mop or a fan in a clean-up job in The Bank (1915), ladders were a constant nemesis in The Pawnshop (1916), and flowerpots had a habit of falling on his head as in Easy Street (1917). Many later comedians have imitated Chaplin's classic scenes of trouble with folding chairs, as in A Day of Pleasure (1919). Kavelerov, analogously, tells us more than once, that "Things don't like me."[75] "Furniture," he says, "tries to trip me. Once some sort of laquered corner literally bit me. With my blanket I always have complex interrelations. Soup which is served me never cools. If some kind of trinket--a coin or a cuff link--falls off the table, it usually rolls under some piece of almost immovable furniture. I crawl along the floor and, raising my head, I see how the sideboard is laughing."[76]

Ivan Babichev is also, like Kavalerov, imbued with many chaplinesque traits. These traits go significantly beyond the matter of his physical similarity to Chaplin's screen character. Ivan Babichev's reaction to the new order of things is epitomized by his phobia for machines. Perhaps Olesha's view of Chaplin's machine-oppressed toiler in Work (1915) prompted his depiction of Ivan Babichev's

---

[75] Ibid, p. 22. This quote is very often cited from its earlier occurrence in the novel (see next note).

[76] Ibid, p. 4.

antimechanical panacea, Ophelia. In <u>Behind the Screen</u> (1917) as well as in the later film, <u>Modern Times</u> (1936), Charlie tries to "throw a monkey wrench" into the mechanical world. The curious emotive quality of Charlie's expressions and gestures in <u>Behind the Screen</u> tells us that he knows just one pull of the machine's control lever will "foul up the works." At first he revels in this power, but, at last, he succumbs to the temptation with, of course, disastrous results for himself. Ivan Babichev, too, can't resist the temptation of trying to "foul up the works." He tells Kavalerov to "...make a scandal...leave with a bang. Slam the door as they say. There's the main thing: to leave with a bang. So that a scar remains on the mug of history-- show off, devil take you! They won't let you in there anyway. Don't give in without a fight!"[77] And, like Charlie, Ivan's attempt to actualize his philosophy by creating Ophelia fails when Ophelia, who is also, after all, a machine, turns on Ivan and pins him to the wall with its "sparkling needle."[78]

Another similarity between Chaplin's portrayals and Olesha's characterizations is found in Charlie's relations with women. In short, Charlie was a failure. He often sentimentally regarded the object of his affections from afar, idealizing her, placing her on an unattainable pedestal in his mind. In his dreams, she floats above the ground in airy costumes, is even given wings. In <u>Sunnyside</u> (1919), Charlie dances in a dream with his love in the Elysian Fields surrounded by scantily clad wood nymphs. In reality, however, he brings flowers to her door, serenades her with his violin, but when she comes out he is abashed and tongue-tied, and suddenly very vulnerable and helpless.

---

[77] Ibid, p. 77.

[78] Ibid, p. 113.

Tragically, he watches her leave with some brutish character. Deep down, we all know that Charlie is the better man, but he is unable to communicate this strange sort of superiority, this greater sensibility, to his love. We are torn inside by the tragedy of the situation, having perhaps, had similar experiences ourselves.

Olesha was fascinated by this kind of relationship with women. He had, in fact, had an experience very similar to those expressed by Chaplin in his youth. In <u>Not a Day Without a Line</u>, Olesha tells us that he once witnessed a performance of three acrobats, two men and a girl. He fell in love with the girl, with the way her hair flew in the breeze. Several days later he saw the same two men on the street. With them, however, was no girl, but a young unattractive boy of bad complexion who spat, and whom Olesha at first took for an assistant. Suddenly he realized that this was the "girl" with whom he had fallen in love. And, Olesha adds, he remained in love with her all his life"[79] In <u>Envy</u>, we find this same type of relationship. Harkins has made a good case for the contention that "Olesha's male characters in <u>Envy</u> are all sterile."[80] Aspiring to Valya, Kavalerov is forced to accept the gross Annechka Prokopovich, who, he says, is "a symbol of my humbled masculinity."[81] Furthermore, from Kavalerov's point of view, Valya is romantically idealized in the extreme. His love for her is, of course, never realized, and,

---

[79] This anecdote from Olesha's <u>**Ни дня без строчки (Избранные произведения, стр. 106)**</u> is retold by William E. Harkins, op. cit., p.293

[80] William E. Harkins, ibid, p. 294.

[81] Yuri Olesha, <u>Envy</u>, (Andrew R. MacAndrew translation), (Garden City: Doubleday, 1967), p. 20. This translation is preferred here.

in fact, despite his being almost crazy with love for her, he never even manages a decent attempt at winning her. In the end, she goes off with Volodya Makarov, unaware of Kavalerov's existence. This is just the sort of love frustration that Charlie Chaplin so often depicted. Ivan Babichev encounters similar frustration also in his attempts to get back into his daughter's good graces. Just as Charlie so often tried, Ivan Babichev approaches his daughter from the street outside her apartment. But she doesn't come out, despite Ivan's having brought her her childhood pillow. And he also fails in his attempt to discredit his brother, her fiance Volodya's benefactor. Valya herself, like the heroines in Chaplin's films, is seen, especially by Kavalerov, as an ethereal character. Kavalerov says: "She was lighter than a shadow, the very lightest of shadows—the shadow of falling snow could envy her..."[82] At the soccer game he approaches her and blurts out his feelings. "Valya," he says, "I've been waiting for you my whole life. Take pity on me...." "But she didn't hear. She ran, undercut by the wind."[83]

There are, in summation, many chaplinesque themes in Olesha's Envy. The masking of serious problems by humor based on empathy, and the resorting to fantasy and the absurd can be viewed as examples of Chaplin's influence, through the cinematic medium, on Olesha's writing. The fate of the "little man," sensitivity in an insensitive world, old values versus new requirements, man versus machine, and romantic love frustrated in asexual characters are all themes in Envy whose similarities to Chaplin's portrayals are reinforced by the physical similarities of Olesha's characters to Chaplin's film character. In light of this

---

[82] Yuri Olesha, Envy, (T. S. Berczynski translation), p. 39.

[83] Ibid, p. 109.

evidence, then, it is easy to view Olesha's <u>Envy</u> as an early instance of profound cinematic influence with Charlie Chaplin as the primary source of inspiration.

Alicia C. Baehr at Lenin's Mausoleum on Red Square in Moscow, 2006.

Linguistics, Memory, and Teaching
By:
Shane C. Sarlo

Shane Craig Sarlo was born and raised in Logan, Utah. His study of Russian language and culture began during his junior year at Logan Senior High School where he graduated in 1998. After completing high school, Shane worked as a university ambassador and continued his study of Russian at Utah State University after receiving the Presidential Leadership scholarship. In 1999, Shane moved to Rostov-na-Donu, Russia, where he served as a religious and humanitarian missionary throughout various cities of southern Russia (Rostov-na-Donu, Volgograd, Taganrog and Tuapse). Upon returning to the U.S. in 2001, Shane relocated to Phoenix, Arizona, to pursue a bachelor's degree in Russian at Arizona State University. He is the author of the story, "Not the Way I had Planned," in the 2008 Capstone Publications book, RUSSIA: The Missionaries' Tales (ISBN 978-1-4357-1264-5, see www.Russianaz.org under "sponsors"). He was inducted into the Epsilon Epsilon Chapter of the Доброе Слово National Slavic Studies Honorary in the spring of 2008. He currently resides in Tempe, Arizona and is employed as a Guest Recognition Coordinator at The Ritz-Carlton, Phoenix. Shane will graduate from ASU, with honors, in May 2009.

PRESENTATION:

Prof. Croft has written to me that he considers this his most impactful article…doing the most to establish him as a leading scholar in the linguistic and psychological "niche" of iconicity and being cited more often by other scholars than any of his other articles until this millenium. He says that he is proud of it because it is his most original work, springing forth more primarily from his own mind than several of his other works that are more dependent upon the previous works of others. And, even in this anthology, we have other subsequent articles (e.g. see the article by Alicia C. Baehr further on) by Prof. Croft on the topics of linguistic iconicity and its usefulness in language and literarature pedagogy that are based upon this first seminal article. When the journal it is published in, Slavic and East European Journal (SEEJ …see the earlier article by Megan Plachecki), a leading scholarly organ in Prof. Croft's field and the journal of the American Association of Teachers of Slavic and East European Languages (AATSEEL) to which he has belonged since 1969, celebrated its "Thirtieth

Anniversary Issue" in 1987 (cf. Vol. 31, pp. 202-3), editors Ann Weiler Perkins and Catherine V. Chvany, in their overview of "Language Pedagogy," termed this article a "notable application of psycholinguistics." It is also the basis for Prof. Croft's association with other scholars of linguistic iconicity. He is one of 300 or so members of the Linguistic Iconism Association and serves on the review board of this organization's scholarly journal, <u>Iconicity in Language</u> (see. www.trismegistos.com/MagicalLetterPage/). Prof. Croft's article is republished here with the permission of the editors of the <u>Slavic and East European Journal</u>, where it was previously in Vol. 22 (1978), No. 4, p. 509-18.

THE MNEMONIC USE OF LINGUISTIC ICONICITY IN TEACHING LANGUAGE AND LITERATURE

By:

Lee B. Croft
Arizona State University

The psycholinguist Roger Brown has recorded his study of a memory syndrome familiar to many of us. As he describes it, "You cannot recall a word, even though you know it perfectly well, and a kind of intensive search is set up in your brain, a search that tosses up a succession of words which are not the one sought, but which are tantalizingly close."[84] In this study Brown and his associates

---

[84] Roger Brown, "The Tip of the Tongue Phenomenon," in <u>Psycholinguistics</u> (New York: Free Press, MacMillan, 1972), pp. 274.

used the "wrong words" tossed up by the mind, later comparing them to the "right" word, in order to draw inferences about the way in which lexical items are stored or "filed" for ease of recall. Similarity factors such as first letter ("I know it starts with 'i-' ..."), number of syllables ("No, 'solidly' is too short..."), syllabic stress ("It goes 'da DA da da'..."), chunking of suffixes ("It's an *–ably* word, or *-ibly,* or..."), and semantic proximity ("Let's see...permanently, inalterably, unchangeably ...") emerge as determining factors in the search, as well as contextual syntactic factors ("It goes in the sentence: 'The word was ... impressed in his mind'").[85] From this, we can see that the search uses all linguistic levels at once: phonological, morphological, syntactic, and semantic.

This type of research has led to a number of significant discoveries about the way the mind stores linguistic information. For example, it appears that, on the level of sound, the constituent phonemes of recalled words are stored separately from their respective phoneme orders– that is, in trying to recall "ambergris" we may come up with "Seagram's," which contains most of the appropriate phonemes, but in a different order (notice also the subtle association of "ambergris," a whale product, with "sea," part of the recalled "wrong" word). It also appears that, on the level of sense, the mind categorizes and makes hierarchies in ways amenable to analysis by what psycholinguists call "dendrograms," an example of which can be shown here from an article by George Mandler.[86] Here we can see how

---

[85] By now the reader has guessed that the word sought here is "indelibly."

[86] George Mandler, "Words, Lists and Categories: A Experimental View of Organized Memory," in <u>Thought and Language</u>, J.L. Cowan, Ed. (Tucson: University of Arizona

the more general categories break down in stages to the more specific:

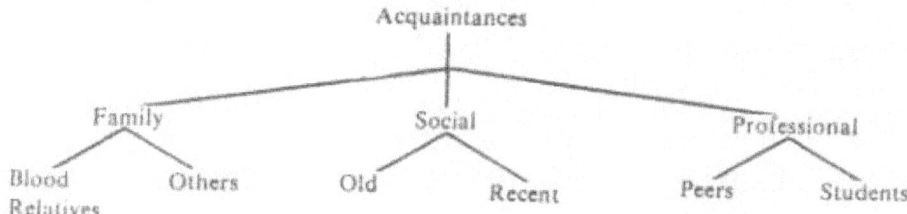

The mind not only categorizes and makes hierarchies, but it also serializes. When using a dictionary it is easiest mentally to run through the entire alphabet to discover the relative place of the letter entry sought. Even more important, the mind associates one "filed" entry with another in a variety of ways: with place ("That ad is on a lower, right-hand page"), with time ("Let's see, he mentioned it to me right after lunch"), with person ("It was the jeweler who told me, that's how I remember"). In short, the mind stores linguistic information in a variety of multi-level, overlapping ways. It is important to stress here that both *sense* and *sound* are involved, and that in categorizing, making hierarchies, serializing, and associating, the mind seeks conventions to connect the two.

One of the most important implications of this research into mnemonic structure is that the person with the best memory is the one who has "filed" the item to be recalled under the most categories or in the most ways. This person can then bring the item forth with the greatest facility. Brown illustrates this with a story:

Press, 1970), pp. 99-132. Evidence here is adduced from the speech errors of aphasics who sometimes confuse lexical items within a given category.

"One evening, a group was trying to recall the name of the well-known philosopher Nelson Goodman. Everyone knew the name but at first no one could recall it. In the end someone did. The names proposed during the search showed the usual main effects: for example, someone thought the first name might be Nathan. However, when we had finished and looked back over the record we found an unexpected effect. The names proposed by those present who were Jewish were all Jewish names; the names proposed by non-Jews were not all Jewish. What does that mean? It may mean that the Jews present had in their memories an ethnic tag "Jewish" on the lexical entry for Nelson Goodman, a tag missing from the memories of the non-Jews, and a tag that was accessible when the name was not."[87]

Thus the Jewish participants were able, because of the ethnic identity "tag" which they assigned to the name when they initially "filed" it, to make a mnemonic association, which the other participants could not make.

The mnemonic structure so far described has serious consequences for the science of pedagogy in general and for the art of teaching language and literature in particular. The process of facilitating recall in the mind of another is a major aspect of teaching. How best to present material to our students so that they can bring it forth when they need it? It follows that the best teaching method is the one which enables the student to "file" the material to be recalled in the most ways. We must maximize the number of mnemonic "tags" we give to our students in every explanation.

There is an especially effective family of mnemonic tags which because of prevailing linguistic doctrine is often scorned, but which has a special relevance to the teaching of

---

[87] Roger Brown, op. cit. pp. 275.

language and literature. This family of mnemonic tags is related to the linguistic concept of iconicity.[88] The term iconicity refers here to any non-arbitrary relationship between a linguistic form and its real-world referent.[52] When such a relationship is found, the linguistic form serves as an icon to the experience it represents in that the connection between form and referent is motivated by factors of inherent similarity which stand apart from semantic assignment by mere social convention. The most straightforward example of iconicity is onomatopoeia, in

---

[88] Iconicity was popular in linguistic scholarship of the late nineteenth century, especially with regard to questions of glottogenesis. These endeavors are looked down upon today because of their subjectivity. Linguists today, striving for empiricism in their science, leave little room for this kind of speculation and interpretation. Speculation and interpretation are, however, entirely appropriate to the study of literature and teaching.

[52] A good explanation of the concept is Michael Shapiro, Aspects of Russian Morphology: A Semiotic Investigation (Cambridge, Mass.: Slavica, 1969), especially 1-15. The best total treatment is Roger Wescott, "Linguistic Iconism," Language, 47 (1971), 416-28. For the general use of iconicity in literature, see Roman Jakobson, "Linguistics and Poetics," in Style and Language, ed. Thomas A. Sebeok (Cambridge, Mass.: MIT Press, 1966), 350-77. See also I. A. Richards, "Functions of and Factors in Language," Journal of Literary Semantics, 1 (1972), 25-40. These scholars use phrases such as "sound symbolism" and "grammatical parallelism" for the phenomenon wherein literary form identifiably mirrors literary content. The symbolic function is not obviated by terming this relationship "iconicity."

which the linguistic form itself (the English "bang" and "crash," and the Russian "**Бац**" and "**Цап**") imitates the sound of the real-world event it represents. Literary examples involving entire sentences abound, as in Tennyson's line, "The murmuring of innumerable bees in immemorial elms," or Axmatova's "**Змейным свистом срезывает серп**." In teaching either language or literature, we should mention when such an obvious iconic relationship exists, and actively seek less obvious examples of iconicity in material to be covered. There are two reasons for doing this. First, the student will be given one more category under which to "file" things in the mind. Thus the tag "iconic" will be added to the student's repertoire of mnemonic tags just by virtue of the fact that the teacher mentions it. Second, and more important, the iconic tag has a particular relevance because it provides the student with a ready-made associative tie between the realms of sense and sound, which other tags do not have and which plays an important part in the recall of linguistic material.

More complex and interesting tags can and should be referred to in the classroom. Relational or "horizontal" iconicities, for example, abound in language. Carl Abel demonstrated the palindromic formation of antonyms in Coptic and Demotic Egyptian. In his example, opposite phonological order signifies opposite meaning, as in: [kar-] "wise" and [rak-] "foolish," [mer-] "right hand" and [rem-] "left hand," [mes-] "darkness" and [sem-] "to become visible," and [tek-] "to flow" and [ket-] "to become stationary."[53] This relationship can also be found in the

---

[53] Carl Abel, <u>The Ilchester Lectures on Comparative Lexicography</u> (London: Trubner and Co., 1883), 123. Able lists several other Egyptian examples of this type. The journal <u>Word Ways</u>, 7 (1974), 241, contains discussion of this and similar phenomena. The term "horizontal" iconicity

Indo-European languages, as in Lithuanian [*ker*-as] "to be dumb, unable to speak" and [*rek*-ti] "to speak, talk." By showing students this type of opposite-sound, opposite-meaning relationship in a pair like Russian "**раб**" [*rab*-] "slave" and "**барин**" [*bar*-in] "lord, master" (English "*rab*-ble" and "*bar*-on"), we can aid their recall of this vocabulary.

A different type of motivated relationship between sound and meaning may be found in Russian by examining the presence of the vowel [-o-] in certain relational adjectives. Each pair of adjectival antonyms, for example, has one member that is correlated to a certain type of psychological neutrality. A good test for determining just which member of an antonymal pair this is, is to see which member, in the most neutral circumstance of context, a person will put in the syntactic frame: "How _____ is it?" That is, we always ask how big something is, and not how small, even though the object we have in mind may be quite small. In neutral circumstances, we ask how heavy, not how light, how old, not how young. It is interesting that in Russian the member of the antonymal pair which is correlated with this neutrality is very often signaled by the presence of stressed [-o-], as in:

Большо́й	Big	**Ма́ленький**	Small
Высо́кий	High	**Ни́зкий**	Low
Широ́кий	Wide	**У́зкий**	Narrow
Глубо́кий	Deep	**Ме́лкий**	Shallow
Гро́мкий	Loud	**Ти́хий**	Quiet
Тёмный	Dark	**Све́тлый**	Light
То́нкий	Fine	**Гру́бый**	Crude

is used by Thomas V. Gamkrelidze, "The Problem of 'l'arbitraire du signe,'" <u>Language</u>, 50 (1974), 102-11.

Notice that few counter-examples (like **старый-молодой**) present themselves and that several apparent counter-examples (like **трудный-лёгкий**) can be explained by the fact that one member may have more than one antonym (as **лёгкий-тяжёлый**).[54] And, it can hardly be coincidental that [-o-] predominates in the neutral circumstance of question words which are meant to correct a no-information situation (**что, кто, какой, который, сколько**), or that as a verbal desenence it signals agreement with relatively unmarked entities of all kinds (neuter nouns, general or impersonal subjects, infinitives). These facts are disquieting evidence that semantic increments of meaning ("sense") are non-arbitrarily correlated to sound at levels well below the morpheme, and that only the inability to identify this correlation in concrete terms has heretofore prevented teachers from imparting this kind of "feel-for-language" to their students.[55]

Several scholars, including Edward Sapir and Otto Jesperson, have commented on the non-arbitrary tie between the vowels of human language and impressions of magnitude. These comments have focused on the vowel [-i-] which connotes smallness (as in "itsy-bitsy," "teeny-weeny," "little") in contrast to the more open vowel [-a-]

---

[54] This interesting observation about adjectival antonyms was made to me by fellow Cornell University graduate student James Cradler who credited it in turn to Hugh Olmsted.

[55] See Roman Jakobson, "Quest for the Essence of Language," <u>Diogenes</u>, 51 (1966), 345-59, and Dwight Bolinger, "Rime, Assonance, and Morpheme Analysis," <u>Word</u>, 6 (1950), 117-37. See also Bolinger, "The Atomization of Meaning," <u>Language</u>, 41 (1965), 555-73.

which connotes expansiveness (as in "large," "grand," "awesome"). A well-known test illustrates how this type of iconicity is felt by most of us: "If your language has only two words, 'ping' and 'pong,' with which to represent an elephant and a mouse – which word would you pick for each animal?" The majority of people, regardless of their cultural origins, will easily choose "pong" for the elephant and "ping" for the mouse, because they feel the non-arbitrary association of magnitudinal impression and sound.[56] A teacher of Russian would do well to bear this relationship in mind when contrasting the small amount of time represented by the word "миг" (an "instant") to the larger amount of time represented by "год" (a "year").

---

[56] See Edward Sapir, "A Study in Phonetic Symbolism," Journal of Experimental Psychology, 12 (1929), 225-29, and Otto Jesperson, Language: Its Nature, Development and Origin, 11th ed. (London: George Allen and Unwin, 1959), especially 396-412. See also "The Symbolic Value of the Vowel -i-," Selected Writings of Otto Jesperson (London; Allen and Unwin, 1962), 557-78; David R. Heise, "Sound-Meaning Correlations Among 1000 English Words," Language and Speech, 9 (1966), 14.; Ronald C. Johnson, "Magnitude Symbolism of English Words," Journal of Verbal Learning Behavior, 6 (1967), 508-11; I. Taylor and M. M. Taylor, "Phonetic Symbolism in Four Unrelated Languages," Canadian Journal of Psychology, 16 (1962), 344; and A. E. Horowitz et al., "Phonetic Symbolism in Natural Languages," Journal of Abnormal Social Psychology, 50 (1955), 338. These journals offer many insights into magnitude symbolization. One good source for examining its literary use is Percy G. Adams, "The Historical Importance of Assonance to Poets," PMLA, 88 (1973), 8-18.

Similarly, most people feel a non-arbitrary relationship between kinetic and tactile impressions and sound. The following test to demonstrate this is similar to one used by Gestalt psychologist Wolfgang Kohler in 1947. Of the following shapes,

one is represented by the word *ooloómu* and the other by the word *taakáate*. Which word goes with which shape? Most of us know the answer because we feel the tie between the smoothness and roundness of the kidney-bean shape and the word "oolóomu," and between the sharp points of the star shape and the abrupt consonantal stops of "taakáate."[57] A more subtle example can be demonstrated by performing a similar test on the Russian words "вилка" (*vílka*... "fork") and "ложка" (*lóžka*... "spoon"), words which, if examined phonologically, are really very similar. In a sampling taken by this author, a clear majority of students polled could match the correct word to the appropriate picture of a fork and a spoon, even when they knew no Russian. No doubt they felt the contrast between the small points of the fork (symbolized by the smallness-connoting vowel [i]) and the roundness of the spoon (symbolized by the roundness of the

---

[57] Wolfgang Kohler, <u>Gestalt Psychology: An Introduction to New Concepts in Modern Psychology</u> (New York: Liveright, 1947).

spoon (symbolized by the roundness of the vowel [o]). Obviously, if this iconicity is pointed out to students when these words are introduced ("The small, sharp points in "**вилка**" and an [i] and the round spoon, '**ложка**," with a round [o]…"), then their recall of these lexical items in the proper relationship will be considerably facilitated. This will be so, significantly enough, even for those students who are unable initially to match the right sound with the right picture since the teacher will now have furnished them with a very special kind of mnemonic tag which they can subsequently use.

Anthony Burgess mentions that one author who has made effective literary use of this relationship between sound and kinetic or tactile experience is Vladimir Nabokov. Nabokov's use of this iconicity is especially easy to see in the first sentence of Lolita: "Lolita, light of my fire, fire of my loins. My sin, my soul. LO-LEE-TA: the tip of the tongue making a trip of three steps down to the palate to tap, at three, on the teeth. LO-LEE-TA."[58]

Sound, then, is capable of conveying sense not just by conventional semantic assignment, but by iconicity, the sound's inherent relation to external reality. This capacity, though not previously formalized in these terms, has been called the "naturalness" or "expressivity" of language, and it is just this capacity of sound to convey increments of meaning apart from the conventional semantic assignment which is used by poets to distinguish their art form from ordinary discourse. In testing this capacity, we would expect to find general agreement as to the "sense" of "sounds" which are completely meaningless by the standards of conventional semantic assignment. Several careful studies

---

[58] Anthony Burgess, Language Made Plain (London: English Universities Press, 1964). 8-9.

of this type have been completed both in the Soviet Union and in the West. In these studies, subjects are asked to define in various ways (often by choosing alternatives from arrays of conceptual antonyms) word-length segments of sound which are unfamiliar to them. Often, surprising degrees of consensus are observed. This author, for example, has received much propaganda value from a talk to potential students entitled "You Already Know Russian," wherein they choose spontaneously for meaning after hearing and several time repeating the word "**Штанга**" (*štánga*): "*Štánga* . . . heavy or light? *Štánga* . . . shallow or deep?" Most students are surprised and impressed to learn that they can make these kinds of "grammatical" judgments in Russian despite their unfamiliarity with the language. That is, most students quickly choose "heavy," not "light," "deep," not "shallow," "masculine," not "feminine," (even when some are preconditioned from other languages to think of -a ending words as feminine in gender). This agreement (and it really does not matter which choices the agreement centers on, although in this case the word's lexical meaning of "barbell" seems in line with the choices made), running in this author's sampling of eighty students to approximately eighty-five percent, can only mean that people do feel non-arbitrary ties between sound and the real world it represents independently of lexical assignment.[59] It

---

[59] For the Soviet scholarship in this phenomenon see three articles entitled "**О восприятии звуков**" by **Г. Н. Иванова-Лукьянова** (sound correlated to judgements of darkness and lightness), **Е. В. Орлова** (synopses of definitions of unfamiliar sound segments), and **М. В. Панов** (literary uses of this phenomenon in poetry), in **Развитие фонетики современного русского языка**, ред. С. С. Высотский, М. В. Панов, и В. Н. Сидоров, (Москва: Наука, 1966, стр. 136-63. See the study by

is common sense to make use of these ties in our teaching whenever we can. Once a student is told about the iconicity of the Russian word "**пушка**" (púška..meaning "cannon"), how it starts with an explosion ("p") and has a rush of smoke ("š") and then an impact ("k"), he never forgets it.

The non-arbitrary connection between sound and the realm of tactile or kinetic perception has already introduced a synaesthetic aspect into this investigation. Another synaesthetic iconicity involves the phenomenon of *audition colorée* or acoustic-chromatic synopsia, in which a person hears a sound and simultaneously envisions an associated color. These impressions, which have a rough universal conformity, are said to exist in all of us at birth, but they become psychologically subordinated in later life. Examples of this non-arbitrary connection between the visual world of color and the linguistic world of sound are to be found in the color lexicon of the world's languages (as English light colors "yellow," "red," "silver" having front stressed vowels and the darker colors "blue," "black," "brown" having more back stressed vowels). People who feel this iconicity strongly have used it to mnemonic effect and at least one educational theorist, Caleb Gategno, has long advocated the color-coding of sounds to aid in the visual aspect of foreign language instruction.[60] This type of iconicity has also been

---

Dina Crockett, "Secondary Onomatopoeia in Russian," Word, 26 (1970), pp. 107-13, and also Erik Fudge, "Phonological Structure and 'Expressiveness,'" Journal of Linguistics, 6 (1970), pp. 161-88.

[60] Synaesthesia is considered under the rubric of iconicity here because the key element is the non-arbitrary relationship of sound to the other sensory experience. For the color terms, see Brent Berlin and Paul Kay, Basic Color Terms: Their Universality and Evolution (Berkeley, Cal.:

put to artistic use in literature by such artists as Rimbaud ("A noir, E blanc, I rouge, U vert, O bleu: voyelles, / Je dirai quelque jour vos naissances latentes"; "Voyelles," 1871) and Vladimir Nobokov, who describes his color impressions of sound very interestingly in his autobiographical work, *Speak, Memory*. He relates, for example, that the letters of his childhood alphabet blocks were the "wrong colors."[61]

In addition, sound has been associated with various states of emotion. High vowels [i] and [e] are said to connote "light," "happy," "stable" moods, whereas low vowels [u]

Univ. of California Press, 1969), p. 178. (Reviewed by George A. Collier, in Language, 49 (1973), pp. 245-58). The scholarship on acoustic-chromatic synopsia is very interesting. See A. N. Pierce. "Synaesthesia," Psychological Bulletin, 1 (1911), p.157, and Roman Jakobson, "Agreement Between the Systems of Sound and Color," Child Language, Aphasia, and Phonological Universals (Janua Linguarum, 72; The Hague: Mouton, 1968), pp.82-84. To document the use of this iconicity for mnemonic effect, see Gladys Reichart, Elizabeth Weith, and Roman Jakobsen, "Language and Synesthesia," Word, 5 (1949), pp.224-35. See also David I. Masson, "Synesthesia and Sound Spectra," Word, 8 (1952), pp. 39-47. For pedagogical color-coding, see Caleb Gattegno, Teaching Foreign Languages in Schools: The Silent Way, 2nd ed. (New York: Educational Solutions, 1972), 144.

[61] Vladimir Nabokov, Speak, Memory (New York: Grosset and Dunlap, 1967), pp. 15-17. These artistic uses are detailed in a fine article by D. Barton Johnson, "Synaesthesia, Polychromatism, and Nabokov," Russian Literature Triquarterly, No 3 (Spring 1972), pp. 378-98. Interesting also is T. Alajouanine, "Aphasia and Artistic Realization," Brain, 71 (1948), pp. 229-41.

and [o] connote "dark," "gloomy," "unstable" moods. Palatal [m] and [l] (called in Russian "**ласковое**" or "caressing" [l]) are felt to connote "security," "coziness," and "affection."[62] Once this has been pointed out, students in Russian language courses have little difficulty remembering words like **угрюмый**, "sullen," or **милый**, "dear." This type of iconicity has its literary repercussions, of course. Nils Ake Nilson has an analysis of Blok's poem "**На поле Киликовом**" based on the dominance of different vowels in successive stanzas as the mood changes.[63] A shorter example of this may be found in Jurij Ivask's (**Юрий Иваск**) poem, significantly titled "The Vowels" (**Гласные**, 1970), wherein the mood changes from happy to tragic as the vowels, set in similar consonantal environments, change from high-front to low-back, with the final line's dominant [-a-] expressing the poet's empathy:

Пели, пели, пели,

Пили, пили, пили,

Поле, поле, поле,

Пули, пули, пули,

Пали, пали, пали.

---

[62] **Юрий Иваск**, "Волшебные звуки," <u>Новый журнал</u> 75 (1964), **стр.** 157-64.

[63] Nils Ake Nilson, "Blok's 'Vowel Fugue,' A Suggestion for a New Interpretation," <u>International Journal of Slavic Linguistics and Poetics</u>, 11 (1958), p. 150. See also Kiril Taranovskij, "The Sound Texture of Russian verse in Light of Phonemic Distinctive Features," <u>International Journal of Slavic Linguistics and Poetics</u>, (1965), p. 114.

Critical approaches to literature have also been influenced by iconicity. Much debated have been literary analyses of an anagrammatic nature wherein the sound texture of the work involved imparts to the reader through its iconicity a message which stands apart from, although it very often strongly reinforces, the conventional semantic content of the work. This type of approach was concretely initiated by James J. Lynch, who analyzes Keat's poem, "On First Looking into Chapman's Homer," by pointing out that the most frequently used sounds in the poem (the high-front vowels [i] and [e], the consonants [s], [l], [t], and [n]) may be arranged in the fashion of an anagram to spell out the otherwise unmentioned key theme word of the poem, "silence." This critical methodology has been used also by Catherine Chvany in her "Analysis of a Poem by Teffi." One can easily imagine how students' appreciation of Konstantin Simonov's poem, **Жди меня** ("Ždi menja"), might be enhanced once it is pointed out that the dominant sounds of the poem, "ž," "i," and the dentals "d" and "t," subtly call out to the reader the main theme of the poem, that the hero wants "to live," (**жить**), even though the word **жить** itself is never mentioned in the poem as such.[64]

Due to the way the mind stores linguistic information for recall, then, teachers would be well advised to use explanations involving iconicity when they can. This, of course, is not always easy to do. Iconicity is not always easy to see. It could be that every linguistic form has its iconic

---

[64] See James J. Lynch, "The Tonality of Lyric Poetry: An Experiment in Method," Word, 9 (1953), pp. 211-24, and Catherine V. Chvany, "Analysis of a Poem by Teffi," in Studies Presented to Professor Roman Jakobsen by his Students, ed. C. E. Gribble (Cambridge, Mass.: Slavica, 1968), pp. 61-69.

aspect, an aspect we are just not seeing. More probably, as Roger Wescott speculates, the iconic elements are held in some kind of delicate and constantly changing equilibrium with the arbitrary elements in language.[65] One convenient aspect of iconicity, which results from the possibility of its unperceived universality, however, is that counter-examples cannot refute its existence, but instead, often lead to further evidence. For example, Christine Tanz, in an article entitled "Sound Symbolism in Words for Proximity and Distance," points out that very often words expressing proximate distance from ego are shorter than, and very often included within, the corresponding words which express a greater distance from ego. This, of course, shows a word relationship which is iconic to the real-world spatial relationship of proximate distances being included within the more distant. Examples of this are constituted by the following words for "here" and "there," which themselves for an orthographic example:[66]

	here	there
Amharic	[*izzi*]	[*izzi*ja]
Arabic	[huna]	[*huna*ka]
Woleolan	[iga]	[*iga*la]
Japanese	[soko]	[a*soko*]

In answer to this fine example of iconicity, the skeptic will say "What about French *ici* and *la*, or English

---

[65] Roger Wescott, op. cit. (see note 52), pp. 427-8.

[66] Christine Tanz, "Sound Symbolism in Words for Proximity and Distance," <u>Language and Speech</u>, 14 (1971), p. 260.

(phonetically judged) "here" and "there," or Russian здесь (*zdes'*) and там (tam)? Or, expanding the refutation to the demonstratives, what of the fact that Russian proximate этот, эта, это are "bigger" words than the corresponding distant тот, та, то? Iconicity is where one finds it, however, and these just add more fuel to the clever iconicist's fire. In the French, Russian, and English words for "here" and "there," we have an iconicity of a different kind – one of the magnitudinal symbolizations like the one discussed above with the ping-pong test. The small distance from ego is represented by the words with high front vowels which are contrasted to the words with low, back vowels which represent greater distance. As for the demonstratives like этот and тот, they too represent an iconicity of a different kind. These words are used to point to objects which can be visualized. Visible objects which are closer to ego appear larger to the eye and must, therefore, be represented by the larger word этот. The further objects appear smaller and are reduced images of their closer counterparts, just as they are represented by the smaller, reduced form тот. Thus can apparent counter-examples be turned to pedagogical advantage in the mnemonic sense, especially since the mere discussion of how such lexical items relate in an iconic way to reality will serve to cement them properly into students' memories.

In recalling linguistic material, the mind, according to the evidence at hand, uses many overlapping ways to link sense with sound. When this link between sense and sound consists, as we have seen that it does, of more than a mere convention, it may be perceived as an example of iconicity – sound imitating in a multitude of ways the very reality it represents. This type of relationship finds its way into our languages and our literatures. As teachers we can use this special relationship as a mnemonic device to implant factual material in the minds of our students in such a way that they will be able to recall it with ease.

Hayden L. Croft among the Generals at Moscow's Museum of the Battle of Borodino (1812)—Photo by Lesley Hoyt Croft, 2002.

TRANSLATING THE FORM AS WELL AS THE CONTENT
BY:
JAIME R. NIELSEN

Jaime R. Nielsen was born and raised in Mesa, Arizona. She graduated from Westwood High School in May of 2005. She then went on to attend Colby College in Waterville, Maine, pursuing a Russian degree. In 2006, she transferred to Arizona State University where she continues her work in the Russian language. She was inducted into ASU's Epsilon Epsilon Chapter of the **Добро Слово** National Slavic Studies Honorary in April 2007 (see her in the group photo in Lee B. Croft, et. al. <u>Russian in Arizona: A History of Its Teaching</u>, IIHS, Tempe, Az/Perm, Russian Federation, 2007, pp. 245). She married Steven Nielsen in December of 2007. After her planned graduation in May of

2009, she plans to attend medical school where she will pursue a career as a family practice physician.

PRESENTATION:

This article was originally published in the 17th issue of Hayden's Ferry Review in 1995 by Editor Salima Keegan, who enlisted the aid of ASU Russian student Gary Walker to typeset the Russian Cyrillic version of Alexander Pushkin's poem together with Prof. Croft's facing verse translation. Prof. Croft explains the twenty-year gap of time between his translation (1975) and its publication (1995) by saying that his work was being considered for inclusion by the scholars and editors of the internationally funded "Pushkin Project" into the Complete Works of Alexander Pushkin in English (a fourteen-volume set published by Milner and Company Ltd. Publishers, Norfolk, UK, 1999). When his translation was at last rejected in favor of another, he submitted his translation to Editor Keegan at Hayden's Ferry Review, where it beat the other into print by four years. This notable and national journal, produced here at Arizona State University, has published works from John Updike, T.C. Boyle, Richard Ford, William Kittredge, Joseph Heller, and Pulitzer Prize-winner Rita Dove. This particular issue marked the beginning of national distribution both textually and online, and articles announcing its release named Prof. Croft's verse translation of an early poem by the great Russian poet Alexander Pushkin as the highlight. ASU's own Melikian Center Director Stephen Batalden remarked that "any translation of Pushkin is important" and "I think it's a great coup." The article features an introduction discussing the translation's preservation of Russian aspects of form along with the poem's meaning into the English version. Prof. Croft is a strong advocate of form as the defining essence of poetry…not merely as a decoration of the thoughts expressed, but as a mnemonic device so that the thoughts can be more easily committed to memory. One of his first professional publications was a collection, entitled <u>Russian Symbolist Poetry: Verse Translations from the Silver Age</u> (Four Continent Books, New York, 1976…a single copy of which is currently for sale on www.amazon.com for $100.00!). This collection, which published the translations of twelve ASU Russian language students and one University of Arizona graduate student, has a review comment on the back cover by Prof. Andrew Zigelis of the University of Georgia saying: "This little collection provides a sampling of the works of the major Russian Symbolist poets, Balmont, Briusov, and Blok, and includes several less well-known figures as well. *The attempt to give a verse translation of each poem will add substance to the arguments of those who feel that in poetry translation form should be preserved as well as the content* (Italics mine…JN)." And, twenty years later, in his RUS-211/212 textbook, <u>Russian Through Poems and Songs</u> (Alternative Copy Service, Tempe, AZ, 1995) Prof. Croft discusses the conflict of form and meaning in the translation of poetry in several places. On page 85, for example, he reports having engaged in a formal debate in February of 1981 entitled "Form Versus Content in Poetic Translation" with University of Texas-Austin Professor Sidney Monas, who was visiting ASU as a Distinguished Professor of Russian History. After taking his courses, we can easily guess that Prof. Croft took the side in this debate of the necessity of preserving the form in poetic translation.

Pushkin's '*Romance*:'
A Translation Preserving Form
By:
Lee B. Croft
Arizona State University

With all the translations and the studies of Alexander Pushkin's (1799-1837) work, you might think that all his work has been translated, that all his work has been thoroughly studied. This is not true. There are still many parts of Pushkin's large body of work untranslated and unstudied. Here is an example of a Pushkin poem never before translated into English. Pushkin wrote it in 1814 while still a high-school student in the Tsar's Village Lyceum. The original version had eight verses (cf. <u>А. С. Пушкин: Полное собрание сочинений в шести томах, М А. Цявловский, глав. ред., Москва, Ленинград, 1937, том 1, str.</u> 66/660), but only six found their way into subsequent publications of the poem (e.g. <u>А. С. Пушкин: Полное собрание сочинений в десяти томах. Д. Д. Благой и др. ред., Издательство Художественной литературы, Москва, 1959, том 1, стр.</u> 259-260) after its first printing in 1827. During Pushkin's life the poem was put to music in three different versions and was very popular, due in all probability to its topic of the tragedy of "illegitimate" birth. Pushkin's sympathetic adoption of the personna of the unfortunate mother in this early poem indicates that a later event in his life must have troubled him severely. In 1826 Pushkin sired an out-of-wedlock child with a serf, Olga Kalashnikova, the daughter of his father's steward on the family estate (Henri Troyat's <u>Pushkin</u>

(Translated from French by Nancy Amphoux) Minerva Press, NY, 1975 pp. 300-302).

In my translation I have tried to preserve the ABABCDCD rhyme scheme of the eight-line stanzas as well as the iambic *(-1-1-1-1)* tetrameter. The dominant sounds of the poem, the spirants "С" and "З," the dentals "Т" and "Д" and the vowel "Ы" and "И," anagrammatically spell out its theme—*"стыд"* ("shame"). Pushkin's more mature works have been perceived by scholars to include such anagrammaticality (cf. three fascinating articles in <u>Slavic and East European Journal</u>: Lauren Leighton's "Gematria in the 'Queen of Spades': A Decembrist Puzzle, "21:4 (1977), pp. 455-469; Dora Burton's "The Theme of Peter as Verbal Echo in <u>Mednyj Vsadnik</u>," 26:1 (1982), pp. 12-26; and Sergej Davydov's "The Sound and Theme in the Prose of A. S. Pushkin: A Logo-semantic Study of Paronomasia," 27:1 (1983), pp. 1-18). On occasion I have made equivalent alliteration (e.g. the "с/s" in ". . . К' страданью присуждает нас " =="... has sentenced us to suffering sore").

Alexander S. Pushkin 1814 Poetic Creation	Lee B. Croft 1975 Verse Translation
Романс	**Romance**
Под вечер, осенью ненастной, В пустынных дева шла местах И тайный плод любви несчастной Держала в трепетных руках. Всё было тихо—лес и горы, Всё спало в сумраке ночном: Она внимательные взоры Водила с ужасом кругом.	In autumn on a rainy evening, A maiden walked deserted lands. Poor fruit of secret love's conceiving She carried in her trembling hands. All was quiet—hills and forest, All reposed in gloom of night; Directed she in terror sorest To every side her cautious sight.
И на невинном сём творенье Вздохнув, остановила их... "Ты спишь, дитя, моё мученье,	On her creation innocent, Having sighed, she fixed her gaze... "You sleep, my child, my torment,

Не знаешь горестей моих.	Unaware of my malaise.
Откроешь очи и тоскуя,	You'll open eyes, so sorely missing
Ты к груди не прильнешь моей.	That to my breast no more you'll press.
Не встретишь завтра поцелуя	No more to meet the morrow's kissing.
Несчастной матери твоей.	No more poor mother's dear caress.
Её манить напрасно будешь!	Futile will it be to beckon!...
Мне вечный стыд вина моя,--	To me my guilt is shame always,--
Меня навеки ты забудешь:	You'll me in time forget to reckon;
Но не забуду я тебя!	But I'll forget you not one day!
Дадут покров тебе чужие	You will share some others' home
И скажут: 'Ты для нас чужой!'	And they'll relate you're alien.
Ты спросишь: 'Где мои родные?'	You will ask: 'Where are my own?'
И не найдёшь семьи родной.	But will not find your native kin.
Несчастный! Будешь грустной думой	You'll, luckless one, w' sad'nd mind
Томиться меж других детей!	Among the other children languish!
И до конца с душой угрюмой	For mother's caresses having pined
Взирать на ласки матерей:	In spirit to the end in anguish.
Повсюду странник одинокой,	When everywhere a lonely stranger,
Всегда судьбу свою кляня,	Always cursing your hard fate,
Услышишь ты упрёк жестокий...	You will hear cruel jests of anger,
Прости, прости тогда меня...	Forgive me then, my child, too late!
Ты спишь, позволь себя, несчастный,	You sleep, allow y'rself, my poor one
Прижать к груди в последний раз.	To press yourself to breast once more!
Закон неправедный, ужасный	A fearsome law of unjust moral
К страданью присуждает нас.	Has sentenced us to suffering sore.
Пока лета не отогнали	For a time the years won't drive away
Невинной радости твоей.	Your childhood's innocent joy of life.
Спи, милый! Горькие печали	Sleep, my dear one!—Quiet day
Не тронут детства тихих дней!"	Will chase away the bitter strife!"
Но вдруг за рощей осветила	But sudden did through groves the moon
Вблизи ей хижину луна...	Cast its light on nearby hut…
Бледна, трепещуща, уныла,	Pale and shaking, eyes cast down,
К дверям приближалась она:	She approached the door tight shut.
Склонилась, тихо положила	Bent she down then, softly placing
Младенца на порог чужой.	The infant on the threshold there,
Со страхом очи отвратила	With fear aback her eyes a'tracing,
И скрылась в темноте ночной.	Then faded into night's nowhere.

Why Memorize?
By:
Jeremy Ecton

Jeremy Ecton was born in Bountiful, Utah, November 2, 1983, but grew up in Gilbert, Arizona. Shortly after his graduation from Highland High School in May 2002, Jeremy was called to serve a two-year mission for The Church of Jesus Christ of Latter Day Saints to the Ukraine, Kiev Mission. Upon his return, Jeremy enrolled into the Chemical Engineering and Russian programs at Arizona State University. He was inducted into the Epsilon Epsilon chapter of **Добро Слово** (Dobro Slovo), the National Slavic Studies Honorary in Spring 2007 (see him in the group picture in Lee B. Croft, et. al. Russian in Arizona: A History of Its Teaching, IIHS, Tempe, AZ/Perm, Russian Federation, 2007, pp. 245). His article, "Our Ukrainian

Landlady," was published in the earlier capstone book, <u>Russia: The Missionaries' Tales</u> (Lee B. Croft, et. al., Capstone Publications, Phoenix, AZ, 2008, pp. 104-110...see www.Russianaz.org under "sponsors"). After his graduation in May of 2009, Jeremy plans to pursue a doctorate in Chemical Engineering.

PRESENTATION:

Prof. Croft reports that the material in this article was originally included in a scholarly presentation entitled "The Neuromnemonic Case for Rote Memorization" that he gave at the national convention of the American Association for the Advancement of Slavic Studies' (AAASS) Slavic Languages Pedagogy section in Honolulu, Hawai'i, in November of 1993. Much of the information in it about the workings of the human brain stem from Croft's research and teaching in the field of substance-abuse education. From 1981 to 1983, Croft taught ASU's controversial course, "Marijuana and Man," under Health Science (HES-) and general Liberal Arts (LIA) listings, later using his expertise and gained authority as the basis for a private drug counseling and testing business, Croft Consultants, that his wife, Dr. Lesley Hoyt Croft, headed. He remembers that the reaction to his call for the pedagogical use of rote memorization was NOT positive by his AAASS audience. One scholar, the lead author of a widely-used beginning Russian language textbook, upbraided Croft for "recidivist" pedagogy and decried his "making students memorize and recite material they couldn't yet understand."

Prof. Croft's University of Arizona colleague, Prof. Delbert D. Phillips, was also at the 1993 AAASS convention in Honolulu and he suggested that Croft submit a textual version of his presentation to him and the Russian editors of Sintaksis Publishers in Moscow for inclusion into the two-volume anthology **Методика преподавания русского языка и литературы в Америке** (**Д. Филлипс, ред., Синтаксис, Москва, Россия, 1996, том 2, стр. 113-127**). This was a very significant collection of articles on the teaching of Russian language and literature in America that was published in Russia in the early post-Soviet days…the first of its kind. Here, of course, Croft's article appeared in Russian as "**Нейромнемонический процесс заноминания через повтор**" ("The Neuromnemonic Process of Memorization by Repetition"). But, while this Russian article was in editorial process in Russia, Croft decided that he wanted to include it *bilingually* into his own textbook for ASU's Basic Russian Conversation course (RUS-211/212) that he was preparing during his sabbatical-leave year of 1994-5. Prof. Phillips gave his permission for this, and the article was published, with Russian marked-stress text paralleling English text on the same page, titled as "Why Memorize?—The Neuromnemonic Case for Rote Memorization" in Croft's **Russian Through Poems and Songs** (now available at Alternative Copy Center, Tempe, AZ ,1995, pp. 5-20). As things turned out, the bilingual publication of the article in Croft's text preceded by a year the publication of the original Russian version in Moscow. But both versions have been well received in the profession (see also the article by Alicia C. Baehr), and Croft's text is used to this day at GRINT, the institute in Moscow that hosts the students of Prof. Phillips' renowned University of Arizona Russian Abroad program. I have prepared here the English version of the bilingual edition from Prof. Croft's text, as opposed to translating the Russian from Prof. Phillips' anthology, but have included, of course, the Russian titles and sources in the Russian Cyrillic.

The Neuromnemonic Case for Rote Memorization
By:
Lee B. Croft
Arizona State University

"Repetition is the mother of learning"
"Повторение-мать учения"

The aim of this paper is to provide the foreign language teacher with a model of mnemonic process, which may be useful in the structuring of learning activities for students. At the outset, let me describe the particular context in which I have used this model to structure my students' learning activities.

I teach a course called Basic Conversational Russian to monolingual speakers of English at a large American university. This course is intended for students who have studied the Russian language for one year. This assumes a basic mastery of the alphabet, a useful lexicon of 500-1000 words, and a previous systematic scanning of Russian grammar: the aspects and tense of the verb, the cases of nouns, adjectives ad pronouns. The course is meant to be an enjoyable complement to our second-year mainstream grammar course.

The main text is S. Khavronina's <u>Russian as We Speak It,</u> and we proceed through this text in its intended order. All activities are oral; there is no written homework, although there are written exams. I give all instructions in Russian and endeavor to avoid any English grammatical explanations. In class the students read aloud and translate into English the introductory reading of each chapter. They read and translate each dialogue and try to reenact each one without reference to the text. We then work our way orally through the exercises at the end of each lesson, translating the short anecdote there if one is given. This textbook in its various editions has served me well for many years. Whenever I have tried something else, the results have forced me to return to Khavronina. I would certainly welcome a post-Soviet revision of this text at this time.

The problems that I have encountered in teaching this course over the past twenty years have been many, but most are derivative of the fact that I have, for largely budgetary reasons, too many students in the class. And this class represents, for many of them, their only exposure (three hours per week) to spoken Russian. Indeed it is not rare for me to have thirty-five students in a class. And this is obviously not optimum size for building conversational skill. Subdividing the class has proven ineffective without competent guidance of the subgroups. We have no faculty aides, no student helpers, no graduate assistants, but only over-worked and underpaid faculty. And so I have devised some strategies to require oral preparation work of the students--that is, songs and poems.

We sing in the classroom. No matter that my voice is not a particularly good one. No matter that many students may be shy about singing in front of their cohort. Nevertheless we sing, not individually, but chorally, as a group. I direct and urge the students on ("**Живо...с выражением, господа!**" "Lively now…with expression, ladies and gents"). We sing those stereotypical pieces which every American identifies with Russia: **Подмосковные вечера** ("Moscow Nights"), **Катюша** ("Katiusha"), **Очи чёрные** ("Dark Eyes"), **Калинка** ("Kalinka"), **Эй, ухнем** ("Eh, Ukhnem"), **Тонкая рябина** ("The Slender Mountain Ash"), **Бородино** ("Borodino"), and a dozen or so others. I persuade my students that these songs are important, not only as common cultural ground with the Russians who all know them, but for psycholinguistic reasons. Even people with severe speech pathologies, stutterers, for example, can sing smoothly. The U.S country-and-western singer Mel Tillis is a good example. And so the students sing, and they are asked on the written exams for each of the lessons in the Khavronina text to answer in Russian questions about the content of the songs (we "cover" two songs per lesson, which takes us six sessions or two weeks). An example question from "Moscow Nights" would be: **Почему певец хочет, чтобы его милая была добра ему?** ("Why does the singer want his darling to be kind to him?") Almost *any* grammatically correct answer is considered correct and the subsequent discussion of various answers occasions much class mirth and builds rapport.

The activity which is more central to the topic of discussion in this paper, however, is the memorization and recitation of Russian poetry. The students are required to memorize and recite, without reference to text, one poem or series of quotes every other week throughout the year-long course. In order to thwart that old demon, procrastination, I have laid down a schedule of recitations, which mandates that the recitations be completed by a given date if an "A" grade is desired. The poem which is currently scheduled is read at least once in every class either by me or by one of the students, usually at the beginning of the hour. The students do not have to recite these poems in class, though many do. They may recite them to me or to my faculty colleagues in the office, in the hall, on the mall or the street (but NOT over the telephone)—anywhere where they are sure the feat will be properly recorded in my gradebook. There are, in chronological order: two poems on immortality by Gavril Derzhavin ("**Река времён**" ("The River of Time") and the formidable "**Памятник**" ("Monument"));

three poems by Alexander Pushkin ("**Ты и Вы**" ("Thou and You"), "**Я вас любил...**" ("I Loved You Once…"), and "**К *****" ("To ***")); three poems by Mikhail Lermontov ("**Ангел**" ("The Angel"), "**Парус**" ("The Sail"), and "**Выхожу один я на дорогу...**" ("Alone I walk out on the road…")); a trio of prose quotations (Denis Fonvizin on human ignorance from <u>The Minor</u> ("**В человеческом невежестве...**"), Ivan Turgenev on the "Russian language" ("**Во дни сомнений, во дни тягостных раздумий о судьбах моей родины...**") and Leo Tolstoy's "The hero of my tale…is truth." ("**Герой же моей повести, которого я люблю...**"); two poems by Fyodor Tiutchev ("**Накануне годовщины 4ого августа 1864 года**" ("On the Eve of the Anniversary of August 4th, 1864") and the Latin titled "Silentium" ("**Молчи, скрывайся, и таи...**")); a poem by Alexander Blok ("**Ночь, улица, фонарь, аптека...**" ("The night, the street, the streetlight, the drugstore…")); the farewell suicide poem by Sergei Esenin ("**До свидания, друг мой, до свидания...**" ("Good-bye, my friend, goodby…")); two poems by Anna Akhmatova ("**Когда в тоске самоубийства...**" ("When in anguish of suicide…") and "**Мужество**" ("Courage")); and, finally, a poem by Boris Pasternak ("**Гамлет**" ("Hamlet") from <u>Doctor Zhivago</u>). The selection of these pieces was dictated by the same logic which motivates the choice of songs. At the second-year level of study, the students are continuing to form the bases of a common understanding of culture. They need the "classics" in order to do this. Moreover, the discussion of these poets and their lives gives the students an opportunity for a deeper view of Russian history. In subsequent years of their study, at higher levels of coursework, I ask the students to memorize and recite things of their own choosing and I learn much myself from their choices.

Despite the difficulties of this course requirement (both for the students and for myself), I do not apologize for equipping an entire generation of my university's Russian language students with these masterpieces of literature. I tell my students that poetry is especially valued within the Russian culture (at least among educated Russians). I tell them of the large audience in Russia for poets, who declaim their poetry at amazing lengths from memory, and about how it baffles the Russian audiences when our visiting American poets have to read their own poetry from a book.

It might interest my Russian colleagues to know that many American students attain university levels of study without ever having memorized or recited anything at all. American education in the modern era (since the 1960s, at least) has backed away from requiring the committal of factual material to memory. Compensatory focus has been directed to the learning of attitudes and (more desirably) "how to" skills. Polling my own classes reveals that over twenty percent of my students can not recall ever being asked to memorize or recite anything at all: not lines in a play, not multiplication tables, not even our alphabet. This is why my requirement that they memorize and recite Russian poetry comes as a shock to them. But it is also why their satisfaction of the requirement eventuates in such pride and gratitude.

Before I go on to examine the psychological underpinnings of this memorization, let me share with you an anecdote about my poetry requirement. One spring in the 1970s a female student asked if she could bring her grandmother with her to class. The grandmother, she said, was very recently bereaved of her husband of many years and was so grieved that the family members were afraid to leave her alone. The old woman spoke only a little English. She was a Lithuanian who had subsequently learned

German. But she had studied Russian in school before World War I. I consented to her attendance and she sat silently with her granddaughter through several classes of my Basic Conversational Russian. One day, as usual, I began the class with the question: "**Кто хочет читать сегодня?**" ("Who wants to recite today?"). To the surprise of all present, the old woman responded: "**Я хочу**" ("I want to."). She then recited in Russian with few mistakes Tiutchev's touching lament about his lost love, "On the Eve of the Anniversary of August 4th, 1864." And then she explained in halting English that she had been required to memorize that very poem sixty-five years before and that she was grateful to me for requiring her granddaughter to memorize it too—so that she would be similarly consoled in the event she too would lose someone close to her. The class was so moved, as was I, that we were unable to continue the lesson that day.

Recently, as part of a program evaluation, I had the opportunity to survey more than a hundred of my alumni of the past twenty years on their opinions about the value of what they learned at my university and how they learned it. Very prominent in their mention, and always positive, was my requirement of poetry memorization, inasmuch as it gave them "something to say in Russian." This positive evaluation even came from students who received a grade of "incomplete" in the course because they did not do the required number of recitations (I allow them to choose one to drop in each semester, but they must complete the rest to get a grade, and all the poems are included, similar to the songs, on the exams). The alumni favorites are Pasternak's "**Гамлет**" ("Hamlet") and Tiutchev's "Silentium,"—not at all the easiest to memorize, though they say that, when "something in Russian" is requested of them, they most often recite the first one, Derzhavin's shorter "**Река времён**" ("The River of Time").

Because of my experience with the students in my Basic Conversational Russian course, I have reflected a great deal on the task of memorization, and specifically on the task of memorizing things in a foreign language, which both my students and I agree is more difficult than memorizing things in one's own language. Physiologically, the memorization of material in a foreign language necessitates the "opening up" of new neural pathways to areas of the brain untouched in the process of native-language recall. Studies of aphasic patients reveal that non-native language skills stem from different loci of memory storage in the brain. People whose native language ability is severely impaired by stroke or by brain trauma are often able to communicate in sequentially acquired non-native languages.

I like to imagine the human neuron, or brain cell, as a kind of wire through which an electrochemical charge runs in order to complete a neurological circuit. These neurons link together across their trillions of synapses to form these circuits, called by one school of memory experts "engrams." And these engrams provide the physical basis of our memories, through which all thought process, including the understanding and production of language, must work.

For illustration, let us imagine that a tennis ball is bouncing toward us. The human eyes take in light reflected from the surface of the approaching tennis ball and convert this light into an electrochemical charge (or "action potential"), which is sent from the retina across the optic chiasmus in the central brain to the occipital lobe in the rear of the brain where visual information is stored. From here the charge runs through diverse neuronal "wires" to other loci within the brain. In order to describe the circuit, or engram, traced by the charge, we need to describe the loci involved. One way we can do this is to consider a matrix of distinctive features uniquely describing a tennis ball relative to our individual realities. For example, the ball has shape (+ three dimensional, + spherical) and texture (+ fuzzy, or, if you want, - smooth). These qualities of shape are registered in the somato-sensory area of the brain, found along both sides of the parietal sulcus at the top of the head. This is because the perception of shape, if you think enough about it, is a vicarious or secondary, perception of touch-feel. And so, we might easily surmise that the neurological engram representing the tennis ball runs from the occipital lobe to the parietal sulcus. We might also, for further example, guess that the tennis ball, as opposed to say, a peach, which is similarly sized, shaped and textured), is considered non-edible (-edible), and thus the engram runs to the locus, perhaps in the cerebrum above the hippocampus, where engrams may be routed to the limbic system for possible satisfaction of the primary drive, hunger. But in this case it does not so continue (being non-edible) but instead runs upward into the outer cortex of the cerebrum where higher-level associations are made. We can imagine individual variations to the engram, the brain storage process being surprisingly "plastic" (things learned in association are stored in association and the connection thus becomes reality), the tennis ball running through the loci where Martina Navratilova's image is registered, or through the locus where a particular personal pain is found. But, eventually, the engram runs to the cerebellum, where the brain's taxic control center instructs the body's musculature to respond in such a way as to hit back the approaching tennis ball with a racket.

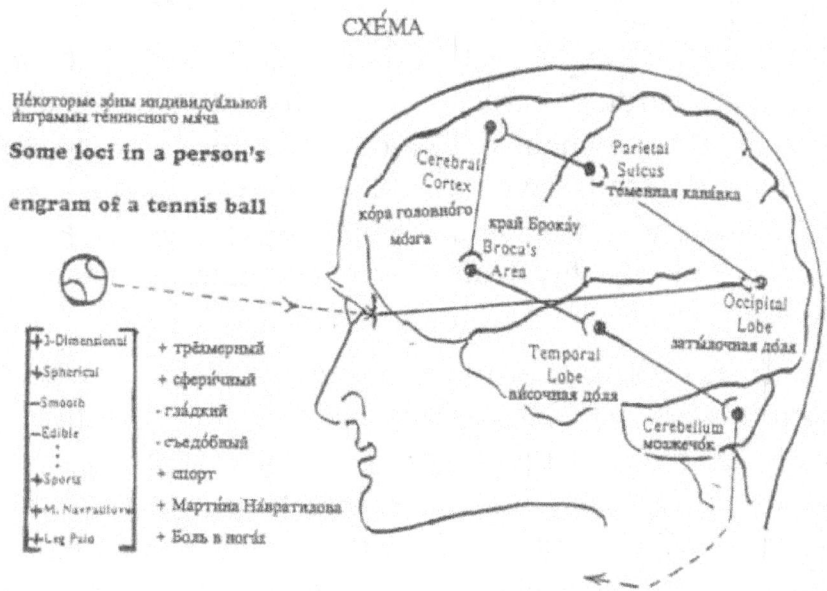

If we think of it in this way, an approaching tennis ball is neurologically represented in milliseconds in the brain by a wondrously complex but probably unique engram, or circuit (see accompanying illustration).

    This circuit, of course, necessarily runs through the brain's language center, Broca's area below the left temple (in right-handed people) for the processing of the requisite sounds sorted in the adjacent temporal lobe. This is how we know to say "tennis ball" in English. And, of course, the engram may also run to some foreign language registry for the equivalent translation. Indeed, in a millisecond the charge may run through millions and millions of brain loci in order to form the individually unique neurological circuit which constitutes its psychological reality, wherein mine may be different from, but is hopefully similar enough for recognition to, yours. With regard to learning, we mainly need to ask: "How does the charge know which way to run?" And, for us teachers: "How can we make it run, in the minds of others, the way we want it to run?" In order to understand this, we need to examine the way in which an individual neuron "learns." Neurologists tell us that a neuron is a cell which, unlike other bodily cells, does not reproduce. Instead, the neuron "learns." The neuron uses its genetic material, its DNA and RNA, to regulate the amount of its resistance to the electrochemical charges to which it is exposed[1].

With successive transitions through it of the charge, the neuron lowers its electrochemical resistance so that the charge runs more easily through it in successive turns. That is, it offers less and less resistance to successive similar charges. This, of course, means that the more times the circuit of these particular neurons is run, the easier it is to run. At each synapse, or junction between adjacent neurons, the charge "knows which way to run" since it is following the neuronal path of least electrochemical resistance to the established (already) associated locus. With this understanding we can see how the apprehensive traces we call "short-term memory" become transferred into the brain's permanent storage. Repetition is, indeed, the mother of learning.

Many people are unable, after they have been told an unfamiliar telephone number, to dial it again after an hour, or a day has passed. This is because they retained the number in their short-term memories only as long as they needed it for the initial dialing. The memory, if you will, lasted only as long as its engram was actually being run for the first time by the electrochemical charge which entered their ears with the sound of the informant's voice. When the circuit's resistance overcame the charge, the memory was lost.

There are several strategies which one can use, however, to transfer the short-term memory to permanent storage. One way is to deliberately "mark" the item to be remembered for special urgency in some way, often by associating it with other material already stored in permanent memory and easily accessed. Indeed, as teachers we should be aware that items stored in association with the most items already in storage are the ones which are the easiest to recall. Always explain things in several ways, give a multitude of synonyms and contexts of usage, tell the item's history, relate its previous usefulness to you, etc. These are things that good teachers do naturally, of course, without needing to be instructed in it. Nevertheless, a formulation of the neurological rationale for it can be useful in other regards as well.

Consider that the apprehension of all speech first comes through short-term memory. We are constantly bombarded with speech utterances, which are unique to our present personal situation that we have never encountered before. Yet the elements of which this speech is composed: phonological, morphological lexico-semantic, sentential, discoursive, are present in permanent memory storage. It is the content of our permanent memory storage that enables us to understand and respond to the unique utterances which come to us through our short-term memories. The implication of this conception is that, as teachers, we should be requiring the maximum possible transfer of information into permanent storage. Conversely, in the interest of time we should avoid pedagogical strategies which focus on transitory situations in which students operate only within short-term memory to accomplish some communicative task. This statement is not meant to contend with the strategies of my colleagues who would ask the student to manipulate a small extant lexicon to, say, get an automobile tire changed, or even buy a ballet ticket. I admit that these strategies have their place as well. My point is simply to give a sound neurological basis to those old, too-often-scorned methodologies of our pedagogical predecessors who helped us get to where we are. We should certainly have more than one method in our arsenal.

My teaching philosophy is twofold: 1) require the students to work harder than they thought they could, and 2) praise and reward them, both individually and collectively, for every small success gained. The task of memorizing and reciting offers ample opportunity for both aspects of my philosophy. When I ask my students how they manage, in two weeks' time, to memorize and recite in Russian such a difficult poem as Derzhavin's "**Памятник**" ("Monument") their answers invariably include that main and primary way in which short-term memories are transferred into permanent storage--that is, repetition. They read it over and over, they write it out, translate it, listen to it on tape, make mental milestones at the stanza breaks and separately memorize these. Then they start to recite it aloud—the first line, then the second, then the first and the second together, then the third, then the first, second and the third, and so on. Many try to eliminate top-to-bottom repetitional bias by starting up from the end successively by lines. Finally, by forcing the memory transfer through repetition, they get the job done and recite the entire poem smoothly. They notice as they approach closer and closer to the completion of the memorization they are able to focus their attention on ever finer details of understanding and of proper pronunciation and emotional nuance. The final result is praiseworthy indeed.

The final insight to share concerns the student consensus that the poems get easier and easier to memorize and recite as the year wears on. This is also explainable by the neurological model presented. The engrams of one poem are already in place as the engrams of the other are stored.

And there is an "overlap" which means that less and less new neural pathways have to be made in order to effectuate the storage. Thus the rote memorization of poetry, or any other information, adds to the material permanently stored, and thus enables us to handle the myriad unique short-term situations we encounter every day. Rote memorization, embodying the important element of repetition, is thus a pedagogical strategy both effective and rewarding. We in American education should return it to our repertoire.

NOTE:

1. The fact that these neurons do not reproduce themselves has other significance as well. In an ordinary 1350-gram human brain there are estimated to be several score billion of these neurons. Throughout life, a person learns by making associative connections among them. This ever increasing number of possible connective networks (the engrams) is necessary in order to compensate for the neurons' absolute attrition at an ever increasing rate beginning in the thousands per day at a person's maturity. A person of ninety years is thought to have only about two-thirds the number of neurons that a person of twenty has. And in old age the loss of so many neurons ultimately upsets the integrity of the engrams, causing the detriment of recall and the slowing of mental processes.

Of course, disease (e.g. Alzheimer's Syndrome) or drug use (e.g. Korsakoff's Syndrome) can dramatically accelerate the loss of neurons or, even in a young person, interfere with the neurons' ability to regulate their electro-chemical resistance. A neuron which is exposed to lipid solutions of even very dilute amounts (as dilute as 5 nanograms per milliliter) of delta-9-tetrahydrocannibinol (the most studied psychoactive ingredient of marijuana) offers 40-60 percent more resistance to the action potential required for engrams to be run. Such interference results in the skew storage of information processed through the senses. New engrams are not formed and learning essentially stops, and even worse, skew, or improper, associations are made thus negatively effecting recall. One can imagine the electrochemical charge not running the correct neural pathway entirely, finding all or part of it chemically blocked, but running instead down some other, incorrect, path of lesser resistance.

Recent studies indicate that as many as a quarter of Americans of the 18-25 year old age group, the group which comprises most of our undergraduate students, are users of psychoactive drugs (drugs which cross the blood-brain barrier to impact on neuronal membrane dynamics.) These drug users often differ from consensus on tests of subtle sound-sense associations (see, for example, the "**Штанга**" test in my SEEJ article, included here in the article by Shane C. Sarlo and also in the one by Alicia C. Baehr). As a substance-abuse counselor, I had a client, a long-time daily marijuana smoker, who showed the effects of this skew information storage in his capacity for lexical recall. He had become a virtual exhibit of malapropism, uttering phrases like: "We need an office in *promiscuity* (proximity) to the hospital," and "You can buy a new car, you're *effluent* (affluent)" until his speech bordered on incoherence. The message is clear—we should tell our students that if they want to learn and to develop mentally, they should cease and abstain from the use of such psychoactive substances.

Sources:

Beaty, Jackson. Introduction to Physiological Psychology: Information Processing in the Nervous system. Brooks/Cole Publishing Co., Monterey, Ca, 1975

Croft, Lee B. "The Mnemonic Use of Linguistic Iconicity in Teaching Language and Literature," in Slavic and East European Journal. Vol. 22 No. 4 (Winter 1978), pp. 509-518.

Croft, Lee B. "Triplicity and Textual Iconicity: Russian Literature through a Triangular Prism," in Syntactic Iconicity and Linguistic Freezes: the Human Dimension; Marge E. Landsberg, ed;, Walter De Gruyter Publishers, Berlin, 1995.

Croft, Lee B. Poems and Songs for Basic conversational Russian. 5th ed., Alternative Photocopy, Tempe, Az., 1993.

Croft, Lee B., TOADIES: THE Explanation of Toxicomania in American Society (published in both Russian and English). Sintaksis. Moscow. 1992.

Hubel, David H. Eye, Brain and Vision. Scientific American Library, Series No. 22, New York, 1988.

Keller, Howard H. "Memory: Poetic and Neurophysiological Descriptions," in Slavic and East European Journal. Vol. 26 No. 1 (spring 1982), pp. 77-85.

Khavronina, S. Russian As We Speak It. Russky yazyk Publishers, Moscow, any of several editions have been used 1973 through 10th ed., 1989

Mann, Peggy. Marijuana Alert. McGraw-Hill book Company, New York, 1985 (note the mention on pp. 76 of my drug education efforts at ASU).

Mann, Peggy. "Dogged Crusader Against Drugs" (about Dr. Gabriel G. Nahas, see below) in Reader's Digest. May 1989, pp. 102-106.

Nahas, Gabriel G. Keep Off the Grass. 3rd ed., P. Eriksson Publishers, Middlebury, Vermont, 1985.

Smith, C.U.M. The Brain: Towards an Understanding. Capricorn books, New York, 1972.

Patrick J. Heuer at Boris Yeltsin's grave, Moscow, 2007

The Professor and the Pushkin Pornographer
By:
Vadim S. Kagan

Vadim S. Kagan was born in Minsk, Belarus. His family immigrated to Phoenix, AZ in February 1990. He grew up in Mesa, AZ and graduated from Mesa High School in 2002. He enrolled in Arizona State University for his freshman year of college, but then went to nursing school. After realizing that nursing was not his true calling, he came back to ASU and indulged his growing interest in the culture of his personal heritage by choosing to major in Russian. He was inducted into ASU's Epsilon Epsilon chapter of the **Добро Слово** ("Dobro Slovo," The National Slavic Studies Honorary) in Spring 2008, and, in the summer of 2008, he studied in Russia as a participant of the University of Arizona's Russian Abroad Program under the direction of U. of AZ Distinguished Professor of Russian Delbert D. Phillips.

PRESENTATION:

This publication is not, strictly speaking, a scholarly article. It is a review written by Prof. Croft that was published in the journal World Literature Today (WLT) in 1995 (Vol. 69, No. 4, pp. 816-7). Prof. Croft had been on the review staff of this journal since the 1970's when it bore the title Books Abroad. He had written more than thirty reviews that were published there, specializing in writing about Russian poetry and Russian poets, both native and emigre.

Mikhail Armalinsky (1947-) is a controversial figure in the literature of the Russian diaspora…arguably the *most* controversial figure in this literature today. His history is that he was allowed to leave the Soviet Union as part of the 1970's "third wave" of emigration, largely of dissident Jews. He came to the United States in February of 1977 and settled in the unlikely location (for a Russian émigré) of Minneapolis and began to publish Russian-language poetry of his own and others of an explicitly erotic nature, founding his own publishing house named M.I.P. (the initials of his real name, Mikhail Izrailevich Peltsman) Company (cf. www.mipco.com) in 1984. When Prof. Croft reviewed for WLT (63:4, pp. 701) an M.I.P. Company published collection of poetry (**Черновик отваги** or "Outline of Valor") by a "Leningrad poet named **Алексей Шельвах**" in 1989, the erotic themes and explicit descriptions of sex in the work struck Croft as too similar to the previous works of publisher Armalinsky (e.g. Armalinsky's 1988 **По обе стороны оргазма** ("On Both Sides of the Orgasm")) to be coincidence and he hinted in his review that **Шельвах** and Armalinsky might be the same man. This drew a scoffing letter to him from Armalinsky who assured him that "the Leningrad author" **Шельвах**, struggling as "a lathe operator" in his factory job and living in his communal Soviet apartment with a wife and two children, would be "interested to learn of your opinion that he doesn't exist." This was the beginning of a long relationship by mail and, more recently, by email between Mikhail Armalinsky and Lee B. Croft.

By the time this happened, Armalinsky had already become known as the "Pushkin pornographer." This was because of M.I.P. Company's publication, in 1986, of a small booklet entitled **Тайные записки: 1836-1837 годов** by none other than **А. С. Пушкин** (<u>Secret Notes of 1836-1837</u> by A(lexander) S(ergeevich) Pushkin). This work purported to be the rumored-to-exist diary of the great Russian poet Alexander Pushkin's final year of life before his death in a tragic duel. And the work, written in the most graphic modern Russian idiom, was extremely explicit in detailing the poet's sexual dalliances with not only his wife, but her sisters and a number of others singly and in groups…in short, it was modern western "porno" in Russian. In the "Necessary Foreword" to it, Armalinsky relates as its publisher the circumstances by which he came to possess the work. A Leningrad historian, an "acquaintance of an acquaintance" of his, known to him only by the first-name/patronymic "Nikolai Pavlovich," gave to him for the purpose of getting it out of the USSR the manuscript of the historian's translation into an equivalent modern Russian vernacular of Alexander Pushkin's personal notes from the last year of his life. Nikolai Pavlovich had, he said, deciphered these notes from Pushkin's original encryption based on the 19th century French (Pushkin's "second language"). Armalinsky, after settling in Minneapolis, managed to type the historian's Russian manuscript into a printed text. But then, Armalinsky reports in his foreword: "I left on an extended business trip and *Nickolai Pavlovich's manuscript disappeared* (italics mine…VSK). I can say no more." But Armalinsky then (in 1986) edited and had his M.I.P. Company publish the **Тайные записки 1836-1837 годов** (the Russian version of the "Secret Notes") under the name of "A. S. Pushkin." So shocking to the Russian literary establishment in the USSR was the publication in America of such a work, besmirching the hallowed character of their national poet and icon, that Moscow's Pushkin Institute scholar of authority who was quickly entrusted to "debunk" the work based on those "sure-to-be-there" internal inaccuracies about Pushkin's life, **Проф. Илья Зильберштейн** (Prof. Ilya Zilbershtein), is alleged to have gone into a such a fit of apoplexy when he saw it, realized its pornographic nature, and concluded that he could not debunk it, that he had to be removed from his office to the hospital…and that he soon thereafter died. His opinion that this was "the most malicious and impudent falsification that has ever been" ("**И должен прямо сказать, что такой подлейшей и наглейшей фальшивки ещё никогда не бывало**") and that no other work in over a hundred years of forgeries "went to such deliberate lengths to besmirch Pushkin" ("**(такие)…не доходили до таких пределов, до сознательного стремления опорочить Пушкина**") was published in the leading popular magazine **Огонёк** (1987 No. 12 edited by **Виталий Коротич** (Vitalii Korotich)) with a sidebar by a noted Soviet international lawyer, **Ф. РЕШЕТНИКОВ**, (**доктор юридических наук, профессор, специалист по уголовному закону зарубежных государств**—"F. Reshetnikov, Doctor of Juridical Sciences, Professor, Specialist on Criminal Law of Foreign Governments"), stating that, for publishing such a demeaning calumny of Pushkin, Mikhail Armalinsky's host Americans should apply to him "their traditional remedy for sexual perversion—CASTRATION! (caps mine…VSK)"

Later in 1986 Armalinsky's M.I.P. Company brought out an English translation of the notes under the title of SECRET JOURNAL, 1836-1837 and purportedly written "by Alexander Pushkin" (translated by Mikhail Armalinsky and Tjody Aän). In this version, Armalinsky made so bold as to give more fodder for potential debunkers by providing a number of explanatory annotations about the characters and events mentioned therein. The review of this English version by American Prof. Richard Gregg of Vassar College in Slavic Review (Vol. 46 (1987), No. 3/4, pp. 642-643) parallels the reaction (see above) by Russian scholar **Илья Зильберштейн** in **Огонёк.** Gregg ridicules the work's "pseudo-history" of publicational circumstances, calls it "sovporn," and a "forgery." But the work remains undebunked, because, Gregg admits, "the author has done his homework." At the end of his review he writes: "…these pages produce an effect that is not so much erotic as emetic. Well wishers (I am not one) can only hope that Armalinsky, who has done his best to dishonor the name of Russia's greatest poet, will find a niche in a publishing enterprise more worthy of his talents. May I suggest the editorial staff of Hustler magazine?"

For much of the next decade (1987-1997) Armalinsky's publication of "Pushkin's Secret Notes" was largely shunned by the mainstream literary establishment…especially in Russia. The apparent hope of the literary establishments of both worlds was that the scandal associated with the pornographic "Pushkin Notes" would just fade away and that the notes themselves would be forgotten. But the scandal, fueled by Armalinsky's continuing and very persistent efforts, did not fade away. In the 1990's with the dissolution of the Soviet Union and the rise of the world-wide web and internet communications, Armalinsky was able to use the less restricted Russian press and the new communications technology to see the notes published in language after language and to see their sales increase. The count is now at 24 languages, and includes

The Bi-lingual Записки/Journal Cover

even a marked-stress facing-pages version in both Russian and English (this was suggested to Armalinsky by Prof. Croft) to aid the world's Russian language learners toward mastery of otherwise arcane vocabulary and phraseology (cf. Retro Publishing House, St. Petersburg, Russia, 2006).

Daring the Russian literary establishment to publish an M.I.P. Company sanctioned version of the notes in Russia, Armalinsky paid to have challenges ("**СЛАБО́!**" or "I dare you!") published in Russian newspapers. The Russian Wikipedia entry on Mikhail Armalinsky (search alphabetically at http://ru.wikipedia.org) terms him an "internet activist" ("**сетевой деятель**") and "the first active Russian spammer" ("**первый активный российский спамер**") for being an early and very adept internet and email advertiser of the notes (the U.S. Slavicists' professional email listserve group SEELANGS has recently banned him for violations of its advertising policies). One of the ways Armalinsky assures that the associated scandal remains in the public eye is to publish associate David Baevsky's collections of reactions from all over the world entitled **Парапушкинистика** ("Parapushkinistika") 1996, 1998, 2004 and **Парапушкинистика II**, 2007.

In this third millenium (2000-), Armalinsky has seen the notes published in Russia. Moscow's Scientific Publishing Center Ladomir ("**Ладомир**") published it in 2001 as part of its series "**Русская потаенная литература**" ("Russia's Secret Literature"). And Ladomir also published, in 2002, a collection of Armalinsky's own selected poetry and prose entitled **Чтоб знали! Избранное 1966-1998** ("So that they'd know! Selected works of 1966-1998"). This 860-page tome has an introduction by **Ольга Воздвиженская** (Olga Vozdvizhenskaya) entitled "**Соитие Ленинграда с Миннеаполисом, или преодоление несовпадений (о сочинениях Михаила Армалинского)**" ("The

Copulation of Leningrad and Minneapolis, or the Overcoming of Discordances"). This introduction is accessible separately in a translation by Prof. Croft at www.mipco.com/English/introVozd.htm. And, Armalinsky has personally seen a play derived from the notes performed on the stage in Paris, France. A one-man show entitled <u>Pouchkine: Le Journal Secret</u> starring French actor Manuel Blanc debuted at the Théâtre du Marais in Paris on September 27, 2006. In December of 2007 a pictorial feature on Armalinsky appeared in the Russian version of <u>Penthouse</u> magazine. It mentions some of his notorious antics—using an American flag he once drew for the New York City sexual tabloid <u>Screw</u>-- with the stars and stripes rendered in penises and vulvas, as his corporate logo; creating an online religion of genitality accessed through a site called www.templeofgenitals.com that he then tried to sell on eBay for a million dollars; and so on.

In 1995, Armalinsky submitted a collection of his personal poetry entitled **Вплотную...** ("Close to…," M.I.P. Company, Minneapolis, 1994) to be reviewed in <u>World Literature Today</u>. The Associate Editor there, William Riggan, assigned the review to Prof. Lee B. Croft at ASU, informing him that he would be allowed a double-length review if he would, in the course of reviewing **Вплотную...**, address the nature and genuinity of "Pushkin's <u>Secret Notes</u>" in the pages of <u>WLT.</u> That's what follows here, reprinted by permission of <u>World Literature Today:</u>

World Literature Today
69:4 (Autumn, 1995)

Review of Armalinsky, Mikhail. **Вплотную...** ("Close to..."). M.I.P. Company, Minneapolis, MN, 1994.

Mikhail Armalinsky is a Russian émigré poet and publisher now based in Minneapolis who has scandalized Russian literary circles since his 1986 publication of Alexander Pushkin's "Secret Notes" from 1836-37, the last year of the great poet's life. The pornographic nature of these notes, clearly of a modern Western stripe, drew apoplectic reaction from the Soviet literary authorities who first encountered them. One legal authority, in a sidebar to an article on this "hoax" in **Огонёк** magazine, suggested that Armalinsky be castrated for so besmirching the hallowed name of Pushkin. But, of course, the sales of these "Notes," now translated and published in English, Italian, German, and French, are guaranteeing the financial viability of Armalinsky's M.I.P. Company, which might otherwise struggle to continue its production of Russian "erotica" (original Russian verse, prose, and translations of works by the Marquis de Sade). Currently, Armalinsky is publicizing his "dare" to Russian publishers to issue a full and MIP-sanctioned version in Russian, where to date the press has only published unrecompensed excerpts. Pushkinists worldwide have yet to address the authenticity of the notes *per se*, as if they feared the consequences of being unable to find a flaw.

Any credence the putative "Pushkin Notes" might have is due to the formidability of Armalinsky as a literary scholar and as a poet himself. His formidability as a literary scholar is established by the notes' lack of glaring errors in the reflected detail of Pushkin's last year of life. It is not, after all, an easy matter to fictionalize Pushkin's well-researched life without making substantive errors, as witness Wayne State University Press's factually flawed (and with uncredited poetry translations) 1989 publication of John Oliver Killens's <u>Great Black Russian</u>. In 1986, when Armalinsky published the English edition of the "Secret Journal" (as the English version was titled), he added a number of textual explanations which offer yet further challenge to prospective debunkers within the community of Pushkinists. Still the challenge is untaken. Yet it is Armalinsky's formidability as poet, well reflected here in the collection **<u>Вплотную</u>** (Close To), which offers the best explanation of the matter: his clear feeling of "kinship" with Pushkin and his adoption of Pushkin's personna to gain attention for his own literary endeavors, which have, especially since his emigration to the United States in 1977, taken on a pornographic character strikingly similar to the notes he attributes to Pushkin. And it is this similarity which most erodes the credibility of the notes' authenticity. Surely the same mind created both the notes and the poetry here... and it wasn't Pushkin's.

The title of the present collection, "Close To," serves as an indication that the majority of the poems herein deal with various aspects of human intimacy, as indeed do Armalinsky's other nine books by the same publisher (see for example, Vytas Duka's review of his prose collection **<u>Двойственные отношения</u>** in <u>WLT</u> 68:2, p. 389). There are three subtitled sections here: "Antiquarian Things," "Used Things," and "Things Afresh"--with the poems arranged chronologically throughout. The poems of the late 1960's and early 1970's muse considerably on the passage of time, with calendar division (days of the week, months of the year) serving as the main metaphor. Even then, however, problematic human relationships can be seen in

Armalinsky's poetry. He likens other people to "mosquitoes, like vampires… who suck my blood," and he writes that he would like "to kill them, with impunity, like mosquitoes." By 1981 his problematic human relations take on a decidedly misogynistic character, a reflection, it is easy to opine, of the obsession with Western pornography he acquired after his emigration the U.S. This obsession, an addiction clear and simple, leads him to objectify women as sexual objects and to equate them with their genitalia. Evidence of this is rife in the later sections of the collection, in the poems written after his emigration.

As mentioned above, one is struck by the similarity of Armalinsky's own observations with those his publication of the notes has attributed to Pushkin. His "Gospel from Me" mentions that he "feels sorry for Jesus Christ," who was crucified because he "didn't take to fucking" the harlot Maria who offered herself to him. This reminds one of the notes' discussion of how "Christ was ignorant of lust. …And if he did not commit adultery, it is only because he aimed to fuck her but she did not excite him." Later he states that "women are good only for fucking… all to one person the same, only different by pussy." This disjunction of a woman from her genitalia is similarly expressed in the notes where "Pushkin" expresses the opinion that a woman's "soul resides in the pussy and in the heart."

What we have here is a very expressive poet, and one very competent in form. He is capable of innovative rhyme, as in the macaronic Russian "s mysl'iu" ("с мыслью," meaning "with the thought") and the English "I miss you." He experiments in five-line stanzas and in cleverly syncopated sound textures. His message is never opaque and is arrestingly expressed. However, he has let a modern illness, pornography addiction, cause him to take his poetic expression to places most of us do not want to go. He apparently has ambivalent feelings about this. On the one hand he takes pride in the scandal he has caused, writing of his creative rationale: "They were reading for fun, / My life they didn't notice- / Tongues held behind their teeth. / So I beat them out of it/ So they couldn't be silent." This same pride motivated Eduard Limonov, in his **Дневник неудачника** ("Diary of a Loser") (see, for example, my review in WLT 58:2, p. 334), to write the one-line poem "They were singing an opera, and I came in," itself a conceited formal parody of Valerii Briusov's famous one-liner (from Chefs d'oeuvres, 1897) "O close thy pale legs." On the other hand, there is some internal indication that Armalinsky realizes the nature of his addiction when he writes: "I feel that I've fallen into a circle, like a cell, the repetitions of which there is no way out of." It should be noted that Armalinsky's disease is our disease, and that since it infected Armalinsky it has spread to his homeland as well. Let's hope for his sake, and ours, that a cure is found soon.

--Lee B. Croft
Arizona State University

So, soon after this review appeared in WLT, Prof. Croft received a letter (dated December 23, 1995) from Mikhail Armalinsky on M.I.P. Co. stationery saying that "(I) really appreciate your *advertisement* (italics mine...VSK) of my books in the WLT," and offering "a couple of factual comments," among which is comment number 4: "Pornography is not a disease, it is a cure for the disease."

.

A Russian Biography of an American Scientist

By:

Patrick J. Heuer

Patrick J. Heuer is a senior who will soon be graduating from Arizona State University. He will be graduating with two Bachelors of Arts degrees: one in International Political Economy and one in Russian. After graduation he will be attending law school, studying international commercial arbitration. His adventurous spirit and curiosity for international culture has taken him all over the world. From the jungles of Puerto Rico to the backstreets of Naples to the rolling plains of the Russian steppe he has cultivated a truly global perspective and attained fluency in three languages. But, he retains the strong values and a commitment to hard work that he learned growing up in a large, loving family in Prescott, a small town in northern Arizona.

PRESENTATION:

Prof. Croft has always had a special interest in biographies, so that he has written many, producing reference-work biographical entries on Russian literary figures like Mikhail Lermontov, Nikolai Gogol, Boris Pasternak, and Anna Akhmatova, on Russian generals like Alexander Suvorov, Mikhail Kutuzov, Semyon Budyonnyi and Andrei Vlasov, and on Russian sports figures like Vasilii Alexeev, Lev Yashin, and Valerii Brumel, whom he once met. He is the author of a book on the life of <u>Nikolai Ivanovich Kibalchich: Terrorist Rocket Pioneer</u> (IIHS, Tempe, AZ/Perm, Russian Federation, ISBN 978-1-4116-2381-1, 2006), the man who invented the concussion-detonated hand grenade used to kill Tsar Alexander II in 1881, and then, while in a jail cell awaiting execution for his involvement in this assassination, drew the design of the first rocket-powered human-piloted flying device. But Prof. Croft admits that, despite his background in Mathematics and Science, he had "never heard of the American scientist Irving Langmuir," until he was told about him by his colleague, Prof. Valentin Fyodorovich Olontsev. Prof. Olontsev is a world-class chemist, toxicologist and historian of science who worked on the secret development of the Soviet military's gas mask for most of his professional career in the "closed city" of Perm in the Russian Ural Mountains. After the dissolution of the Soviet Union in

1991, he was able to find positive utilization of his technical skills in air filtration by founding the Institute of Sorbent and Ecological Technology in Perm, which is engaged in environmental rehabilitation. He is considered the "father of the Soviet gas mask" and has now written the definitive book on that subject entitled **Противогаз** ("The Gas Mask"). Prof. Olontsev is active in the Ural Division of the Russian Academy of Natural Sciences (**Российская Академия Естественных Наук**...cf. www.raen.ru) and was instrumental in seeing Prof. Croft awarded this organization's "Ten Years of RAEN Silver Medal in the name of V. I. Vernadsky" for Croft's "collaborative research and for thirty years of teaching and administering a leading American University's (ASU's...PJH) academic program in Russian Language and Culture" in 2005.

Prof. Olontsev had long admired the American scientist Irving Langmuir, winner of the Nobel Prize for Chemistry in 1932. Langmuir was known as the father of high-vacuum radio tubes, of gas-filled incandescent light bulbs (and influential in the creation of flourescent lighting), of high-temperature atomic hydrogen welding, of wartime smoke screens, and of peace-time cloud seeding to create rain in times of drought. As he explained Irving Langmuir's many scientific contributions to Prof. Croft, proposing that they collaborate to produce a Russian biographical treatment of Langmuir, Croft was struck by one aspect of Langmuir's character that reminded him of what he had often told his students of Russian at ASU: "Don't ever ask 'Why do I have to know this?' You don't know what the future might require you to know. You simply should try to KNOW EVERYTHING." This is the way Langmuir saw the world of science. One of his online English biographies (see www.woodrow.org/teachers/ci/1992/Langmuir.html) begins with this thought: "Irving Langmuir would never have thought to ask the question 'when will I ever use this?' His scientific inquiries sprang from a curiosity that saw a purpose in everything. That practical applications flowed from his theoretical wanderings was to him the 'icing on the cake'."

So, Prof. Croft helped Prof. Olontsev to find access to some American research sources on Irving Langmuir and helped Prof. Olontsev, whose English is more limited, to understand these sources. And Prof. Olontsev wrote the Russian versions of several works on Langmuir, published in Russia under both Professors' names. One of these, a booklet published by the Ural Division of the Russian Academy of Natural Sciences in 2001, is presented here in my translation into English. Notice how the Russian Olontsev relatively neglects the specifics of Langmuir's voluminous and multifarious scientific work to focus on Langmuir's general thought as expressed in the intermediary quotations. By this Prof. Olontsev tries to transmit the more basic inspiration of Langmuir's thought to the reader.

Other collaborative projects by Profs. Olontsev and Croft have followed—biographical research into the life of American scientist Linus Pauling, a collaborative foreword to ASU honors graduate Melissa Archibald's book, <u>Nuclear Non-Proliferation Retraining in Post-Soviet Russia</u> (IIHS, Tempe, AZ/Perm, Russian Federation, ISBN 978-1-4357-1542-4, 2008) entitled "The Legacy of 'The Beard': Igor Kurchatov and the Russian Nuclear Bombs," and research into the role of the railroad in the economic and social development of Russia and the United States.

The Lad from Schenectady-Irving Langmuir
By:
Valentin F. Olontsev
Lee. B. Croft

Irving Langmuir (1881-1957)
General Electric Company **photo taken
in Langmuir's Nobel Prize year of 1932**

January 2001, marked the 120th anniversary of the birth, and 16 Aug, 2002 - marked 45 years after the death of the prominent American scholar of physics, chemist, and Nobel laureate, Irving Langmuir. This publication is dedicated to his memory.

"Science as fundamental knowledge was the greatest factor in the liberation of our minds from preconceived opinions and superstitions, come down to us from the depths of centuries."

--I. Langmuir

In the history of the world of science there are people who leave an indelible mark in many branches of knowledge. In fact, some do it with academic pedantry, and others - with engineering practicality. And there is a special group of scientists who combine in themselves both of these aspects. One of these geniuses was the American scientist and engineer - Irving Langmuir.

Langmuir was born on the 31st of January, 1881, in aristocratic Brooklyn, in a small borough with gabled steeples and tree-lined streets. At fourteen, he enrolled at the Pratt Institute in Brooklyn, and, when he was seventeen, he became a student at the School of Mines at Columbia University. In 1903 he successfully graduated, and in 1906 received a doctorate in physics at Göttingen University. Until 1909 Langmuir taught chemistry at the Stevens Institute of Technology in Hoboken (New Jersey).

"Through basic research sometimes problems, whose existence was unknown, are solved."

--I. Langmuir

In 1909 the director of the company *General Electric* (GE) decided to organize a network of scientific and technological laboratories, which could make a significant contribution to the existing status of basic scientific knowledge. When, in the same year, Langmuir first came to Schenectady, he had a very vague idea of what he would do. The directors of GE suggested to Langmuir that he should not distress himself over any time limit, see the laboratories and find out what kind of problems they are studying, and then choose a topic on which he would like to work. Langmuir's chosen field of study, which then seemed insignificant, has opened paths in many directions.

"I always wanted to find my own way rather than listen to what they told me."

    --I. Langmuir

    The consequences of his work led to dramatic changes in basic and engineering studies for many years to come. These include:

1) The development of the science of adsorption and surface chemistry;

2) significant improvements in conventional electric bulbs;

3) development of a theory of elements in chemical compounds;

4) development of the science of the special two-dimensional world of the plane and its application in chemistry, physics and biology;

5) explanation of the remarkable phenomenon of catalysis;

6) broad meteorological experiments to create artificial rain.

    During his long career he has never took the path of research directly pursuing a practical purpose. All the benefits were by-products of studying fundamental mysteries of nature.

"My favorite endeavor – was to understand the workings of simple and well-known phenomena in nature."

    --I. Langmuir

Two centuries earlier Horace Walpole termed the art of finding advantage in unexpected circumstances "Serendipity." Langmuir's talent in that very art for half a century brought him many opportunities to amuse himself and indulge his curiosity, but, at the same time, it brought him numerous honorary degrees, medals, and in 1932 - the Nobel Prize, crowning twenty-three years of hard work.

"Difficulties exist so that we overcome them, rather than in order to circumvent them, in order to take them to heart, hoping, if possible, to resolve them."

I. Langmuir

Langmuir was the third American to receive the Nobel Prize, and the second in chemistry. He opened to the world more exciting approaches to new areas of knowledge than any other of his compatriots and American contemporaries. His creativity is amazing. He always made, in his diary, entries and labelings of detailed design ideas and elaborations of entire theories with specific calculations. In over 37 years of work in the laboratory his diaries accumulated 54 volumes of 330 pages each. Langmuir advanced 138 applications for patents for his inventions, 63 of which were granted.

"The secular scientific spirit is the greatest driving and creative force that brings us closer to the civilized world for which we fight and we pray today".

I. Langmuir

In all of his numerous works Langmuir's characteristic method of chemical thought is shown. And it is this method by which many various problems were solved. And the theories advanced by his method bear names from the world of chemistry, even if actually, as it occurred subsequently, they reflect purely physical phenomena. This is how the term "valence" came into being, and the term "plasma." And so it was with the most famous discovery by Langmuir - adsorption theory, which was understood by him as a consequence of the existence of residual valence in a film on the surface of a supporting substance. The famous adsorption isotherm of Langmuir and the theory of monolayer molecular adsorption were the result of his thought about purely chemical concepts. His work led to a new understanding of surface adsorption on films as thin as a single molecule, and had positive consequences for the dynamics of living cellular membranes and for the measuring of the molecular sizes of penetrating viruses and other toxins. A change to the study of adsorption on the surface layers of liquids, especially non-polar fluids on the surface of support medium, led to the invention of Langmuir weights and the discovery of Langmuir's equation of state for two-layer surface films.

"All hobbies encourage individual activities, and many help to develop a healthy curiosity. A child should acquire them sooner, and our educational system should encourage them."

    I. Langmuir

A passion for mountaineering and skiing led Langmuir to take an interest in meteorology and led him to explore the creation of artificial rain and snow, and attempts to explain their mechanism.

Langmuir preferred to work with a small number of staff, although the amount of experimental research was very impressive. He was awarded many academic awards: the Nichols medals (1915, 1920), Hughes (1919); Rumford (1921), Perkins (1928); U. Gibbs (1930), Franklin (1934); Faraday (1944), etc. He has received the honorary title "pioneer of modern industry" (1940).

In addition, he was a foreign member of the Royal Society of London, a member of the American Physics Academy, Honorary Fellow of the British Institute of Metals and Chemical Society (London). He served as President of the American Chemical Society (1929) and President of the American Association for the Advancement of Science (1941). Honorary doctoral degrees were awarded to Langmuir from the following colleges and universities: Northwestern, Union, Edinburgh (Scotland), Colombia, Princeton, Harvard, Oxford, Johns Hopkins, Queens (Canada), and the Stevens Institute of Technology where he once taught.

In June of 1945, while the battlefields in the west had not yet cooled and the war in the Far East continued, the USSR Academy of Sciences organized the International Science Congress (around its 220-year anniversary) and invited the outstanding scientists of Great Britain, USA and other countries. Among the participants in these celebrations was Irving Langmuir. Many of their thoughts he then described in the article "Competition of nuclear weapons and its alternative."

"Russia," he wrote "has enormous human and material resources. In addition, during the period from 1934 to 1940, Russia, rather than follow a policy of 'appeasement' like other allied countries, launched an extensive program of military training, not for aggression but to defend against German aggression. "

Langmuir noted the deep devotion of the Soviet scientists to science, and stressed that Soviet scientists, even during the war, were able to conduct such research, which would have been impossible in the United States. He also said that people, whom he met in the USSR, clearly were seeking a long period of peace and security.

"Their plans indicate that they hope and believe that this is possible. They expect to rebuild what had been destroyed in the devastated areas and, at the same time, lay the foundation for a future standard of living equal to or even higher than in the USA. Science, pure and applied, plays a crucial role in that program."

At the same time, Langmuir warned that the Soviet people did not relate carelessly to their future. He warned that if the world begins a nuclear arms race and if the international situation changes so that the Soviet Union feels increasingly threatened, then it might begin a program of production of atomic bombs.

Such a view Langmuir connected, in particular, with the fact that the Soviet Union was used to executing large projects of technological innovations. Langmuir's prediction was justified in full. In human terms, Langmuir was characterized by accessibility and attentiveness to the people, sincerity and candor, straightforwardness and being goal-oriented. He married Marion Mercer in 1912. They had two children-- a son named Kenneth and a daughter named Barbara. Then they had two grandsons; Tom and Roger. On the 16th of August, 1957, after a brief illness, Langmuir died.

In 1962, the publisher Pergamon Press, assisted by *General Electric,* implemented a 12-volume publication of the scientific works of Irving Langmuir. In 1999, Langmuir's grandson, Roger Summerhayes, created the video documentary Langmuir's World, in which is collected a large body of material on his famous grandfather. In conclusion, it is fitting to remember the words of the American poet, Henry Wadsworth Longfellow, from his "Psalm of Life:"

> "Lives of great men all remind us
> We can make our lives sublime,
> And, departing, leave behind us
> Footprints on the sands of time."

A Chronology of Langmuir's Life

Born   January 31, 1881

Parents

     Charles and Sadie Comings Langmuir

Attended

Public Schools Brooklyn	1887-1892
Boarding School, Suburban Paris	1892-1895
Chestnut Hill Academy, Philadelphia	1895-1895

Graduated

Manual Training High School, Pratt Institute	1898

Received Degree

Metallurgical Engineer, Columbia University	1903
Doctor of Philosophy, University of Gottingen	1906

Taught

Stevens Institute of Technology	1906-1909

Married

Marian Mersereau	1912

Children
  Son, Kenneth
  Daughter, Mrs. H. R. Summerhayes

Research Scientist

General Electric Research Laboratory	1909-1950
Associate Director	1929-1950
Consultant	1950-1957

Honorary Degrees Awarded

D.Sc. Northwestern University	1921
LL.D Edinburgh University	1921
D.Sc. Union University	1923
D.Sc. Columbia University	1925
D.Sc. Kenyon University	1927
D.Sc. Princeton University	1929
LL.D. Union University	1934
LL.D. Johns Hopkins University	1936
D.Sc. Harvard University	1938
D.Sc. Oxford University	1938
D.Sc. Rutgers University	1941
D.Sc. Queens College (Canada)	1941
LL.D. University of California	1946

Medals Awarded

Nichols Medal American Chemical Society	1915, 1920
Hughes Medal Royal Society of London	1918

Award	Organization	Year
Rumford Medal	Am. Assoc. for the Advancement of Science	1920
Stanislao Cannizzaro Award (Rome)	Royal National Academy of Linnaeus	1925
Perkins Medal	Society Chemical Industry	1928
Chandler Medal	Columbia University	1929
Willard Gibbs Medal	Am. Chemical Society	1930
NOBEL PRIZE	Swedish Academy	1932
Popular Science	Popular Science Monthly	1933
Franklin Medal	Franklin Institute	1934
Holley Medal	Am. Soc. of Mech. Engineers	1934
John Scott Medal	Philadelphia Board of Directors of City Trusts	1937
Faraday Medal	Chemical Society London	1938
Egleston Medal	Columbia University Engineering Schools Alumni Association	1939
Modern Pioneer	National Association of Industry Manufacturers	1940
Silver Beaver	Boy Scouts of America	1942
Faraday Medal	Inst. of Elect. Engineers	1943
Medal of Merit	U.S. Army and Navy	1948
Mascart Medal	Academy des Sciences, Societe Francaise des Electriciens	1948
John J. Carty Medal	Nat'l Academy of Science	1949
Silver Buffalo	Boy Scouts of America	1950

Died

August 16, 1957 in Woods Hole, Massachusetts

Patrick J. Heuer at St. Petersburg's "Church of the Savior on the Spilt Blood" (Спас на крови)...The site where Tsar Alexander II was assassinated in 1881.

Putting Meaning Into the Memory
By:
Alicia C. Baehr

Alicia C. Baehr is a native of Phoenix, Arizona. She was born there in 1986. She graduated from Phoenix Central High School in 2004 where she was first introduced to the Russian language under the instruction of Dr. Nicholas Vontsolos. Alicia began her higher education at Arizona State University after receiving an ASU Provost's scholarship, beginning her studies in Political Science. After her freshman year, Alicia switched her major to the Bachelor of Arts program in the Russian language, while keeping a minor in Political Science. She studied Russian language and culture in St. Petersburg in 2006 through the University of Arizona's Russian Abroad program, working primarily at St. Petersburg State University. Alicia has also traveled to Italy, Austria, Switzerland and France as an Ambassador with People to People. In the spring of 2007, Alicia was inducted into ASU's Epsilon Epsilon Chapter of the **Добро Слово,** National Slavic Studies Honorary. After graduating Summa Cum Laude in December 2008, Alicia is joining the U. S. Air Force to work in military intelligence with hopes of eventually becoming a diplomat for the State Department.

Presentation:

The article "Mnemonotactics and Linguistic Iconicity" by Prof. Lee B. Croft first appeared in the anthology by Olga Kagan and Benjamin Rifkin with Susan Bauckus titled <u>The Learning and Teaching of Slavic Languages and Cultures</u>. This anthology of scholarly articles, solicited and edited by leading American professors in the field of teaching Russian language and culture, was published in 2000 by Slavica Publishers, then of Bloomington, Indiana. Parts of this article had previously appeared in Russian in the earlier pioneering two-volume Russian anthology, <u>**Методика преподавания русского языка и литературы в Америке**</u> ("The Methodology of Teaching Russian Language and Literature in America") edited by University of Arizona Distinguished Teaching Professor of Russian, Delbert D. Phillips…the Director of the University of Arizona Russian Abroad program. Specifically, part of the article **"Опыт мнемонического использования лингвистической образности"** ("Testing the Mnemonic

Utility of Linguistic Iconicity" by Prof. Croft and Patricia Bailey Cossette, who was a former student at Arizona State University) is included in the English-language publication of the article presented here. This article and the other articles of the Phillips anthology, the first such publication in Russia, are reviewed by Prof. Betty Lou Leaver at www.clover.pitt.edu/~aatseel/book-reviews/phillips.html and an overall review may be seen at www.aatseel.org/book-reviews/Phillips.html. The 2000 Slavica anthology edited by Profs. Kagan and Rifkin that includes this article (cf. www.slavica.com/teaching/contents.html) won a national scholarly prize in 2001.

Mnemonotactics and Linguistic Iconicity

By:

Lee B. Croft

Foreign language teachers of the twenty-first century should become effective mnemonotacticians. One of their key considerations should be presenting material so that students can bring it forth from their memories when they need it. In earlier articles (Croft 1978, 1996), I described the mnemonic utility of calling students' attention to non-arbitrary connections between sense and sound, those iconic relationships between the phonological representation of words and the character of their referents, to facilitate student recall. I contend that focusing on these connections is useful because students' minds are already, perhaps unconsciously, associating sense and sound in their own language. They can be helped in their recall when they attempt to learn a foreign language by calling on those same connections.

An example of linguistic iconicity suggesting the existence of neuronal connections between different cerebral realms is the non-arbitrary relationship between the vowels of human language expression and impressions of magnitude, which may universally connect the realms of sound and sight. This tie is evidenced by the prominence of the vowel [-i-], which connotes smallness (as in "itsy-bitsy," "teeny-weeny," "little") as contrasted to the articulatorily more open vowel [-a-], which connotes expansiveness (as in "large," "grand," "awesome"). A well-known test suggests that most of us perceive this type of iconicity: "If your language has only two words, 'ping' and 'pong,' with which to refer to an elephant and a mouse—which word would you choose for each animal?" Most people will easily choose "pong" for the elephant and "ping" for the mouse because they feel the non-arbitrary association of size and sound. Is this association a universal, which transcends cultural differences? That is, do the Lapps, the Hottentots and the Inuits agree with the Jivaro and the Djirbal that small objects generally ought to be represented by words in which articulatorily "small" vowels appear in contrast to the large objects, which are represented by words with articulatorily "large" vowels? My research leads me to believe that *all* language speakers have neuronal connections associating small sounds with small sights, and large sounds with large sights. This hard-wiring in the human species, in my view, predates language split (differentiation) and finds its origin in the sound-imitative aspects of language etiology (cf. Wescott, 1971). A teacher of Russian would be operating soundly on this universality when stressing to students how the word "миг" ([mig]) could easily be remembered as meaning an "instant" (a vowel-symbolized "small" amount of time) as opposed to the word "год" ([god]) which means a "year" (a vowel-symbolized "large" amount of time). Of course, I admit that there are exceptions to this universal tendency. I try to mark them in the students' minds as exceptions, knowing that the understanding of an exception presupposes an understanding of the rule. An example of this kind of exception is the "tiny" Russian word "кит" ([kit]) which, contrary to the characteristic pattern of sound-sense associations, means "whale." When I ask any sample of non-Russian-speaking students (mostly English or Spanish speakers so far) to match the sounds "kit" (as in Russian "кит") or "galúba" (a nonsense word made up by one of my children who thought it a fitting word to describe a whale) with pictures of the animals "minnow" or "whale," most people choose "galúba" for "whale."

Most students will similarly perceive a non-arbitrary relationship between kinetic and tactile impressions and the sounds of language. The following test to demonstrate this is similar to one used by Gestalt psychologist Wolfgang Kohler in 1947. Of the following shapes one is represented by the word "ooloomu" and the other by the word "taakaate."

Which word goes with which shape? Most of us know the answer because we feel the relationship between the smoothness and roundness of the kidney-bean shape and the word "ooloomu," and between the sharp points of the star shape and the abrupt consonantal stops of "taakaate." This understanding is a manifestation of a neuronal connection between the area of the brain where the sounds are stored and sights are registered, and the area where somato-sensory inputs such as touch are processed (since shape can be considered a vicarious touch). A more subtle example can be demonstrated by performing a similar test on the Russian words "**вилка**" ([víl-ka]) and "**ложка**" ([lózh-ka]), words which, if examined phonologically, are similar—they have the same number of syllables, the same position of word-stress, identical ending syllables, and differing vowels only between resonant consonants in the first stressed syllable. In repeated samplings, however, I have found that a clear majority of students polled will match the correct word to the appropriate picture of a "fork" *(***вилка***)* and a "spoon" *(***ложка***)*. No doubt they feel the contrast between the small points of the fork (symbolized appropriately by the smallness-connoting vowel. [-i-]) and the roundness of the spoon (symbolized appropriately by the roundness, both articulatorily and graphologically, of the vowel [-o-]). If this iconicity is pointed out to the students when these lexical items are introduced ("The small, sharp points in **вилка** with an [i] and the round spoon, **ложка**, with a round [o]..."), then their recall of these words will be considerably facilitated.

Several studies (cf. **Иванова-Лукьянова** 1966; **Орлова** 1966; Crockett 1970; Fudge 1970) in Russia and the West have sought to find a universal consensus on the "sense" of linguistic sounds that are meaningless by the standards of conventional semantic assignment. In these studies, subjects are asked to define in various ways (often by choosing alternatives from arrays of conceptual antonyms) word-length segments of sound, which are unfamiliar to them. My own experiments along this line have involved the word **штáнга** ([štánga]), which I ask students who know no Russian (or German) to repeat and then to choose: "**штáнга** ... big or small? ... shallow or deep? ... heavy or light? ...

wide or narrow? ... male or female?"... and so on through a battery of up to thirty antonymal choices. Most students, usually over eighty percent, will spontaneously choose "big," "deep," "heavy," "wide," "male," (overruling their knowledge from other languages that words ending in [-a] are usually feminine) and so on. Although "**штáнга**" means "barbell" in Russian, the consensus on the antonymal character of this sound from people who know no Russian suggests that people sense connections between the sounds in words and those words' referents independently of lexical assignment and, moreover, that these ties cross language barriers.

Teachers would be well advised to use explanations involving iconicity whenever possible. The students' transfer of information from short-term to long-term memory can be abbreviated by the teacher's presentation. Once the students are told about the iconicity of the Russian word "**пýшка**" ([púš-ka], meaning "cannon"), how it starts with an explosion (the sound [p-]) and has a rush of smoke (the sound [-sh-]) and then a following impact (the sound [-k]), they never forget it.

Cross-linguistic iconicity can be found in the relationships between words and also grammatical categories. An example is the sound symbolism to be found in the world's words for proximity and distance (cf. Tanz, 1971). Often words expressing proximate distance from the speaker are shorter than, and often included within, the corresponding words expressing a greater distance from the speaker. This shows a word relationship which is iconic (i.e. it serves as a verbal simulacrum) to the real-world spatial relationship of proximate distances being included within the more distant. Examples of this are constituted by the following words for "here" and "there," which themselves form an orthographic example only:

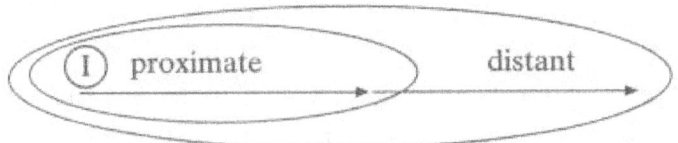

	Word for "here"	Word for "there"
Amharic	[izzi]	[izzija]
Arabic	[huna]	[hunaka]
Woleolan	[iga]	[igala]
Japanese	[soko]	[asoko]

In response to this example of relational iconicity, the sceptic will say "What about French *ici* and *là*, or English (phonetically judged, as opposed to orthographically) "here" and "there," or Russian здесь and там*?* Or, expanding the attempted refutation to the demonstratives, what of the fact that Russian proximate этот, эта, это, meaning "this," are "bigger" words than the corresponding (and counterlogically included within) distant тот, та, то, meaning "that"*?* To this, the iconicist can respond that the French, English, and Russian words for "here" and "there" exhibit an iconicity of another kind—one of the magnitudinal symbolization like the one discussed above with the ping-pong test. The short distance from the speaker is represented by the words with the "small" symbolizing high front vowels *(ici,* "here," and здесь,*)* whereas the words for greater distance from speaker use the "bigger" vowels *(là,* "there," and там*).* As for the demonstratives of the этот/тот, эта/та, это/то variety, they also represent a different kind of iconicity. These words typically place an object into an interlocutor's field of vision. Visible objects that are closer to the speaker appear larger to the eye and are therefore represented by the larger words этот/эта/это.

The more distant objects appear smaller in the visual field and are, moreover, reduced images of their closer counterparts, just as they are represented by the smaller and reduced form тот/та/то. This is how apparent counterexamples can often be turned to pedagogical advantage.

The notion that iconicity is where you find it, or manufacture it, brings up a discussion of the omnipresence of iconicity in language. Indeed, it could be that every linguistic form has an iconic aspect that we do not see. More probably (cf.Wescott, 1971) there is a mass-consciousness mechanism which holds the iconic elements of language in equilibrium with the arbitrary elements of language. Submorphemic increments of meaning (cf. Bolinger, 1950, 1965) in words transcend their individual reconstructed etymologies, causing us to ask: "Just what can we say the sequence 'um' means, the sequence 'ka,' the consonant 'b'?" (cf. Magnus, 1993), and would it, if we pinned it down correctly, mean the same to the Lapp, the Hottentot, the Inuit, the Jivaro, and the Djirbal?"

Attempting to define a "meaning" of the vowel [-o-] from Russian data may be enlightening in this regard. This vowel often appears in Russian adjectival antonyms that express psychological neutrality. A test to determine which member of an antonymal pair this is, is to see which antonym, in the most neutral circumstance of context, will most often be placed in the syntactic matrix: "How____is it?" That is, we usually ask how "big" something is, and not how small, even if the object we have in mind is quite small. In most neutral circumstances, we ask how heavy, not how light, how old, not how young, how soon, not how late. In Russian the member of the antonymal pair, which is correlated with this neutrality is often signaled by the presence of the stressed vowel [-o-], as in:

большо́й	"big"	**ма́ленький**	"small"
высо́кий	"high"	**ни́зкий**	"low"
широ́кий	"wide"	**у́зкий**	"narrow"
глубо́кий	"deep"	**ме́лкий**	"shallow"
гро́мкий	"loud"	**ти́хий**	"quiet"
тёмный	"dark"	**свет**	"light"
то́нкий	"fine"	**гру́бый**	"crude"

Notice that a few counter-examples (such as **ста́рый**/"old"—**молодо́й**/"young") present themselves, that some pairs of frequent use give both members the stressed [-o-] (such as **хоро́ший**/"good"—**плохо́й**/"bad"), and that the words in several apparent counter-examples (like **тру́дный**/"difficult"—**лёгкий**/"easy") may have more than one antonym (as **лёгкий** /"light"—**тяжёлый**/"heavy") (cf. Croft, 1978, footnote 7…i.e. the earlier article presented by Shane C. Sarlo, footnote 54, p. 120…ACB). And, it can hardly be coincidental that the vowel. [-o-] predominates in the neutral circumstance of interrogative words, which are meant to correct a no-information situation (i.e. Russian **что**/"what," **кто**/"who," **како́й**/"which," **кото́рый**/"which," **ско́лько**/"how much,"), or that as a verbal and adjectival desinence it signals agreement with relatively unmarked entities (neuter nouns, general or impersonal subjects, infinitives). These characteristics indicate that semantic increments of meaning are correlated to sound at levels well below the morpheme. My English language response to this can only be: "Oh?," registering cognizance but no commitment of opinion. I wonder what other language speakers would say.

To test the hypothesis that iconic pedagogical

presentations have a special mnemonic utility, a colleague and I devised the following experiment (cf. Croft and Bailey Cossette, 1996). Six Russian verbs were presented to students of first and second-year Russian language classes at Arizona State University. The students were typical American undergraduates, predominately monolingual speakers of English, in their 26th week (the first-year students) or 58th week (the second-year students) of Russian language instruction, who met for five hours per week. The students were told that they "had to know" these verbs. The verbs and their English glosses were: **клониться** (to bow, bend), **шевелиться** (to move one's body, stir), **сутулиться** (to stoop, slouch), **улыбаться** (to smile), **хмуриться** (to frown, be overcast), and **морщиться** (to become wrinkled, contract, pucker) (cf. Katzner, 1984). These verbs are all of similar length, and are all reflexive and imperfective. With the exception of **улыбаться** (to smile), these are verbs of similarly low frequency of use (cf. **Засорина**, 1977), but they fall into two semantic categories: verbs of body movement *(***клониться**, **шевелиться**, and **сутулиться***)* and verbs of facial expression *(***улыбаться**, **хмуриться**, and **морщиться***)*. None of these verbs had previously appeared in the students' learning material.

An advanced student, who did *not* know the study's purpose at the time, presented the verbs to the students in class. The verbs were presented in random order and explained similarly. First, the infinitive was given to the class with its English meaning. The class was asked to repeat the infinitive and the verb's conjugation in unison after the student presenter. Then the verb and its conjugation was printed in Russian on the blackboard for the students to copy cursively onto sheets of paper which were subsequently removed (in an attempt to eliminate the consultation of notes as a variable). Then a Russian pattern sentence using each verb was given orally to the students, one of whom was asked to translate the sentence into English for the others.

At this point an arbitrary fact of usage was given to the students concerning the body-movement verbs, such as "Being a reflexive verb with the suffix '**-ся**,' this verb will never take an accusative direct object." For the facial-expression verbs, however, an *iconic* explanation was given. The students were told that in order to pronounce these verbs they had to make the facial expression represented by them, as in "You have to 'pucker' in order to say **морщиться**." Finally, the students were asked to repeat again the infinitive of each Russian verb aloud.

The hypothesis predicts that, following the presentation, the students will be able to recall the facial-expression verbs more successfully than the body movement verbs because of the greater pedagogical efficiency of the iconic explanation.

After ten days, which included the spring semester break, the students were given a test. First, they were asked to write the Russian verb associated with the given English meanings (an active skill test). Then they were given a list of the Russian verbs and told to write the English meanings (a passive recognition test). The first-year students' active success rate averaged 33.3 percent on the facial-expression verbs (allowing reasonably for mistakes in Russian spelling) as opposed to 24.2 percent for the body-movement verbs. The passive success rate was 66.6 percent on the facial-expression verbs as opposed to 54.5 percent on the body-movement verbs. The second-year students' data showed a 26.9 percent to 12.8 percent success rate superiority on the facial-expression verbs on the active test, and a 69.2 to 44.7 percent superiority on the passive test. The first-year students generally outperformed their second-year counterparts, perhaps because they had recently been studying reflexive **-ся** verbs. But the overall success rates show a 30.5 percent to 19.4 percent success advantage to the iconic explanation in the active test and a 67.7 percent to 48.6 percent success advantage in the passive test.

These results indicate that the presentations containing iconic explanations were superior in helping students recall the lexical material, thus supporting my hypothesis that linguistic iconicity has a special pedagogical utility which can be of significant aid to the mnemonotactically sophisticated foreign language teacher.

Works Cited

Atkinson, Richard C. "Mnemotechnics in Second-language Learning." American Psychologist August 1975: 821-8.

Atkinson, Richard C. and Michael R. Raugh. "An Application of the Mnemonic Keyword Method to the Acquisition of Russian Vocabulary." Journal of American Psychology: Human Learning and Memory 2 (1957): 126-33.

Bialystok, Ellen and Kenji Hakuta, eds. In Other Words: The Science and Psychology of Second-language Acquisition. New York: Basic Books, Harper Collins, 1994.

Bley-Vroman, Robert and Craig Chaudron. "Elicited Imitation as a Measure of Second-language Competence." Research Methodology in Second Language Acquisition. Ed. Elaine E. Tarone, Susan M. Gass, and Andrew D. Cohen. Lawrence Erlbaum Associates, Publisher. Hillsdale, New Jersey, 1994. 245-61.

Bolinger, Dwight. "Rime, Assonance, and Morpheme Analysis." Word 6 (1950): 117-37.

———. "The Atomization of Meaning." Language 41 (1965): 55-73.

Brown, James E. "Recognizing and Recalling Russian Words." Russian Language Journal *165-67* (1996): 63-82.

Crockett, Dina. "Secondary Onomatopoeia in Russian." Word 26 (1970): 107-13.

Croft, Lee B. "The Mnemonic Use of Linguistic Iconicity in Teaching Language and Literature." Slavic and East European Journal 22.4 (1978): 509-18.

Крофт, Ли Б. "Мнемоника, языковая образность и преподавание языка и литературы." Методика Преподавание русского языка и литературы в Америке. Дельберт Д. Филлипс, ред. Том 2. Москва: Синтаксис, 1996, стр. 127-140.

———. "Нейромнемонический процесс запоминания через повтор" См. Филлипс, стр. 109-127.

Крофт, Ли Б. и Бэйли Коссет, Патрисия. "Опыт Мнемонического использования лингвистической образности." См. Филлипс, стр. 141-144.

Danesi, Marcel. "Applied Psycholinguistics and the Second Language Classroom." A Case for Psycholinguistic Cases Gabriela Appel and Hans W. Dechert, eds. Philadelphia and Amsterdam: John Benjamins, 1991. 123-43.

Fudge, Erik. 1970. "Phonological Structure and 'Expressiveness'." *Journal of Linguistics* 6 (1970): 161-88.

Гаспаров, Борис М. Язык, память, образ: Лингвистика языкового существования. Москва: Новое литературное обозрение, 1996.

Ingram, Frank L. "Auditory Memory and Visual Memory: Relating the Teaching of Russian to the Learner's Overall Language Aptitude." <u>Proceedings of the Kentucky Foreign Language Conference: Slavic Section</u>. Vol. I, No. 1 Richmond, KY: Department of Foreign Languages, Eastern Kentucky University, 1983. 40-44.

___. 1984. "Analysis and Synthesis in Reading Russian." <u>Kentucky Proceedings</u> Vol. II, No. 1l. 25-30.

___. 1984. "Why Johnny Can't Read Russian." <u>Russian Language Journal</u> 38 (1984): 63-76.

___. 1986. "Russian Words and Memory: Considerations of Vocabulary Acquisition Efficiency." <u>Proceedings of the Kentucky Foreign Language Conference: Slavic Section</u>. Vol IV, No. 1. Richmond, KY: Department of Foreign Languages, Eastern Kentucky University, 1983. 183-92.

___. 1996. "L-1 and L-2: Friends or Foes in Foreign Language Acquisition?" <u>Russian Language Journal</u> 44 (1996): 217-23.

Иванова-Лукьянова, Г. Н. "О восприятии звуков." Развитие фонетики современного русского языка. С. С. Высоцкий, ред. Москва: Наука. 1966. 136-43.

Jauregi Ondarra, Kristi. 1997. "Research into Foreign Language Classroom Processes." <u>Collaborative Negotiation of Meaning: A Longitudinal Approach</u> Kristi Ondarra Jauregi, ed. Utrecht Studies in Language and Communication, II. Amsterdam and Atlanta: Rodopi, 1997.

Katzner, Kenneth. <u>English-Russian, Russian-English Dictionary</u>. John Wiley and Sons. New York, 1984.

Keller, Howard H. "The Role of a Common Semantic Denominator in Russian Root Structures." <u>Russian Language Journal,</u> 96 (1973): 95.

———. "Memory: Poetic and Neurophysiological Descriptions." <u>Slavic and East European Journal</u> 26.1 (1982): 77-85.

Kimenyi, Alexandre. "Reduplication and Binomial Expression in English." <u>The Semiotic Bridge: Trends From California</u>. Ed. Irmengard Rauch and Gerald F. Carr. Approaches to Semiotics 86. Berlin and New York: Mouton de Gruyter, 1989. 347-53.

Kohler, Wolfgang. <u>Gestalt Psychology: An Introduction to New Concepts in Modern Psychology</u>. New York: Liveright, 1947.

Kopstein, F. and S. Roshal. 1954. "Learning Foreign Vocabulary from Pictures Versus Words." <u>American Psychologist,</u> 9 (1954): 407-08.

———. "Method of Presenting Word Pairs as a Factor in Foreign Language Vocabulary Acquisition." <u>American Psychologist</u> 10 (1955): 354.

Magnus, Margaret. <u>What's in a Word?: Evidence for Phono-Semantics</u>. Mt. Vernon, New Hampshire: Circle Publishers, 1993.

McKenna, Kevin J. " Associative Mnemonics in Russian Vocabulary Building." <u>Russian Language Journal</u>. 48, Nos. 145-6 (Spring-Fall 1989): 37-59.

Meara, Paul. "The Classical Research in L-2 Vocabulary Acquisition." <u>Words, Words, Words: The Translator and the Language Learner</u>. Ed. Gunilla M. Anderman and Margaret A. Rogers. Topics in Translation Series 7.

Clevedon, Philadelphia and Adelaide: Multilingual Matters, Ltd., 1996. 27-41.

Merril, Floyd. <u>Sensing Semiosis: Toward the Possibility of Complementary Cultural 'Logics'</u>. New York: St. Martin's Press, 1998.

Moss, Kevin. "A Russian Culture Course Based on a Semiotic Pattern." <u>Russian Language Journal,</u> 47 (1993): 3-15.

Орлова, Е. В. "О восприятии звуков." <u>Развитие фонетики современного русского языка.</u> С. С. Высоцкий, ред. Москва:Наука. 1966, 144-54.

Филлипс, Дельберт Д. <u>Методика преподавания Русского языка и литературы в Америке.</u> 2 тома. Москва: Синтаксис. 1996.

___. "Utilizing Language Acquisition Theory to Improve the Results of Instruction in Russian." <u>Proceedings of the Kentucky Foreign Language Conference: Slavic Section.</u> Vol. LEI, No. 1. Richmond, KY: Department Of Foreign Languages, Eastern Kentucky University, 1985, 83-91.

Pinker, Steven. <u>Language Learnability and Language Development</u>. Cambridge: Harvard University Press, 1984.

_____. <u>The Language Instinct: How the Mind Creates Language</u>. New York: William Morrow and Co., 1994.

_____. How the Mind Works. New York and London: W.W. Norton and Co., 1997.

Pressley, Michael, Joel R. Levin, and Harold D. Delaney. "The Mnemonic Keyword Method." <u>Review of Educational Research</u> 52.1 (1982): 61-91.

Pressley, Michael, Joel R. Levin, Nicholas A. Kuiper, Susan L. Bryant, and Sarah Michener. "Mnemonic Versus Non-mnemonic Vocabulary-learning Strategies: Additional Comparisons." <u>Journal of Educational Psychology</u> 74.5 (1982): 693-707.

Pressley, Michael R. "Comparing Hall (1988) with Related Research on Elaborative Mnemonics." Journal of <u>Educational Psychology,</u> 83.1 (1991): 165-70.

Prestel, David K. "An Aid for Vocabulary Acquisition in Russian." <u>Proceedings of the Kentucky Foreign Language Conference: Slavic Section</u>. Vol. V, No. 1. Richmond, KY: Department of Foreign Languages, Eastern Kentucky University, 1988. 25-35.

Raugh, Michael R., Richard D. Schupbach and Richard C. Atkinson. "Teaching a Large Russian Language Vocabulary by the Mnemonic Keyword Method." <u>Instructional Science,</u> 6 (1977): 199-221.

Schnelle, Helmut. "Language and Brain." <u>Origins of Semiosis: Sign Evolution in Nature and Culture</u>. Winfried Noth, ed. Approaches to Semiotics 116. Berlin And New York: Mouton de Gruyter, 1994. 339-65.

Sebeok, Thomas A. <u>I Think I Am A Verb: More Contributions to the Doctrine of Signs</u>. Topics in Contemporary Semiotics. New York and London: Plenum Press, 1986.

Tanz, Christine. "Sound Symbolism in Words for Proximity and Distance." <u>Language and Speech,</u> 14 (1971): 260.

Tarone, Elaine E. "Summary of Research Approaches." <u>Research Methodology in Second-language</u>

Acquisition. Ed. Elaine E. Tarone, Susan M. Gass and Andrew D. Cohen. Hillsdale, New Jersey: Lawrence Erlbaum Associates, 1994. 323-37.

Von Uexkull, Thure. "From Index to Icon: A Semiotic Attempt at Interpreting Piaget's Developmental Theory." Iconicity: Essays on the Nature of Culture—A Festschrift for Thomas A. Sebeok on his 65th Birthday. Ed. Paul Bouissac, Michael Herzfeld and Roland Posner. Tubingen: Stauffenburg Verlag, 1986. 119-41.

Воронин, С. В. Основы фоносемантики. Ленинград: Издательство ленинградского университета, 1982.

Wescott, Roger. "Linguistic Iconism." Language, 47 (1971): 416-28.

Засорина, Л. Н. Частотный словарь русского языка. Москва:Издательство "Наука." 1977.

WHY SO MANY THREES?
BY:
JON HARRIS

Jon Harris was born in Winnipeg, Manitoba, Canada, but grew up in Chandler, Arizona, USA and graduated from Chandler High School in May 2003. Jon immediately began coursework at Arizona State University seeking a Bachelor of Arts in Marketing from the W.P. Carey School of Business until finding a passion for Russian language, literature and linguistics through introductory courses taken at Arizona State University under Dr. Don Livingston and Dr. Lee B Croft. Jon then switched majors of study and began work on a Bachelor of Arts in Russian language and literature at Arizona State University in 2006. He has studied in Russia as part of the University of Arizona's Russia Abroad program in both St. Petersburg and Moscow at St. Petersburg State University and Moscow Humanities University, respectively, and was inducted into ASU's Epsilon Epsilon Chapter of the **Добро Слово** National Slavic Studies Honorary in April 2007. He has also studied German and French at Arizona State University from 2006 to 2008, Spanish at Chandler High School from 2000 to 2003 and plans to pursue a Master of Arts in Russian language, literature and linguistics at the University of Arizona after graduation in Spring 2009.

PRESENTATION:

The title of the article by Prof. Croft that I am presenting here is **"THRICE TO TELL THE TALE: People in Threes Going Up in Smoke and Other Triplicities in Russian Literature and Culture."** Prof. Croft, long fascinated by the "why" of "things in threes" in Russian literature and culture, submitted the article under this title to the Rocky Mountain Review of Language and Literature, the scholarly organ of the Rocky Mountain Modern Language Association (RMMLA) in 2004. This title, however, was shortened by the editors of the journal who omitted the first five words when they published it textually as pages 29-49 of Vol. 59, Number 2, in 2005. The shortened title also headed the article's online publication in the Rocky Mountain E-Review, accessible through a membership password at www.rmmla.org. I, however, like the former full title, thinking that it more comprehensively reflects the article's contents…here also very slightly amended from the original published version…and, consulting with Prof. Croft, decided to include it in this version. Since its 2005 publication, the article has garnered for itself considerable subsequent citation on the Internet.

Prolific online scholar Dr. Bill Long includes it in his discussion of triplistic aspects of William Shakespeare's <u>Macbeth</u> at www.drbilllong.com/ShakeM/Threes.html. Then, Michael Eck includes it as a "feature" in his comprehensive online <u>Tricyclopedic Book of Threes</u> at www.threes.com/articles/LeeBCroft.pdf. Michael Eck and "Threes Master" Herb O. Buckland (see the acknowledgments at the end of the article) joke by e-mail that Prof. Croft has now joined them as the "Third Triophile." Prof. Croft's work is cited as informing the online Wikipedia's very definition of the meaning of the number THREE (3) at http://en.wikipedia.org/wiki/3_(number). See the "original scholarly articles/reviews about the three" at the IN LITERATURE section of this comprehensive entry. The "spontaneous human combustion" sites also cite this article by Prof. Croft. See http://en.wikipedia.org/wiki/Spontaneous_human_combustion and also http://medlibrary.org/medwiki/Spontaneous_human_combustion in the "references."

THRICE TO TELL THE TALE: People in Threes Going Up in Smoke and Other Triplicities in Russian Literature and Culture

BY:

Lee B. Croft
Arizona State University

"I knew she wasn't Russian when she said she told her husband to honk the car horn four times as a signal that he had arrived outside the studio. If she were really a Russian, she would have told her husband to honk THREE times."

--Dr. Roy Hanu Hart[89]

"Is there a limited number of 'letters' in the language of quantum electrodynamics that can be combined to form 'words' and 'phrases' that describe nearly every phenomenon of nature? The answer is yes: the number is THREE."

--Richard Feynman[90].

---

[89] Dr. Roy Hanu Hart, author of <u>Bitter Grass</u>, <u>The Numbers of Heaven</u>, and <u>Journey of Faith</u>, responded this way (in a personal telephone conversation with the author in 1999) when asked to comment on the genuinity of a television-interviewed "Anastasia" pretender subsequently debunked by a DNA test (cf.also Hart, 2002, pp. 198-200).

[90] Feynman, Richard, 1985, pp. 84 (caps mine). Nobel laureate Feynman uses this statement in the course of explaining "The Strange Theory of Light and Matter."

"What is the artist if he is not a TRIPLE thinker?"

--Gustave Flaubert[91].

In the article, "Triplicity and Textual Iconicity: Russian Literature Through a Triangular Prism," Lee Croft advances a theory of narrative efficiency based on the capacity of the human mind for processing information to explain "the inordinate triplicity in Russian literature and culture."[92]

---

[91] Wilson, Edmund, 1938 (1963 ed.), uses this question, "to Louise Colet" as the epigraph to his collection, The Triple Thinkers: Twelve Essays on Literary Subjects.

[92] Croft, 1995, pp. 249-265. The key works here are Jakobson (1936) and Jakobson (1958) wherein Jakobson describes the semantic structure of the Russian substantival case system as a hierarchy of three semantic features binarily applied. His description uses a two-dimensional graphic representation called a "Prague School Markedness Diagram" (cf. the works of Catherine Chvany, 1984, 1986, for discussion of the model's adaptation into a three-dimensional figure, the cube). In Croft's "model of narrative efficiency" this diagram represents the structure of the encoding capacity of the human mind. The decoding capacity is described surprisingly analogously by Miller (1956) who describes limits on the information processing ability of the human mind within diverse sensory parameters of short-term memory (through which narrative communication flows) as a binary decision raised to the third power...i.e. 8, or "Seven plus or minus two." Miller's description is well amenable to graphic respresentation by a Prague School Markedness diagram like Jakobson's...forming a kind of iconicity between the

Croft argues that the Russian culture is particularly susceptible to seeing things in threes, to tricategorization, to tertiariness of all kinds. In support of this argument he endeavors to go well beyond the triplicity inherent in most cultures--the philosophical religious and physiological/psychoanalytic trinities (father, son, holy spirit; space, time, change; hell, earth, heaven; id, ego, superego; old brain, mid brain, outer cortex), the physical/electrodynamic/genetic trinities (width, depth, height; gravity, time, mass/energy; combinatorial triplets of nucleotides), and semiotic system trinities (icon, index, symbol; perception (stimulus), analysis, response)[93]--to specify more uniquely Slavic/Russian aspects of cultural triplicity. These aspects include the tertiary Russian personal identification by name (first name, patronymic, last name) and the impressively rife tertiariness of Russian grammatical categorization...a reflection of the structure of Russian thought:

"...there are (or were) three numbers (singular, dual, plural), tenses (past, present, future), voices (active, middle, passive), degrees of comparison (simple, comparative, superlative), moods (indicative, subjunctive, injunctive), aspects (durative, iterative, perfective), sentence types (declarative, interrogative, exhortative), genders (feminine, masculine, neuter), persons (first, second, third), types of

---

encoding and decoding structures of the mind, an iconicity essential to successful communication and narration.

[93] These natural and cultural triplicities are further specified in Croft, 1995. This and the others mentioned here are, of course, more universal triplicities, which are present in every culture. What I am doing here is demonstrating (and trying, perhaps, to explain) the special intensity of triplicity in the Russian culture, and, particularly, in Russian literature.

verb (transitive, intransitive, ergative), declensional types (masculine/neuter, feminine I, feminine II), conjugational stress patterns (stem, desinence, switching). Surely the dominance of triplicity in grammatical categorization is not merely fortuitous. It is a consequence of the way (Russians) think..."[94]

Examples of triplicity in Russian literature, and in the forms of oral narration which preceded literature, are especially easy to find. Vladimir Propp, the Russian formalist literary critic who gave us the extremely structured Morphology of the Folktale, devotes an entire section of this seminal work to "trebling" and how it:

"...may occur among individual details of an attributive nature (the three heads of a dragon), as well as among individual functions, pairs of functions (pursuit-rescue), groups of functions, and entire moves. Repetition may appear as a uniform distribution (three tasks, three years' service), as an accumulation (the third task is the most difficult, the third battle the worst), or may twice produce negative results before the third, successful, outcome."[95]

In The Uses of Enchantment: The Meaning and Importance of Fairy Tales, psychologist Bruno Bettelheim writes that "the number three in fairy tales often seems to refer to what in psychoanalysis is viewed as the three

---

[94] This is from Croft, 1995, pp. 251 and synopsizes categorizations from several definitive grammars of the Russian Language, including Vinogradov, 1972. But this is not all. Linguists describe Slavic vocalic phonology on a chart of two articulatory tricategorizations: front/central/back and high/mid/low. They divide the consonants into stops, fricatives, and resonants. (cf. Carlton, 1990).

[95] Propp, 1970, pp. 74.

aspects of the mind: id, ego, and superego."[96] The tales, in Bettleheim's view, are designed to parallel the struggle of these three forces within the developing personality of the young listener. In the tale, the id's unconscious energy seeks release--a primary drive (old-brain or limbic system, physiologically) must be satisfied. Human conflicts result. The tale then introduces elements, which represent the ego's (mid-brain, physiologically) attempts to satisfy the id's demands within the requirements of conscious external reality. These attempts, of course, are doomed to failure without the role of the superego (the cerebral cortex, physiologically), which introduces a sense of moral right and wrong, the uniquely human ability to sacrifice self-interest for the sake of others. The fairytale protagonist, the hero, who eventually succeeds and triumphs in the conflict, is the one who, in contradistinction to others, acts on the level of the superego. This is the very purpose of the fairy tale--to teach the young listener the value of (1) self-sacrificing actions, (2) the value of an over-riding morality, and (3) the sense of right and wrong.[97]

When Russia developed literacy and then literature, the narrative techniques, which had evolved as parts of the oral genres (the byliny and the skazki or fairy tales) were carried over into textual structures. Triplicity, accordingly, became an integral part of the written story.

In the twelfth-century epic Lay of Igor's Campaign, the upstart Prince Igor and his three relative princes, Vsevolod, Oleg, and Sviatoslav, encounter and, unfortunately, disregard a bad omen, an eclipse of the sun, which occurs

---

[96] Bettelheim, 1977, pp. 102.

[97] The numbers in parentheses, both here and later in the paper, are added by the author to point out related triplicities.

three days into their journey of conquest. Sergei Zenkovsky analyzes this very complex early literary work by pointing out that:

"three distinct structural planes can be discerned in the Lay. The first concerns the destiny of Prince Igor, his campaign, defeat, and escape from the Kumans. This plane, the narrative core of the work, is somewhat clouded by invocations to the late bard, Boyan, reminiscences of past glory, and the allusive atmosphere of foreboding. The second plane consists of portents and lamentations over the outcome of the campaign and Russia's fate, such as the dream of Prince Sviatoslav of Kiev and the lament of Yaroslavna, the wife of Igor. The final plane consists of the author's admonition to the princes to unite, and his censure of their fighting ."[98]

We can see here also that Russian critic Zenkovsky's literary analysis is as fraught with triplicity as the literary example itself...his perception of "three (1) distinct (2) structural (3) planes,"...Prince Igor's "(1) campaign, (2) defeat, and (3) escape"...the "invocations to (1) the late bard, Boyan, (2) reminiscences of past glory, and (3) the allusive atmosphere of foreboding." Indeed this kind of meta-triplicity, the product of a subliminal eisegesis or mimesis (if not overtly deliberate), is not rare in Russian literary criticism. Consider Roman Osipovich Jakobson's excursis on an ancient Russian treatise entitled "The Colloquy on Teaching Letters." This work is thoroughly infused with triplicity by an unknown author, likely a monk, trying to make a correlation between the word's relationship with the human soul and human reason and the Son's relationship with God the Father and the Holy Spirit--"a polemic," Jakobson explains, "against the anti-trinitarian sects of the

---

[98] Zenkovsky, 1974, pp. 168.

fifteenth century." But Jakobson begins his "Acknowledgements and Dedication" of this section with the following sentence, composed of three triads of differing (one successive, one elaborative, one specificative, including, like a fairy tale, two negative rejections before the final positive acceptance) trielemental increments:

"The Moscow Linguistic School (a tripartite name), (1) faithful to the (2) precepts of its (3) founder, Filipp Fedorovich Fortunatov (a tripartite name), has been destined to (1) elucidate, (2) substantiate, and (3) develop his view that language is (1) not a mere 'external cover in regard to the phenomena of thought' and (2) not only a 'means for the expression of ready-made ideas,' but (3) first and foremost it is 'an implement for thinking' ."[99]

Was Jakobson influenced to express this triplicity by his analysis of a textually proximate triplistic work? Or was he, a supreme Russian scholar with the narrative goal of edification, subject to the same forces governing the narrative techniques of the authors he studied? The answer is probably both.

In his preface to the second edition of his verse translation into English of Alexander Pushkin's Eugene Onegin, Walter Arndt writes that the great "novel-in-verse" is:

"...concerned, as (Vladimir) Nabokov has put it, with 'the afflictions, affections and fortunes of three young men-- Onegin, the bitter lean fop; Lensky, the tempermental minor poet; and Pushkin, their friend--and of three young ladies-- Tatyana, Olga, and Pushkin's muse'...There are three settings (the country estates, Moscow, St. Petersburg)...and the

---

[99] Jacobson, 1971, pp. 365.

author plays a triple role--that of narrator, of an acquaintance of the hero, and of a character in the poem ."[100]

One might well point out here also that Vladimir Nabokov's characterization of the "afflictions, affections, and fortunes" of a "bitter lean fop" and a "tempermental minor poet" is concomitantly rife with the same triplicity it describes. Surely it is more than merely curious that criticism often mirrors its object. It's simply that the narrative goal of literature and the narrative goal of criticism of literature is the same--maximal message impact on the reader. So it is not suprising that both should share triplicity as a structural aspect.[101]

There is a saying in the Russian culture that some stories are "good enough to tell three times" (**"сказка/история...достойна три раза сказывать"**). But it's three times and three times only...twice is not enough, and four times "exhausts the story" and makes it trite, reflecting poorly on the story-teller. This may be a supersitition, like "spitting three times" (**"Тьфу-Тьфу-**

---

[100] Pushkin, 1963, pp. ix-xxi. Only the 2nd edition of this Dutton publication includes this characterization in its introduction.

[101] Another candidate for exemplification of criticism mirroring the triplicity of Pushkin's Eugene Onegin is that of Edmund Wilson (1938 (1963), pp. 44) who writes: "Pushkin has put into the relations between the three central characters a number of implications. ...they may be said to represent three intellectual currents of the time:(1) Evgenii is Byronism turning worldly and dry; (2) Lensky, with his Schiller and Kant, German Romantic Idealism; (3) Tatyana, that Rousseauist Nature which (1) was making itself heard in Romantic poetry, (2) speaking a new language and (3) asserting a new kind of rights."

Тьфу") over the left shoulder to remove the "hex" or "jinx" of a "**дурной глаз**" (the "evil eye"). But it's evident in Russian literature as well as in oral story telling. If one surveys the collected works of the great poet, Mikhail Lermontov, for example, one finds that he decided to give the title "**Молитва**" ("Prayer") to precisely THREE of his poems: "Do not blame me, Almighty..." (1829), "I, Mother of God, am now in prayer..." (1837), and "In difficult times of life..." (1839)[102]. Three times, and only three times, did Lermontov give this very title to his poems on religious aspects of his life. There are also three poems titled "**Звезда**" ("Star") and three poems with "**Смерть**" ("Death") in the title and three poems with "**Поэт**" ("Poet") in the title. This is not likely to be coincidental...though it may not have been a consciously deliberate act on the part of the poet...and it is not insignificant. A new line of bibliometrics may now be established wherein the oeuvre of the other great Russian literati are scanned for such titular triples.

Nikolai Gogol is an author whose work is rife with triplicity. In his Dead Souls he likens Russia to a "troyka, winged troyka...that none can overtake."[103] He declares that "Lo, the troyka has (1) wings, (2) wings, (3) wings..." and later..."(1) steeds, (2) steeds...(3) and more steeds." Gleb

---

[102] These are the only poems of this title included in the outstandingly comprehensive and definitive **Лермонтовская Энциклопедия** (Мануйлов, ред., **1981, стр.** 283-4...translations available in L'Ami and Welikotny, 1967, and Liberman, 1983). There is also a "**Юнкерская молитва**" (a 'Soldier's Prayer') in Lermontov's oeuvre...but this is not his prayer.

[103] A "troyka" (**Тройка**) or "trio" in this sense is a Russian harness arrangement, referring to a sleigh or carriage drawn by three animals.-author)

Zhekulin, in his article, "Rereading Gogol's 'Viy'," describes Gogol's "favourite...the fundamental device of triplication":

"Three students set out on their journey: Tiberii Gorobets, Khoma Brut, and Khaliava; for three nights Khoma reads in the church--these are the visible, obvious instances of triplication, but there are other, less noticeable instances: on his return to Kiev after his witch-ride, Khoma passed...some three times through the market; the church in which the body of the pannochka-ved'ma was lying had three concical cupolas; the old witch approaches Khoma in the shed three times before she catches him; when Mikita's experiences with the witch are mentioned, three men want to tell the story (this story is treated in a different regard below...-authors); only three of the Sotnik's servants are known to us by their names, Evtukh, Dorosh, and Spirid; and, at the very end of the story, Khaliava, drinking his third tankard, pronounces a eulogy of Khoma: 'He was a splendid man, was Khoma? A magnificent man! And he was ruined for nothing.'"[104]

Zhekulin also points out that Gogol's syntax too "often falls into patterns of three. Thus the young widow who gives shelter to Khoma on his return to Kiev used to sell 'ribbons, rifle-shot and wheels'; the little church was 'wooden, blackened, and carpeted with green moss'." Further, Zhekulin points out three successive permutations of the same sentence, paragraphs consisting of "three sentences of similar syntactical construction," and sentences composed of "three subordinate clauses." He clearly demonstrates that the thematic triplicity, evident in the plot and in the opposition of the characters, is rendered through triads of sentences, many of tertiary syntactical structure, and with triple strings of adjectives. Structure in support of

---

[104] Zhekulin, 1983, pp. 302.

content is nowhere more emphatic than when dealing with triplicity.[105]

By the 1830's Nikolai Gogol had become aware of a particular "story worth telling three times"...the story of spontaneous human combustion. Stories of spontaneous human combustion had entered the literature of the romantic period from sources in France and Italy. The story exists in many cultures. Even in Hawaiian lore, we learn that part of early 19th century King Kamehameha's fear of Kauai's tributary King Kaumualii was based on Kaumualii's knowledge of an incantation, called the "Aneekapuahi" which, if uttered in an adversary's presence, would cause that adversary's spontaneous incineration (Joesting, 1984, pp. 58).[106] Early American literature includes an episode of it. Charles Brockden Brown's popular Gothic romance, Wieland; or the Transformation (1798) includes an episode of spontaneous human combustion, and later descriptions enter the works of Melville and Dickens.[107] In Gogol's particular view, spontaneous human combustion was part of the malicious workings of the Devil. He decided to include an episode of it in his story "St. John's Eve" from the collection, Village Evenings Near Dikanka (1831-2). The character "Petro the orphan" marries the beautiful Pidorka after complying with a demand by the Demon Basavryuk and a witch helper to kill Pidorka's younger brother Ivas in order to acquire a fortune in gold coins. But Ivas reappears when the witch is summoned by Pidorka to cure Petro's dejection of forgetfulness about his heinous act. When Petro sees the witch, he

---

[105] ibid. pp. 303.

[106] Joesting, 1984, pp. 58.

[107] cf. Croft, 1989, pp. 335-347 for the locations and discussion of these examples from Melville's Redburn and Dickens' Bleak House.

"...let out a shreik of laughter that struck fear into Pidorka's heart. 'I've remembered! I've remembered!' he shouted with uncanny glee, and seizing hold of an axe, swung it with all his might at the old woman. The axe sank two inches into the oak door. The old woman disappeared into thin air and a child of about seven, clad in a white shirt, with his head covered by a sheet, suddenly appeared in the middle of the room...the sheet dropped from his head.

'Ivas!' cried Pidorka and rushed across to the boy; but the vision was enveloped from head to foot in blood and flooded the hut with a red light...In terror she ran out of the hut; but then, recovering her senses somewhat, she turned back to help the boy; in vain! The door had slammed shut so hard behind her that she couldn't open it. People came running up; they pounded on the door, and then broke it down, but there wasn't a soul inside. The entire hut was full of smoke, and in the middle, where Petro had stood, lay a heap of ashes, still giving off wisps of smoke. They rushed to the bags of gold--but instead of coins they only contained broken shards of pottery. Their eyes popping from their heads and their mouths agape, the Cossacks stood rooted to the spot, afraid even to twitch their moustaches."

A paragraph later, Gogol's narrator explains "...that wasn't the end of the matter. The very same day that the Devil took Petro to himself, Basavryuk reappeared in the village...he was none other than Satan himself, and had taken human form in order to get his hands on hidden treasure."[108]

"St. John's Eve" is an impactful scary story, and it garnered for Gogol his early reputation as a teller of supernatural tales. The episode of spontaneous human

---

[108] Gogol, 1994, pp. 48-9. Translation here is by Richard Peace.

combustion was an important aspect of his narration, infusing the story with a terrifying manifestation of the "Devil's will."

But Gogol was not done with the story of spontaneous human combustion. He included another episode of it into the story "Viy," from the Mirgorod collection (1835, rewritten in 1842). This is the same story treated above for its triplicity. In "Viy," the seminarian Khoma Brut is asked to pray over the body of the deceased daughter of a local Cossack commander. But this daughter was, according to the three Cossacks, Evtukh, Spirid, and Dorosh, a witch (actually a "gentleman's daughter witch" or "pannochka-ved'ma), as evidenced by their story of what happened to Mikita the Dog-keeper when he dallied with her.

"Once her young ladyship came to the stables where he was grooming a horse. Come here, Mikita, she says, let me put my foot on your shoulder. And--fool that he is--he obliges: don't stop at that, he says, get right up on my back. The mistress raised her foot and the moment he saw her naked, white leg he was completely bamboozled. The silly dolt bent down and, grabbing hold of her naked legs with his two hands, galloped away like a horse across the field, and he hadn't a notion afterwards where they went; only he came home more dead than alive, and from that day on he was withered as a dead stick; then one fine day they went to the stables and what do they find?--a heap of ashes and an empty bucket: he'd burst into flames, and burnt to a cinder. But you ask anyone, there wasn't a better dog-keeper anywhere in the world ."[109]

---

[109] ibid, pp. 391. I have altered Richard Peace's translation slightly here, preferring "Dog-keeper" (or even, as has been used elsewhere, "Dogboy") to render the Russian "псарь" where Peace uses "Huntsman."

Later it is the pannochka-ved'ma ("Gentleman's daughter-witch") who, while Khoma is praying for her soul, rises up from her coffin to summon "Viy," the demonic monster with eyelids drooping to the ground who steals Khoma's soul through eye-contact when his gnome minions lift his eyelids to expose his eyes. Again, the episode of spontaneous human combustion is associated with the work of the Devil.

Gogol's third and last telling of the story of spontaneous human combustion is found in his great novel Dead Souls. His con-man Chichikov is trying to purchase from a host of greedy and incompetent Russian landowners (the real "Dead Souls") the legal titles to the landowners' serfs that have died since the last census. He intends to use these titles as collateral to obtain a large bank loan and then default on the loan and abscound with the money. But the landowners he encounters are reluctant to sell him the titles to their dead serfs, even though the sale would lessen their tax burden. Chichikov asks one of these landowners, Mrs. Korobochka: "Have any of your serfs died?" Her answer shows her to be more concerned with her serfs' services than with their lives:

"Oh, my good friend, eighteen of them!..And they were all such nice people, such good workers. True, since then some new ones have been born, but what's the good of that; they're all so young and yet the tax assessor came and demanded that I pay so much per soul. So the people are dead and I have to pay for them as if they were alive. Last week my blacksmith was burned to death. He was such a good blacksmith and a quite skilled locksmith as well."

Chichikov asks, "Why, did you have a fire?" And Mrs. Korobochka continues:

"God has spared me that calamity--a fire would have been even worse. No, he burned all by himself, the blacksmith. Something caught fire inside him. He had too much to drink, and there was blue flame escaping from him, and he kept smoldering and smoldering and then went all black like charcoal--and yet, what a good blacksmith he used to be! And now I can't go driving--no one to shoe the horses ."[110]

So, Nikolai Gogol thrice and only thrice tells the tale of spontaneous human combustion in his works. Likely, he considered it a most impactful story to tell once, still impactful to tell twice, and even thrice. But, after that, no more. The story's narrative utility was, in his mind, exhausted.

Fyodor Dostoevsky's works are replete with triplicity. His early masterpiece, <u>Notes From the Underground</u>, begins with these three famous sentences: "**Я человек больной. Я злой человек. Непривлекательный я человек.**" Each of these three sentences is composed of three words and each sentence presents these words in three different orders (1. subject, predicate noun, adjective; 2) subject, adjective, predicate noun; and 3) adjective, subject, predicate noun). In his "A Brief Note on the Translation," translator Michael Katz...who states right off that "of all the works of nineteenth-century Russian literature I have translated, without doubt Dostovevky's Notes From the Underground remains the most challenging"...most adeptly relates the peculiar ordering of the words in these first three sentences to the characterization of the work's fictional narrator and to the work's dominant themes: individuality, humanity, and the effects of personal character. After presenting ten previous translations of these three sentences

---

[110] Gogol, 1961, pp. 59-60. The translation here is by Andrew R. MacAndrew.

into English, Katz translates them as: "I am a sick man. ...I am a spiteful man. I am an unattractive man." [111]

Triplicity in Dostoevsky's works is well shown in William Woodin Rowe's article, "<u>Crime and Punishment</u> and <u>The Brothers Karamazov</u>: Some Comparative Observations." This article goes on for five pages of text, detailing the amazing "scope of triplicity" in both of these Dostoevsky novels. Here is a sample of Rowe's description of the plots:

"Perhaps most fatefully of all, triplicity informs the descriptions of murder in both novels. At his 'third meeting' with Ivan, Smerdyakov describes the murder in <u>The Brothers Karamazov</u>. He hit Fyodor Pavlovich three times, he claims, with a paperweight weighing about three pounds. The third blow broke the latter's skull and he collapsed, whereupon Smerdyakov took the 3000 rubles from an envelope closed by 'three large red wax seals'.

Raskolnikov (in <u>Crime and Punishment</u>--author), who has pawned with Alyona a ring 'with three red stones' gains entrance in response to his 'third' ring at his third visit to Alyona's, after which he hits her three times (hoping to steal 3000 rubles). As with Smerdyakov, his third and last blow breaks the skull. Dostoevsky seems intrigued by this 'third-of-three death patterning': in <u>The Brothers Karamazov</u>, Father Ferapont claims to have killed a devil by making the

---

[111] cf. Michael Katz' (ed. and trans.) "A Brief Note on the Translation" (pp. xi-xiv) in Dostoevsky, 2001. The other translators are: C.J. Hogarth (1913), Constance Garnett (1918), Ralph Matlaw (1960), Andrew R. MacAndrew (1961), Serge Shishkoff (1969), Jessie Coulson (1972),Mirra Ginsburg (1974), David Magarshack (1979), Jane Kentish (1991), and Richard Pevear and L. Volokhonsky (1993).

sign of the cross three times; in <u>Crime and Punishment</u>...Svidrigailov kills himself with the third shot of a three-shot pistol."[112]

In his earlier article, "Dostoevskian Patterned Antimony and Its Function in <u>Crime and Punishment,</u> " Rowe states that Dostoevsky "creates antimonic effects by means of a three-stage formulation which may be likened to the swinging of a pendulum from one side to the other and then at least partially back."[113] He cites Leonid Grossman's work, "**Достоевский-художник**" ("Dostoevsky the Artist"), to establish the triplistic nature of this patterning in other works of Dostoevsky.

"Describing what he deems the main characteristic of Dostoevsky's 'structural system,' Leonid Grossman notes a tendency in the novels to reveal a tragic situation gradually 'in three meetings or three conversations of the heroes.' This conduces, he observes, to a careful thematic development 'in a little trilogy,' a 'concise three-act drama' with increasing suspense, horror and revelations."[114]

An example of this tripartite Dostoevskian antimony (i.e. the "pendulum swinging from one side to the other and then part way back") is to be found in <u>Crime and Punishment</u> where the detective Porfirii Petrovich looks at the murderer Raskolnikov and "with a kind of obvious mockery" screws up his eyes "as if winking at him." Here, "both reader and Raskolnikov are led to believe that Porfirii (1) seemed to

---

[112] Rowe, 1974, pp. 338-9. I have been unable to find an actual "three-shot pistol," though I did purchase a collector's model (non-firing) of such a pistol, a 19th century rotating-barrels cap-and-hammer specimen, in Istanbul, Turkey's, central market in 1999.
[113] Rowe, 1972, pp. 287.
[114] op.cit. Rowe, 1974, pp. 341 in notes.

wink, (2) may not have, and (3) probably did" wink, engendering in Raskolnikov the conclusion that Porfirii is "(1) wrong, (2) right, (or) (3) slightly wrong ."[115]

This tripartite antimony is thematically evident in Dostoevsky's novel, <u>Demons</u>, a "novel in three parts." In her article, "The Absence of Historical Time in Dostoevsky's **Бесы**," Dawn Seckler mentions parallel triplistic themes in Dostovevsky's work: life, death, and resurrection (Christ-like behavior of his characters); crime, confession, redemption; paradise, cast out of paradise, return to a partial paradise... In <u>Demons</u>, Seckler writes, Dostoevsky's main character Stavrogin "becomes involved with three of the novel's female characters--Liza Nikolaevna, Darya Pavlovna, and Maria Timofeevna." In the chapters "Night" and "Night (continued)," Dostoevsky describes Stavrogin's "trek from his home (1) to Kirillov's, then (2) to Shatov's, along Bogoiavlenskaia Street, and (3) to the Lebiadkins'" and she comments:

"That there are three, and not two or four, references to the dark and rainy weather is significant. Dostoevsky trebles elements of both description and action: just as references to the conditions outside are made three times in these two chapters, Stavrogin comes into contact with Fed'ka the convict three times. The first, figurative, 'meeting' occurs when Petr Verkhovenskii mentions Fed'ka's presence in town to Stavrogin. The second and third meetings are literal: Stavrogin meets Fed'ka along Bogoiavlenskaia Street on his way to and from the Lebiadkins', meets Fed'ka in exactly the same spot where they had previously parted. Like the rain and the darkness, Fed'ka's presence is sustained in timelessness while Stavrogin engages in other business. When, after each of

---

[115] op.cit. Rowe, 1972, pp. 290.

his three visits, Stavrogin re-enters the darkness outside, he also enters a world where nothing has changed."[116]

Leo Tolstoy once wrote a version of "The Three Bears" in order to help in his project to educate his peasants. In his later years he wrote the didactic tale, "The Three Old Men," to edify a society subject to a church hierarchy he found distasteful. In this story, Tolstoy's archbishop, a passenger on a ship in the cold White Sea, encounters three old men that he hears described by three different sources as being "holy men." One of these sources is referred to in three different ways ("little muzhik," "peasant," and "fisherman"). The archbishop inconveniences the ship's company by demanding that he be taken to the island where these old men live. There, he meets the simple old men and asks them how they pray. They answer naively that they pray to God by saying: "Three are Ye, three are we. Have Ye mercy upon us." The archbishop then spends all day teaching the old men the Lord's Prayer, and leaves their remote island satisfied that he has well carried out God's will. But soon a light on the horizon appears, causing the archbishop to ask the helmsman in triplistic fashion what it might be, "--a boat, or not a boat; a bird, or not a bird; a fish, or not a fish?" The light, of course, materializes as the three old men, who have levitated themselves into the air and soared out over the sea in pursuit of the ship so as to ask the archbishop for further repetitions of his instruction on how properly to pray. Thus Tolstoy's lesson to society about the superfluity of the church hierarchy is perfused with triplicity

---

[116] Seckler, 2003, pp. 62. Dostoevsky-philes can often cite examples of triplicity in almost any work of Dostoevsky's, but most frequently do they cite the triplicities of plot and characterization in the novel <u>Eternal Husband</u>. I am not trying to be exhaustive...only illustrative of the different main aspects of the phenomenon.

for mnemonic effect. After his excommunication from the Russian Orthodox Church in 1901, he is reputed to have synopsized his stance toward organized religion with a rhyme, treating the triune relationship of himself, God, and the Russian Orthodox Church in precisely NINE (3X3) words: "**Бог и я—мы друзья. Мне не нужна религия.**" ("God and I are friends/I don't need religion").[117]

Daniel Rancour-Laferriere is a leading psychoanalytic interpreter of literature, often including Freudian insights (e.g. the triplistic "id, ego, superego") into his work. His recent work on Tolstoy, entitled "<u>Tolstoy on the Couch</u>:..," includes discussion of Tolstoy's "psychopathology" and its effects on his literary works. The title (after a colon) continues, "...(1) <u>Mysogyny</u>, (2) <u>Masochism</u>, and (3) <u>the Absent Mother</u>." In his review of this work, Martin Bidney mentions Rancour-Laferriere's discussion of how the narrator of Tolstoy's "never-finished 'Notes of a Madman'" witnesses "three episodes of punishment," crying at two of them "and, in the third, beats his head on the wall in identification with the tale of Christ's crucifixion."[118] Consideration of this discussion leads to the conclusion that triplistic aspects of Tolstoy's "psychopathology" finds its reflection in the structure of his literary works...and, perhaps derivatively, in the works interpreting them. Again we see another triplicity--the triplicity of Tolstoy's psyche, Tolstoy's work, and Rancour-Laferriere's interpretation of both...the author, the work, the criticism-- the main "stuff" of our literary lives.

According to Temira Pachmuss, the symbolist poet Zinaida Gippius "saw various manifestations of the number 'three' in the composition of the world--the Holy Trinity, the

---

[117] cf. Croft, 1986.
[118] Bidney, 2004, pp.305.

unity of human personality-love-society, or of the spiritual world-man-material world, and so forth." Gippius explained that the essence of her Weltanschauung "can be presented as an all-embracing triangle in the structure of the world and as an uninterrupted merging of the three principles, indivisible and yet separate from one another." Pachmuss has translated Gippius' poetic expression of this idea from the nine-line (3 X 3) poem "**Тройное**" ('Threefold'):

"The world abounds in a three-fold depth.
A threefold depth is given to poets.
And really don't poets speak
Only of this?
Only of this?
A threefold truth--and a threefold beginning.
Poets, trust in this truth.
God thinks only about this:
About Man. Love. And Death."[119]

John Garrard has elucidated the apocalyptic elements in Alexander Blok's innovative narrative poem, The Twelve. He points out that the "simple 'plot' of The Twelve--(involves) the triangle of Petrukha, his prostitute girlfriend Katia, who has abandoned him for a wealthier turncoat Van'ka." Garrard, having studied Alexander Blok's personal copy of the Bible's book of Revelation, elaborates that this "simple plot" "replicates in miniature the narrative of Revelation, in which John of Patmos predicts the fall of Rome and Domitian by way of the coded imagery of the Whore of Babylon and the Beast." Garrard mentions Blok's consciousness that St. John, whom he considered the author

---

[119] Pachmuss, T. 1971. pp. 105.

of three books of the Bible (The Gospel, the First Epistle, and Revelation), three times uses the image of a bride preparing for her wedding to describe aspects of the "three effects upon the world" which will result from Christ's reappearance: "First, the exact moment ('hour') of his coming will be a surprise, no matter how urgently people have been expecting and hoping for it. Second, his coming will cause massive change and destruction. Third, he will be virtually unrecognizable at the hour of his actual appearance." Garrard continues that "Blok's most explicit clue that the subtext for his Christ figure is Revelation lies in the three iterations of the statement that the Twelve Red Guards follow a banner 'with no cross.' The Twelve uses the same line on three occasions quite early in the poem: 'Hey, Hey, with no cross!'." And, Blok made marginalia in the text of his copy of Revelation, drawing lines to connect the jotted names of his characters to characters in the text...for example, drawing a line between Revelation's mention of the "Whore of Babylon" to the jotted name "Katia," an important character in The Twelve. When St. John uses the image of a wedding and a bride three times, Blok "underlines precisely these (three) passages," and "as if the underlining and the parallel lines were not enough, he added three X's in the margin."[120]

---

[120] Garrard, 2003, pp. 45-72 (cf. pp. 50, 58, and 63-4). On pp. 61 Garrard elaborates on the Biblical use of the number twelve. Garrard's insightful mention of the symbolic glyphs here (the three "x's") brings to mind the fact that Russian uses three dots ("...") to mark ellipses. In that regard, Pushkin titled his famous poem, "**Я помню чудное мгновенье**..." ("I remember that wondrous instant...") as "K +++" using three plus marks to signify the absence of his muse's name. And, Lermontov "titles" his poem (later song) "Выхожу один я на дорогу..." ("Alone along the road I'm

Edmund Wilson, the eminent literary critic, had a very high opinion of Nobel Prize laureate Boris Pasternak's novel, Dr. Zhivago. In November of 1958, he wrote:

"Dr. Zhivago will, I believe, come to stand as one of the great events in man's literary and moral history. Nobody could have written it in a totalitarian state and turned it loose on the world who did not have the courage of genius. May his guardian angel be with him! His book is a great act of faith in art and in the human spirit. As for his enemies in his fatherland, I predict that their children, over their vodka and tea, will be talking about the relations between Larisa Fyodorovna and Pasha and Yury Andreyevich (3) as their parents, and I don't doubt they themselves, have talked about Tatyana and Lensky and Evgeni Onegin (3), and Natasha and Prince Andrei and Pierre (3)." [121]

---

walking...") as "***" (*three* asterisks, ostensibly to signal absence of a formal title). The asterisk (Russian "**звёздочка**" or "little star") is perhaps the oldest and most universal glyph of all, dating to the ideogram phase of Mesopotamian cuneiform writing (ca. 3000 BCE, cf. http:\\std.dkuug.dk/jtc1/scz/wg2/docs/n2664.pdf)   and having in modern computer typography both the original six (2X3)-point (Unicode U+2217) and, because of the Muslim perception that the six points symbolise an Israeli Star of David, five-point (Unicode U+066D) versions. Three asterisks arranged in a triangle are called an "asterism" (Unicode U+2042, cf. http:\\en.wikipedia.org/wiki/Asterisk). Of course, the discussion here involves Russian literary uses of THREE tripled glyphs (X,+,*).

[121] Wilson, 1965, pp. 446. The references in the quotation are to characters of Pasternak's <u>Dr. Zhivago</u> ("Larisa Fyodorovna and Pasha and Yury Andreyevich"), Alexander

Wilson discusses the symbolism of the name "Zhivago," associating it with "life" in the life, death, and resurrection triad. He compares the plot structure to an elaborate "Skazka" or "Fairy tale" in which a "miraculous figure" in the person of Zhivago's half-brother Evgraf three times comes to Yury Zhivago's rescue:

"First, when, before Zhivago has taken his family away, he collapses in Moscow with typhus; again, when he is marooned with his family in the Urals, before he has been kidnapped by the partisans; and finally, when, returned to Moscow, unwanted and unassimilable, he is on the point of petering out. On this last occasion, Evgraf induces him to leave for a time his devoted lower-class wife and provides him with lodgings in which to write. We never know what Evgraf is or how he accomplishes his miracles; he is always an important person whose authority is felt at once, never questioned; he can always produce food, secure for his half-brother conditions of leisure. Yet we do not know (1) what office he holds, (2) why he is always so sure of himself, and (3) how he has managed to escape the purges. On his third intervention, he brings death in the flesh. The Doctor, now hidden from his family, does not survive his last creative liberation, but Evgraf preserves his manuscripts, the poems in which Yury lives again."[122]

One of the most emblematic stars of current Russian literature is Victor Olegovich Pelevin. In her <u>Russian Life</u> article, "Victor Pelevin: Genius Temporis," Galina

---

Pushkin's <u>Eugene Onegin</u> ("Tatyana and Lensky and Evgeni Onegin"), and to Leo Tolstoy's <u>War and Peace</u> ("Natasha and Prince Andrei and Pierre")...three characters from each.

[122] ibid, Wilson, 1965, pp. 442. In this quotation we see described the life, death, and resurrection (by virtue of the preserved poems) mentioned earlier.

Yuzefovich writes that: "You cannot understand Russian literature of the past fifteen years without reading Victor Pelevin."[123] And in the works of Pelevin, triplicity is often evident in his relations of time, place, and character. In the tale, "Hermit and Six-Toes" ("**Затворник и шестипалый**"), there are two main characters and a "socium" of others--all gradually revealed through the flow of details to be chickens in a mechanized Russian food factory. As these two, the "Hermit" and "Six-toes," consider their place in their particular "cosmos," three lights are immediately visible in the universe above them. The Hermit states that he has come to this world from the third of five previous worlds where he has been. He and "Six-toes" are then approached by a giant rat named "One-eye." They ask the rat why "if both eyes are in order he is called 'One-eye'." The rat answers that the "one-eye" refers to his third, inner, eye...an eye which is always open. As their eventual fate becomes clear to them by the ninth (3X3) and last chapter, hermit and six-toes escape from three of the "Gods" who attempt to process them into food by pecking them and resorting to their forgotten power of flight. Even the syllabic structure of the work is rife with triplicity...the names (e.g. "**Затворник**," "**Шести** (2X3)-**палый**," and the "Socium") and the most impactful sentences (e.g. "**Сметрь пришла**"..."Death arrived").[124]

In all of Russian Culture, but especially in its preliterate narrative forms through its most sophisticated modern literature, I find a pervasive and intense triplicity--in plot, characterization, and even the wording itself; in source,

---

[123] Yuzefovich, G., 2004, pp. 40.
[124] Pelevin, V. 2001. Cf. 1996 Translation as "Hermit and Six-fingers" by Serge Winitzki and Serge Bratus at www.geocities.com/Athens/Forum/5344/fun/friends.html#translations.

theme, and method; in authors' lives, their relationships, and their resultant treatments by critics. Telling things three times in a triplistic way is a veritable hallmark of Russian literature, which opens diverse aspects of the culture as a whole to further elucidation.

Acknowlegments

Many people have contributed to my study of the "threes" in Russian literature and in literature and culture generally. Mostly, I am grateful to my students for their constant reinforcement of the value of my opinions. And to my colleagues who have tolerated my presentations on this and other topics over the years. And to certain others of my colleagues who have, their own interest piqued, sent related articles, source citations, letters of commentary and suggestions-- like Tatyana Dhaliwal, Tatiana Keeling, Jeanette Owen, John Garrard, George Gutsche and Daniel Rancour-Laferriere, going back to 1985. But I have also appreciated input from diverse "other" sources, including the internet's Threesology Research Journal (see the website at http://cenocracy.topcities.com ...notably pages /cro1- entitled "Examples of Three...beginning,"), an absolutely mind-boggling analysis of "pattern-of-threes" in our lives mostly by triophile extraordinaire Herb O. Buckland (my own favorite page is /cro60a1.html which treats the triplistic aspects of human hearing physiology and music), from Michael Eck and his www.threes.com (which enumerates much triplicity in the American English culture, primarily) and the "Digital Project" of Red Planet Software and from Prof. John A. McNulty, Ph.D., of Loyola University of Chicago's School of Medicine for his amazing "List of Three's in Anatomy:" (cf.www.meddean.luc.edu/lumen/MedEd/GrossAnatomy/Threes.html, but also published in the Threesology Research

Journal...see above). There is much triplicity in the religio-philosophico-psychological work of russophone (1) philosopher, (2) mystic, and (3) teacher George Ivanovich Gurdjieff (1866-1949) and his disciple Peter Demianovich Ouspensky (1878-1947), with the "Law of Three" and the "Three Paths to Awakening," the nine-point "enneagram of personality types" and etc. (see, for example, www.gurdjieff-legacy.org/50bookexcerpts/ouspenskypioneer.htm or www.darkecho.com/JohnShirley/sgurd.html). A Russian website by Alexander I. Stepanov entitled "The Number and Culture. The Rational Unconscious in Language, Fiction, Science, Present Politics, Philosophy, History," including a good list of "Triple Structures" is to be found at www.alestep.narod.ru/eng_bl/. An interesting late find was Brian Stross's article, "Maya Bloodletting and the Number Three," in which a "sonic resemblance" of Mixe-Zoquean words for "three" and the Maya (and earlier Olmec) words for ritual bloodletting is considered the etiology of homonymous iconographs. Also, I am grateful to my mother-in-law, Kathryn Hoyt, for introducing me to the works of Bruno Bettelheim.

SOURCES:

Bettelheim, Bruno. 1977. The Uses of Enchantment: The Meaning and Importance of Fairy Tales. New York. Vintage.

Bidney, Martin. (2004) Review of Daniel Rancour-Laferriere's Tolstoy on the Couch: Misogyny, Masochism, and the Absent Mother in Slavic and East European Journal. Vol. 48, No. 2 (Summer 2004). pp. 305-6.

Carlton, Terrence R. 1990. <u>Introduction to the Phonological History of the Slavic Languages</u>. Columbus, Ohio. Slavica Publishers, Inc.

Chvany, Catherine V. 1984. "From Jakobson's cube as 'objet d'art' to a new model of the grammatical sign." <u>International Journal of Slavic Linguistics and Poetics</u>. 29: 43-70.

Chvany, Catherine V. 1986. "Jakobson's Fourth and Fifth Dimensions: On Recording the Cube Model of Case Meanings with the Two-dimensional Matrices for Case Forms." In R. D. Brecht and J. S. Levine (eds.) <u>Case in Slavic: Studies Dedicated to the Memory of Roman O. Jakobson.</u> Slavica Publishers. Columbus, OH (now moved to Bloomington, IN...cf. www.Slavica.com). pp. 107-130.

Croft, Lee B. 1986. "Tolstoy's Three Hermits." <u>Masterplots II: The Short Story</u>. Pasadena, CA. Salem Press. In Russian the title is "**Три старца**"..."three old men" as in text.

Croft, Lee B. 1989. "Spontaneous Human Combustion in Literature: Some Examples of the Literary Use of Popular Mythology." <u>CLA Journal (Journal of the College Language Association)</u>. Volume XXXII, Number 3 (March 1989), pp. 335-347.

Croft, Lee B. 1995. "Triplicity and Textual Iconicity: Russian Literature Through a Triangular Prism." In <u>Syntactic Iconicity and Linguistic Freezes: The Human Dimension.</u> Marge E. Landsberg, ed. Berlin and New York. Mouton de Gruyter. pp. 249-265.

Dostoevsky, Fyodor. 2001. <u>Notes From the Underground</u>. Edited and Translated by Michael R. Katz. New York and London. Norton Critical Edition, 2nd Edition. W.W. Norton and Company.

Feynman, Richard P. 1985. QED: The Strange Theory of Light and Matter. Princeton, New Jersey. Princeton University Press.

Garrard, John. 2003. "The Twelve: Blok's Apocalypse," in Religion and Literature. Vol. 35, No. 1 (Spring 2003), pp. 45-72.

Gogol, Nikolai. 1961. Dead Souls. (Translation by Andrew R. MacAndrew with a foreword by Frank O'Connor). New York and Toronto. A Signet Classic of the New American Library.

Gogol, Nikolai. 1994. Village Evenings Near Dikanka and Mirgorod. (Christopher English, transl. and ed., with introduction by Richard Peace). Oxford and New York. Oxford University Press's World's Classics series (0-19-282880-0).

Grossman, Leonid. 1959. "**Достоевский-художник**," in **Творчество Ф. М. Достоевского. Н. Л. Степанов, ред. Москва.** (cf. Rowe, 1974, pp. 341).

Hart, Roy Hanu. 2002. Journey of Faith. Alexandria, LA. Menta Publications (Box 8057, Alexandria, LA 71306-1057...0-935688-02-1). cf. chapter 52, pp. 198-200. The epigraph is from a personal telephone to Lee Croft made in 1999.

Jakobson, Roman O. 1936. "Beitrag zur allgemeinen Kasuslehre" in Roman Jakobson's Selected Writings, II: Word and Language. The Hague. Mouton. pp. 23-71.

Jakobson, Roman O. 1958. "**Морфологические наблюдения над славянским сколонением**" in Roman Jakobson's Selected Writings II: Word and Language. The Hague. Mouton. pp. 154-181.

Jakobson, Roman O. 1971. "Toward a Nomothetic Science of Language." in Roman Jakobson's <u>Selected Writings, II: Word and Language</u>. The Hague. Mouton. pp. 154-183.

Joesting, Edward. 1984. <u>Kauai: The Separate Kingdom</u>. Honolulu and Lihue, HI. University of Hawaii Press and Kauai Museum Association, Ltd.

L'Ami, C. E. and Alexander Welikotny. 1967. <u>Michael Lermontov: Biography and Translations.</u> University of Manitoba Press. Winnipeg.

Lermontov, Mikhail Iurievich. 1983. <u>Major Poetical Works: Mikhail Lermontov.</u> Translated and with a biographical sketch, introduction, and commentary by Anatoly Liberman. University of Minnesota Press. Minneapolis.

Мануйлов, В. А. (Глав. Ред.) <u>**Лермонтовская энциклопедия.**</u> **Издательство "Советская Энциклопедия" Москва. Стр. 283-4.**

Miller, George. (1956) "The Magical Number Seven, Plus or Minus Two: Some Limits on our Capacity for Processing Information." in <u>The Psychological Review</u>. 63: pp. 81-97.

Pachmuss, Temira. 1971<u>. Zinaida Gippius: An Intellectual Profile</u>. Carbondale, Illinois. Southern Illinois University Press.

Пелевин, Виктор. 1996 "Затворник и шестипалый" at http://exbicio.boom.ru/library/pelevin/zatvor.htm.

Pelevin, Viktor. 1996. "Hermit and Six-Fingers." translation by Serge Winitzki and Serge Bratus. See

www.geocities.com/Athens/Forum/5344/fun/friends.html#translations.

Pelevin, Victor. 1997. "Hermit and Six-toes." in The Blue Lantern and Other Stories. Translation from the Russian by Andrew Bromfield. New Directions. New York.

Пелевин, Виктор. 2001. "Затворник и шестипалый: Повесть" Вагриус. Москва.

Propp, Vladimir. 1970. Morphology of the Folktale. Translated by L. Scott and edited by L. Wagner. Austin, TX.. University of Texas Press.

Pushkin, Alexander S. 1963. Eugene Onegin. Edited and translated by Walter Arndt. New York. Dutton.

Rancour-Laferriere, Daniel. (1998) Tolstoy on the Couch: Misogyny, Masochism, and the Absent Mother. New York. New York University Press.

Rowe, William Woodin. 1972. "Dostoevskian Patterned Antimony and Its Function in Crime and Punishment." in Slavic and East European Journal. Vol. 16, No. 3 (Fall 1972). pp. 287-296.

Rowe, William Woodin. 1974. "Crime and Punishment and The Brothers Karamazov: Some Comparative Observations." Russian Literature Triquarterly. 10, pp. 331-342.

Seckler, Dawn. 2003. "The Absence of Historical Time in Dostoevsky's Besy." in Studies in Slavic Cultures. Issue IV (Bakhtin) (Sept. 2003). pp. 57-67. Access at the University of Pittsburgh through www.pitt.edu/AFShome/s/l/Slavic/public/html/sisc/SISC4/index.html.

Stross, Brian. 1989. "Maya Bloodletting and the Number Three." Anthropological Linguistics. Vol. 31, Nos. 3-4 (Winter 1989). pp. 209-226.

Виноградов, В. В. 1972. Русский язык. ("The Russian Language"). Москва. Издательство "Высшая школа."

Wilson, Edmund. 1938 (1963). The Triple Thinkers: Twelve Essays on Literary Subjects. New York and London. Oxford University Press.

Wilson, Edmund. 1965. The Bit Between My Teeth: A Literary Chronicle, 1950-1965. New York. Farrar, Straus and Giroux.

Yuzefovich, Galina. 2004. "Victor Pelevin: Genius Temporis." in Russian Life. Vol. 47, No. 6 (November/December 2004). pp. 40-44.

Zhekulin, Gleb. 1983. "Rereading Gogol's 'Vii'." Canadian Slavonic Papers. 25, pp. 301-6.

Zenkovsky, Sergei. 1974. Medieval Russia's Epics, Chronicles, and Tales. New York. Dutton.

The Magic of Alphamagic Squares
By:
Lee B. Croft

  Prof. Lee B. Croft was born and raised in the oilfield town of Cut Bank, Montana, and graduated from High School there in 1964. As a roughneck on the oil rigs, he worked his way through Montana State University, Arizona State University (BA in Math, 1968), the University of Arizona (MA in Russian, 1970) and Cornell University (Ph.D. in Slavic Linguistics, 1973), before becoming an Assistant Prof. of Russian at ASU. He was tenured and promoted to Associate Prof. in 1978, and to (full) Professor in 1994, having served his Faculty colleagues as Coordinator of Russian and Slavic Languages since 1975.

He is now the Head of the Faculty of German, Romanian, and Slavic in ASU's School of International Letters and Cultures (SILC). He is the author, editor, or translator of twelve books and more than 150 articles, reviews, abstracts, entries, and verse translations of poetry. He has a sterling record as a grantsperson and is a founder of the ASU Melikian Center's grant-supported Critical Languages Institute (1991). He has won several awards for excellence in teaching and student mentorship: CLAS Dean's Quality Teaching Award (1978), Golden Key Honorary Student Mentorship Award (1985), the Burlington Northern Foundation National Distinguished Teaching Award (1985), and others. He is the Faculty Advisor of ASU's Epsilon Epsilon chapter of **Добро Слово**, the National Slavic Studies Honorary, and is a member of this honorary in three universities' chapters. He is a recipient (1993) of the Joe Malik, Jr. Arizona Slavic Studies Award, and of the prestigious *V.I. Vernadsky-10 Years of RANS silver medal* for more than thirty years of professional achievement and collaborative Russian research, given by the RUSSIAN ACADEMY OF NATURAL SCIENCES (cf. www.raen.ru). He is married to Dr. Lesley Hoyt Croft, has four grown children, ten grandchildren, and a great granddaughter. Keeping him at work is his love for interacting with his students, the "best and the brightest," as are his co-authors of this book, but he envisions spending part of his eventual retirement in Hawaii.

PRESENTATION:

This article is not like the others in this book in that it is new and has not been published before. It is largely self-explanatory, combining interests in Mathematics and Linguistics with a fascination for Magic. One of the sites on runes cited in it states that human civilization survived and developed for much longer a time with a patent belief in Magic than it has in the brief sceptical days of science since this belief became perceived as mere superstition. Numbers, Words, and Magic…now there's a TRIO for you. See what you think:

Lee and son Hayden Croft at Tchaikovsky's grave in the "Composers' Corner" of the Alexander Nevsky Cathedral necropolis in St. Petersburg, 2002
--photo by Lesley Hoyt Croft

The Search for Russian Alphamagic Squares and Their Translations

By:
Prof. Lee B. Croft
Arizona State University

A **magic square** is a square array of numbers that add to a constant sum in any row, column, or main diagonal. The oldest magic square known is called the ***Lo Shu*** (from the Chinese *shu*, meaning "writing," or "document"). It was reputed to have been revealed on the back of a *Lo* River turtle's shell to the mythical Emperor Yü in the 23rd Century B.C. The symbols on the back of the turtle's shell were represented as in figure 1.

Figure 1.

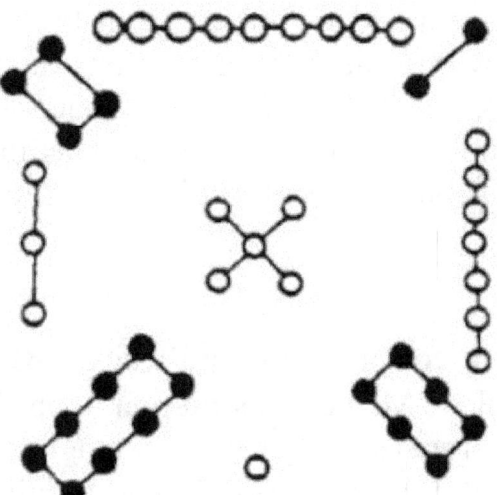

Notice that the dark symbols represent even values and the white symbols represent odd values, and that these values can be represented in our modern number convention as in figure 2.

Figure 2.

4	9	2
3	5	7
8	1	6

Here we see that any column, row, or main diagonal of this array of numbers add to a constant sum of 15, thus making it a "magic" square. This "*Lo Shu*" was thought to have magical properties by the ancient Chinese and several other subsequent cultures as well. Symbols reflecting this array of numerical values were inscribed on amulets and charms in order to protect their owners from misfortune.

In the late seventeenth century the French mathematician Simon de la Loubère returned to France from his post as Ambassador to Siam with a method for the construction of any odd-order (i.e. 3 X 3, 5 X 5, 7 X 7…etc.) magic square with consecutive numbers. This "Siamese method" is difficult to describe,[125] but involves beginning by placing

---

[125] For other methods of construction see Pickover, Clifford A. (2002, chapter entitled "Magic Construction"), pp. 37-64. For the mathematical properties of the 3 X 3 magic square, see Gardner, Martin (2001), pp. 167-173. The terminology (e.g. the necessity to specify "main diagonals" instead of just "diagonals," and the variable definition of a "semi-magic square") is made clear by the definitions in the

the first number of a consecutive series in the center top cell of the array's grid. Then the process involves filling in the cell "up one and over one to the right" with the subsequent consecutive numbers. Let us begin an example by placing the number one (1) into the center top cell of a 3 X 3 grid. When the next number to be placed would fall off the grid, as indeed the first placement of the number two (2) would demand, then the number is instead placed at the extreme opposite end of the intended row or column. IF the number to be placed encounters either another number in its path OR would fall off a corner of the grid itself so that there is no opposite end of a row or column to place it in, THEN the number is placed into the cell immediately below the previous number and the process continues. An example of a third-order magic square created by this process is given in figure 3.

Figure 3.

8	1	6
3	5	7
4	9	2

This is a permutation (a vertical "reflection"), of course, of the *Lo Shu* and has a constant sum of 15. A reinforcive example of a 7 X 7 magic square constructed by Loubére's "Siamese Method" is here in figure 4. By following the consecutive numbers beginning with one (1) through this array, a person can learn De la Loubère's "Siamese method." Figure 4:

"Magic Square Glossary" at Grogono Magic Squares in "Sources."

30	39	48	1	10	19	28
38	47	7	9	18	27	29
46	6	8	17	26	35	37
5	14	16	25	34	36	45
13	15	24	33	42	44	4
21	23	32	41	43	3	12
22	31	40	49	2	11	20

The magic sum here is 175. The general formula for determining the magic sum of any order's magic square of consecutive numbers beginning with one (1) is $Ms = n^3 + n/2$ where n=the number of the square's order. So in the above 7 X 7 (order 7) square, $7^3 + 7 = 343 + 7 = 350/2 = 175$.

The first even-ordered magic square of historical prominence is that of the German Artist Albrecht Dürer (1471-1528) who included the following array of numbers on a grid in his engraving titled *Melencolia I:*

Albrecht Dürer's *Melencolia I*
(Notice square under bell on the wall in the upper right)

This fourth-order square is shown in figure 5:

16	3	2	13
5	10	11	8
9	6	7	12
4	15	14	1

The numbers of this impressive square add to 34 in any row, column, or main diagonal. The four corner values add to 34. The center four values add to 34. The four numbers in each of the four quadrants add to 34, and there are yet further symmetries involving the "broken diagonals." Moreover, the two center cells in the bottom row form the number 1514, signifying the year that Dürer engraved his *Melencolia I*.[126]

Generations of mathematicians and mathophiles have elaborated and refined the study of magic squares. The American renaissance man Benjamin Franklin (1706-1790) was an avid creator of magic squares and wrote in his diaries that he had conceived a method that enabled him to create magic squares almost as fast as he could write. This included a well-published 8th order magic square with numerous additional symmetries and an amazing 16 X 16 square with similar astounding symmetries of sum, but without equal sums on the main diagonals. Franklin reflected in his notes that the creation of magic squares was a pursuit "incapable of any useful application" except that it might train a mind to exactitude and diligence in other spheres.[127] Modern experts on the creation of magic squares—scholars like Martin Gardner, Lee C. F. Sallows,

---

[126] See Holt, Michael (1978, section entitled "Four-Square Magic"), pp. 41-45, for a demonstration of how the Dürer square might be generated with the consecutive numbers, 1-16. The "further symmetries" are to be found in Pickover, ibid, pp. 19-23.

[127] Pickover, ibid, pp. 147-155. The quotation is from a letter Franklin wrote to a Peter Collinson in London, printed in 1769. See Pickover, pp. 148. The 16 X 16 square is on pp. 151.

Ivars Peterson, Harvey Heinz, Ian Stewart, John Robert Hendricks, Eric Weisstein, Clifford Pickover and others (see sources below), have had to contend with the accusation that their mathematical pursuits are not only recondite, but useless and without practicality. But this does not stop them and they remind us that much of current practicality was once considered recondite and useless. That is the nature of science and its progress.

In the early 1980s the Dutch mathematician, Lee C. F. Sallows, examining a mysterious book, published in 1887 and entitled <u>The Origin of Tree Worship</u>, encountered a relation about how a legendary Anglo-Saxon king of Northern England (Sallows records this king's name as "King Mi," but, not being able to find any other record of this king, the author conjectures that it may have been King Ida (ruled ca. 550-571)) came to rule in the sixth century A.D. Taking the throne, this king instructed his young wizard, whose name is unfortunately lost to us, to provide him with a magic charm that would assure him of a long reign and a long life. He gave the wizard three days to come up with the charm. The wizard went into a nearby copse of yew trees for three days and, when he came out, he told the king that the desired charm was to be found on the bole of a yew tree in the center of the copse. Figure 6 represents what the king found inscribed in runes of the Anglo-Saxon Futhorc on the yew tree in the center of the copse, as well as Lee Sallows' first decipherment of these upside-down aettir (three rows) of runes into Old English words.[128]

---

[128] The use of the word "aettir" here may be non-standard, but I believe it is justified as referring to the runes' being structured into THREE rows, thus forming a 3 X 3 magic array. The wizard may have been conditioned to this by the conventional grouping of the twenty-four runes of the

Figure 6.

⟨runic inscription, three lines⟩

Decipherment into Anglo-Saxon period English

⟨runic line⟩
fife tweniitwa ahtatyne

⟨runic line⟩
tweniieahte fiftyne twa

⟨runic line⟩
tuaelf eahte tweniifife

Sallows immediately discerned that these Old English words could be written into modern English as figure 7.[129]

Younger Futhorc into three ("-tir," (or "tier") as related to "-tri," meaning "three" by metathesis) groups of eight ("-aet," signifying "eight"). On the aettir, see www.sunnyway.com/runes. On the "threes," see Croft, Lee B., 2005.

[129] The phonological correspondences here are by the author from various compendia. See www.sunnyway.com/runes or the runes entry from wikipedia. The fact that the set of runes, taken by photocopy and scanner from Sallows' article as reprinted in Guy, Richard K...(1994) pp. 307, is upside-down here is unexplained. The assumption here is that this is how they were originally inscribed on the bole of the yew

Figure 7.

Five	Twenty-two	Eighteen
Twenty-Eight	Fifteen	Two
Twelve	Eight	Twenty-five

And that these words could be transcribed into numbers as in figure 8.

Figure 8.

5	22	18
28	15	2
12	8	25

Sallows soon realized that this is a magic square with a sum of 45 in any row, column, or main diagonal. Surely this meant that the ancient runic inscription was intended by its mysterious creator to give his king advantages of its magic tree by the Anglo-Saxon king's wizard in the fifth century, and not the result of a more modern typographical error.

power. *But then Sallows recalled from his decipherment the number of the Old English letters (represented by the runes) needed to spell each number of the magic square.* Since the number of these letters (e.g. there are FOUR letters needed to spell the number 5, and EIGHT letters needed to spell the number 18,…and so on) do not differ from the Modern English (that is, *the number of runes or, subsequently, letters needed to spell the names of the numbers in English has not changed, despite the obvious historical changes in the number names themselves, for more than 1500 years*), they are written here as in figure 9.

Figure 9.

4	9	8
11	7	3
6	5	10

Notice that the hyphens in "twenty-two," "twenty-five," and "twenty-eight" are not counted (since they weren't there in Old English as reflected in the runes). *But this too is a magic square*, having all rows, columns, and main diagonals sum to 21. **What we have here is an extraordinary confluence of "magic" in the world of numbers with "magic" in the world of words.**[130] This first runic square is

---

[130] To see striking arrays of words alone (especially in Russian) without corresponding numbers, see **Бонч-Осмаловская, Татьяна (2006)**, <u>Курс лекций по комбинаторной литературе</u>, at

doubly magical. It is, as Sallows termed it when he published his analysis of it in 1986, an **ALPHAMAGIC SQUARE**, the first one known. The author's conjecture is that the young wizard, age 21, conceived it as a magic charm for his king (King Ida?), who was 45 years of age, and that the charm worked such magic for the king that his rule and his life extended to the very ripe old age (for those times) of 66 years, the sum of his age and the age of his wonderful wizard (note that the years of King Ida's rule are given as 550-571 A.D.).[131]

In two now classic articles published in the journal Abacus, Sallows investigates the "Alphamagic Squares." He writes: "*Alphamagic* is the word I use to describe any magic array…that remains magic when all of its entries are replaced by numbers representing the word length, in letters, of their conventional written names (thus, one is replaced by

---

www.ashtray.ru/main/texts/bonch_course/14AA.htm on the palindromic structures and

www.ashtray.ru/main/texts/bonch_course/114A.htm on "Магический квадрат" (a famous Latin "Magic Square" of words, also treated in Pickover (2002), pp. 23-4 as the "Templar Magic Square") and other such word arrays in various languages. See www.magic-square-museum.com.

[131] In www.sunnyway.com/runes is the statement that ancient runes were as often imputed to function magically as they were to communicate information, and that mankind has functioned on the assumption that such magic is real much longer than it has functioned in the subsequent, more modern, time of sceptical science that would deny it. With this thought in mind, I keep a copy of this "magic" array of numbers in my wallet and have a copy of the rune set on my office door.

3, since it takes three "Roman" alphabet letters to spell the English name of the number 1 (one))." Sallows then describes a process by which alphamagic squares may be discovered. He defines a "Logorithm" (from Greek root "Logos" for the "word," and "Arithmos" for "number" and as distinct from the more conventional mathematical "Log*a*rithm") as "the letter count of the number word." This means that the English logorithm of 28 is 11 because there are eleven letters in the spelling of the number 28's name ("twenty-eight").[132] Trying to find a third-order alphamagic square in English, he then places the consecutive numbers in a row above each number's respective logorithm. In this array he seeks constant-difference triples of both the numbers and the logorithms that center on a single axis. This is because there is always a constant difference between the three numbers of any line of numbers passing through the center of a third-order magic square. As Ian Stewart describes it: "So a reasonable strategy for finding alphamagic squares is to look for triples of numbers in arithmetic series, such that the corresponding sequence of logorithms also forms an arithmetic series."[133] A partial example is given here in figure 10.

Figure 10.

Numbers: 8 9 10 11 12 13 14 15 16 17 18 19 20 21 22…
Logorithms: 5 4 3 6 6 8 8   7 7 9 8 8 6 9 9…

---

[132] Sallows, Lee C. F. (1986), as reprinted in Guy, Richard K. (1994), pp. 309.

[133] Stewart, Ian (1997), pp. 106.

A study of these correspondences reveals some likely triples in arithmetic series: 8 plus 7 to 15 plus 7 to 22 (8, 15, 22 with constant difference of 7) in the numbers, and the corresponding 5 plus 2 to 7 plus 2 to 9 (5, 7, 9 with constant difference of 2) in the logarithms. Also one can find the number triple of 12, 15, 18 (constant difference of 3) corresponding to the logorithm triple of 6, 7, 8 (constant difference of 1). These two corresponding sets of constant-difference triples center on the number 15, so an attempt is made with 15 in the center in figure 11.

Figure 11.

8		
	15	
		22

Then we add the other triple on the other diagonal, centered on the center value of 15, as in figure 12.

Figure 12.

8		18
	15	
12		22

The other numbers fall into place by mathematical necessity since the magic sum clearly has to be 45. The resultant magic square of numbers is then given in figure 13.

Figure 13.

8	19	18
25	15	5
12	11	22

And to test to see if this is not only a magic square, but an alphamagic square, all we have to do is examine the array of the corresponding logorithms, given here in figure 14.

Figure 14.

Eight (5 letters)	Nineteen (8 letters)	Eighteen (8 letters)
Twenty-five (10 letters)	Fifteen (7 letters)	Five (4 letters)
Twelve (6 letters)	Eleven (6 letters)	Twenty-two (9 letters)

255

And yes, this array of the English logorithms is itself a magic square, with magic sum of 21 in all ways. SO, the above third-order magic square of numbers 8, 19, 18/25, 15, 5/12, 11, 22 IS an alphamagic square. EUREKA! We've found one by a systematic procedure.[134]

Making use of the general formula for a third-order magic square put forth by French number theorist Edouard Lucas (1842-1891) in figure 15,

---

[134] The "Eureka" here is appropriate, as there is indeed a special kind of elation that accompanies making this type of discovery, a discovery involving the personal decipherment or "figuring out" of some aspect of the natural world. In his "Introduction" to Lost Languages: The Enigma of the World's Undeciphered Scripts (2002), pp. 11-48, Andrew Robinson compares THREE "extraordinary achievements of human endeavor" that occurred in the year 1953: Francis Crick and James Watson's discovery of the double helix structure of DNA, Edmund Hillary and Tenzing Norgay's successful ascent of Mount Everest, and architect Michael Ventris' decipherment of the Minoan Linear Script B. Of these, he argues that Ventris' decipherment was the rarest and most singularly striking…an intellectual breakthrough of immediate consequence, changing mankind's understanding of the historic world and its communications. And Clifford Pickover (2002, especially in the introductory pages) gives many citations from diverse cultures and their prominent intellectuals testifying to the "Zen" of discovering striking mathematical symmetries like the magic square.

Figure 15.

A + B	A – B - C	A + C
A – B + C	A	A + B – C
A - C	A + B + C	A - B

and consulting with his colleague Victor Eijkhout, Sallows was able to come up with a computer program in ALPHA.BAS, "a Pascal form," to generate values of "A" that allow for coincidences of constant-difference triples among the numbers and logarithms of English. Using this program he has found numerous other alphamagic squares in English. Confining himself just to magic squares of all-different numerical values from 1-100, he has published "the first ten English alphamagic squares of order 3." The English alphamagic square we constructed above as a demonstration is number two, after number one, that first one found on the yew tree written in runes, the one Sallows has named ***Li Shu*** (n.b.-- not "Lo Shu" like the one on the turtle in China).[135]

Sallows extended his computerized procedure to the finding of alphamagic squares in other languages, and he found and published many. He also defined there to be "translation" relationships of alphamagicality between his discovered squares. Either two different primary magic squares could share the same secondary logarithmic magic square. Or one primary magic square could be alphamagical in more than one language, the two secondary logarithmic squares, though different, both being magic. He pointed out that the concept of alphamagic squares applies to all the

---

[135] Sallows, Lee C. F. (1986) in Guy, Richard K...(1994), pp. 309-312.

alphabetic languages, writing, "Clearly there are many. Besides those like our own employing Roman letters, *there remain others using the Greek, Hebrew, and Cyrillic alphabets* (italics here the author's). The work of collecting and collating alphamagic squares in the various tongues and dialects opens a wide (if decidedly recondite) area of research."[136]

Sallows' inventory of 3 X 3 alphamagic squares composed of different-cell numbers from the numbers 1-100 includes *nineteen Roman-alphabet languages* (he finds that there are none in Latin or Danish). His article informs that there are 6 in Dutch, 7 in English, 6 in Esperanto, 13 in Finnish, 1 in French, 1 in Gaelic, a surprising 221 in German, 3 in Icelandic, 1 in Indonesian, 1 in Italian, 3 in Maltese, 12 in Norwegian, 2 in Portuguese, 9 in Samoan, 14 in Spanish, 11 in Swahili, 5 in Swedish, 17 in Turkish, and 26 in Welsh. His chart entitled "Alphamagic Squares Around the World" states that there are 34 pairs of translation relationships among them, with Welsh being the language to most frequently provide a translation.[137] **Inspired by Sallows' work, and not being able to find any published alphamagic squares in the Russian Cyrillic after more than twenty years of possibility, the author set about to see if he could discover the first Russian Alphamagic Square.**

The author's first attempts were to check all the alphamagic squares in the diverse languages using the "Roman letters" that were published by Lee Sallows to see if any were also alphamagical in the Russian Cyrillic. None of them were.

---

[136] Sallows, Ibid, pp. 314.

[137] Sallows. Ibid, pp. 317-321.

The author then listed the numbers from 1-150 and counted the numbers of Cyrillic letters needed to spell their names in Russian. He then placed all the numbers in the constituency of each Russian logorithm (abbreviated "Rlogo") into tables and checked to see if any third or fourth-order magic squares could be made from the numbers belonging to any one logorithm. This investigation resulted in two encouraging "trivial" cases of Russian Cyrillic alphamagic squares. The first is the result of the fact that the Russian numbers 8, 9, and 10, are the only consecutive numbers (thus having a constant difference of one (1)) all of which are in the constituency of a single logorithm, the logorithm 6 (i.e. the names of these Russian numbers, "**восемь, девять, десять**" all have six (6) Cyrillic letters in their spelling). So, then, figure 16 shows this "trivial" (having repeated numbers in its cells) magic square, having a magic sum of 27.

Figure 16.

9	8	10
10	9	8
8	10	9

And this 3 X 3 array has the corresponding array of Russian logorithms shown in figure 17.

Figure 17.

6	6	6
6	6	6
6	6	6

This is an array with a magic sum of 18, thus proving the third-order magic square of 9, 8, 10/ 10, 9, 8/ 8, 10, 9 to be a Russian Cyrillic alphamagic square, albeit a "trivial one."

Similarly, there are only four numbers in the constituency of Russian logorithm 4. These are "**ноль** (0), **один** (1), **пять** (5), and **семь** (7)." Unlike the third-order square, which needs a constant difference between each of the three numbers in its lines through the center, a fourth-order "trivial" magic square may be constructed of *any* four numbers. So, the following square in figure 18,

Figure 18.

0	1	5	7
7	5	1	0
1	0	7	5
5	7	0	1

having the magic sum 13, has the underlying array of Russian logorithms shown in figure 19,

Figure 19.

4	4	4	4
4	4	4	4
4	4	4	4
4	4	4	4

and this array has a magic sum of 16, thus proving the fourth-order magic square of 0, 1, 5, 7/ 7, 5, 1, 0/ 1, 0, 7, 5/ 5, 7, 0, 1 also to be a Russian Cyrillic alphamagic square, albeit a "trivial one."

A similar "trivial" fourth-order alphamagic square in Russian Cyrillic can be constructed from a set of four numbers all sharing the logorithm 14, as in figure 20:

24 Двадцать Четыре (14)	61 Шестьдесят Один (14)	76 Семьдесят Шесть (14)	111 Сто Один-надцать(14)
111 Сто Один-надцать(14)	76 Семьдесят Шесть (14)	61 Шестьдесят Один (14)	24 Двадцать Четыре (14)
61 Шестьдесят Один (14)	24 Двадцать Четыре (14)	111 Сто Один-надцать(14)	76 Семьдесят Шесть (14)
76 Семьдесят Шесть (14)	111 Сто Один-надцать(14)	24 Двадцать Четыре (14)	61 Шестьдесят Один (14)

Here the magic sum of the numbers is 272 and of the associated logorithms 56.

After much trial and error, the author was able to find what recreational mathematicians call a third-order "*semimagic square*," that is, a square of magic sum of all columns and rows, but with a variance of one (and by other definitions two, which may or may not be the same) diagonal. This is shown in figure 21.

Figure 21.

74	30	62
60	72	34
32	64	70

This array sums to 166 in any column, row, and the right-top-to-left-bottom diagonal, but is only "semimagic" because its numbers in the left-top-to-bottom-right diagonal add not to 166, but to 216 (this should have been a hint…see below). BUT, if we write these numbers out in the Russian Cyrillic we get the array shown in figure 22.

Figure 22.

Семьдесят четыре (Rlogo 15)	Тридцать (Rlogo 8)	Шестьдесят два (Rlogo 13)
Шестьдесят (Rlogo 10)	Семьдесят два (Rlogo 12)	Тридцать четыре (Rlogo 14)
Тридцать два (Rlogo 11)	Шестьдесят четыре (Rlogo 16)	Семьдесят (Rlogo 9)

The logarithmic values of this array are pleasingly different in each cell (consecutive 8-16) and have a magic sum of 36 in each column, row, and both main diagonals. SO, the author managed to discover by trial-and-error a third-order semimagic square that is alphamagic in Russian Cyrillic.

Similarly by trial and error, the author came up with a "close miss" on a fourth-order square in which every cell has a different number. This is in figure 23:

19 Девят-надцать (12)	62 Шесть-десят два (13)	76 Семь-десят шесть (14)	98 Девяносто восемь (15)
83 Восемь-десят три (14)	94 Девяносто четыре (15)	21 Двадцать один (12)	57 Пятьдесят семь (13)
82 Восемь-десят два (14…15)	61 Шесть-десят один (14)	77 Семь-десят семь (13)	35 Тридцать пять (12)
71 Семь-десят один (13)/ 75	38 Три-дцать восемь (14…12)	81 Восемь-десят один (15)	65 Шесть-десят пять (14)

In this array, all the numerical columns, rows, and one main diagonal sum to 255. But the right-top-to-bottom-left diagonal sums to 251…requiring the bottom left cell to be 75. This would result in that cell having the same logorithm of 13. The sums of all the logorithms show that cells nine (left on third row) and fourteen (bottom of second column) are defective of allowing a magic sum of 54, and need to be, respectively 15 and 12 as noted above. So this then is a semimagic square that is almost alphamagical in Russian Cyrillic. Close, but no cigar, as they say.

As the author was unable to make the ALPHA.BAS "Pascal" program published by Lee Sallows work (likely the author's fault), he approached his student, Samuel Comi, a sophomore honors Mathematics major, for advice. Comi readily understood the problem and gave his opinion that he could write a program in Java that would use the Lucas formula to generate third-order alphamagic squares if given the Sallows' logorithms to correlate with the Russian Cyrillic numbers. So equipped, Comi came up with the Java program (see appendix) in a single weekend, and, shown here in figure 24, the first non-trivial Russian alphamagic square.

Figure 24.

74 Семьдесят Четыре (15)	50 Пятьдесят (9)	92 Девяносто Два (12)
90 Девяносто (9)	72 Семьдесят Два (12)	54 Пятьдесят Четыре (15)
52 Пятьдесят Два (12)	94 Девяносто Четыре (15)	70 Семьдесят (9)

The numbers in this third-order square add to 216 in any row, column, or main diagonal, while the associated logorithms (the number of Cyrillic-alphabet letters required to spell the name of each Russian number) add to 36 in any row, column, or main diagonal. **Therefore, the third-order square of 74, 50, 92/ 90, 72, 54/ 52, 94, 70 is a Russian Cyrillic alphamagic square...the first non-trivial one discovered**. Moreover, the computer program shows this to be the *only one* with numbers from one (1=**Один**) to a hundred (100=**Сто**). The author and Samuel Comi call it, in accordance with the tradition established by the earlier "*Lo*

Shu" and "*Li Shu,*" the "**Lee Sam**," which is also a pun on the author's first-name Russian signature, "**Ли сам**," pronounced (roughly) "Lee Sam" and meaning "Lee himself" in Russian. In addition to its alphamagic property, the "Lee Sam" has some other interesting properties. First is the property that the separated digits of its constituent numbers are themselves magical. That is, the first digits of the numbers 74 (i.e. 7), 50 (i.e. 5), 92 (i.e. 9)/ 90 (i.e. 9), 72 (i.e. 7), 54 (i.e. 5)/ 52 (i.e. 5), 94 (i.e. 9), and 70 (i.e. 7), thus forming an array of 7, 5, 9/9, 7, 5/5, 9, 7 form a magic square where the rows, columns and diagonals add to a constant sum of 21. And, the second digits of the constituent numbers 74 (i.e. 4), 50 (i.e. 0), 92 (i.e.2)/ 90 (i.e. 0), 72 (i.e. 2), 54 (i.e. 4)/ 52 (i.e. 2), 94 (i.e. 4), 70 (i.e. 0), thus forming an array of 4, 0, 2/ 0, 2, 4/ 2, 4, 0, form a magic square where the rows, columns and diagonals add to a constant sum of 6. This "divisional digit" property means also that the "digital reversal" array of 47 (from 74), 05 or 5 (from 50), 29 (from 92)/ 09 or 9 (from 90), 27 (from 72), 45 (from 54)/ 25 (from 52), 49 (from 94), 07 or 7 (from 70) forms a magic square whose constant sum on any row, column or diagonal is 81, three times the central cell's digitally reversed value of 27. Neither of these divisional digit squares nor the digital reversal square is alphamagical, however, in either English or Russian.

It turns out that the only other alphamagic square in Russian Cyrillic with non-repeating numbers less than 200 can be constructed merely by adding the digit 1-, signifying 174, 150, 192/ 190, 172, 154/ 152, 194, 170, the numbers of the above square each increased by a hundred (i.e. adding the Russian word for 100, or "**Сто**," with Rlogo of 3). Lee Sallows has termed such an alphamagic square a "second harmonic" of the first. But, if we expand the search into higher numbers there are hundreds of others. The fact that the Russian word for 200 ("**Двести**") has a logorithm of 6—double the logorithm of the word for 100, means that numerous triples of constant difference can be found wherein a sub-100 number is combined with a 100+that number and a 200+that number to form the lines through the center of a third-order square. An example of one of these is given in figure 25.

Figure 25.

154 Сто пятьдесят четыре (18)	48 Сорок Восемь (11)	251 Двести Пятьдесят Один (19)
248 Двести Сорок Восемь (17)	151 Сто пятьдесят Один (16)	54 Пятьдесят Четыре (15)
51 Пятьдесят Один (13)	254 Двести Пятьдесят Четыре (21)	148 Сто Сорок Восемь (14)

The magic sum of the numbers of this third-order Russian Cyrillic alphamagic square is 453 in any row, column, or main diagonal, and the magic sum of the related logorithms (all pleasingly different) is 48. Other even higher numbered squares are likely to result in similar fashion from the fact that the Russian number for 400 ("**четыреста**") has a logorithm of 9, thus making possible numerous triples of concentric constant-difference numbers less than a hundred, with 200+numbers (adding 6 to the logorithm) and

400+numbers (adding 9 to the logorithm). As the number triples increase by 200, the concentric logorithms increase by 3--fertile ground to find alphamagic squares.

Following Sallows' lead in the matter of alphamagic square "translations," the author began an investigation to see if he could find other languages in which the magic square of 74, 50, 92/ 90, 72, 54/ 52, 94, 70 is alphamagical—thus finding a "translation" of the *Lee Sam* Russian Cyrillic alphamagic square into another language. He thought initially to find a translation between a language using the Roman-based alphabet (like English and all the others found by Sallows in his initial articles) and the Russian Cyrillic. So, he looked up the sets of numbers in diverse Roman-alphabet languages in online compendia and counted the numbers of letters to spell these other languages' words for these numbers, checking to see if the resultant logorithmic squares were magical.[138] It was surprising how many of the logorithmic squares had constant-sum rows and columns. The great majority are, in fact, semimagic, but miss having either one diagonal or both diagonals in accord with the prevailing constant sum.

These *four* Roman-alphabet languages have their logorithmic squares on the numbers of the *Lee Sam* Russian Cyrillic alphamagic square with only one main diagonal at variance from magical (i.e. the rows, columns, and one

---

[138] Very useful here is the carefully done compendium of the number systems of the world's languages begun by Shinji Takasugi at http://www.sf.airnet.ne.jp/~ts/language/number.html. In addition, colleagues of the Critical Languages Institute in Arizona State University's Melikian Center for Russian, Eurasian, and East European Studies were most helpful.

diagonal add successfully to the same constant sum): *Albanian, Bosnian-Croatian-Serbian ("latinica" version without compound number intermediary word "and" ("i")), German, and Italian.* So, there is no true translation here.

These *twenty one* Roman-alphabet languages have their logorithmic squares on the numbers of the *Lee Sam* Russian Cyrillic alphamagic square with both main diagonals at variance from magic (i.e. the rows and columns add successfully to the same constant sum, but both main diagonals are different): *Basque, Czech, English, Estonian, Finnish, French, Hawaiian, Latvian, Lithuanian, Nahuatl, Portuguese, Romanian, Seneca, Spanish, Swahili, Swedish, Turkish, Tzotzil, Uzbek ("Lotin" script), Welsh, and Zulu.* In addition, the *Bosnian-Croatian-Serbian ("latinica" version with compound number intermediary word "and" ("i"))* also fails on both diagonals. There is also no true translation here.

An attempt was made to check the Roman-alphabetic rendering of the *Lee Sam's* numbers of *Navajo* to see if the secondary logorithms are magic. Two columns and two rows add to 58, one column and one row add to 60, one main diagonal adds to 60 and the other to 73. Navajo clearly offers no translation of the *Lee Sam* here.

Trying the other-alphabet languages of *Armenian* (rows and columns add to the same constant sum, but both main diagonals are different) and *Georgian* (not even the rows and columns add to a constant sum) does not find a true translation of the *Lee Sam* Russian Cyrillic alphamagic square.

Checking the above twenty-eight Roman-alphabet languages did not result in finding a translation of the *Lee Sam*. So the author resorted to trying the related Cyrillic-alphabet Slavic Language of *Bulgarian* (a South Slavic congener) and found both main diagonals of the logorithmic square different. Similar, but not the same, is the two-diagonal failure in South Slavic *Macedonian.* The Cyrillic version of South Slavic *Bosnian-Croatian-Serbian* yields the same result as the Roman-alphabet version (i.e. the "latinica") with a one-diagonal failure on the version without the compound number intermediary word "and" ("i") and a both-diagonal failure with the intermediary "and." And even the closely related East Slavic language of *Ukrainian* finds the secondary logorithmic square missing a constant sum on one main diagonal. Also, the Cyrillic-alphabet Turkic language of *Tatar* and of Indo-Iranian *Tajik* were found not to provide a translation, as well as the Cyrillic-alphabet version of Turkic *Uzbek*. SO, this meant that 35 languages with diverse (Roman, Armenian, Georgian, and Cyrillic) alphabets were checked without finding a proper translation. The author was about to conclude that the *Lee Sam*, the first third-order Russian Cyrillic Alphamagic Square, might have no true translation in another language or alphabet. But then, Agnieszka Mielczarek of Arizona State University's Critical Languages Institute collaborated with the author to fill out his inquiry form for *Polish*, a West Slavic language that uses a version of the Roman alphabet. The alphamagic result is in Figure 26. It is interesting to speculate that this might be the only true translation (and bialphabetic—Russian Cyrillic to Polish Roman), but the search is not over.[139]

---

[139] Here it might be illuminating to point out that, in literature, a perfect translation is generally considered impossible, given all the variables of language code and cultural context involved, but translations are published every day nevertheless in the interests of communication

Figure 26:

74 Siedemdziesiąt cztery (20)	50 Pięćdziesiąt (12)	92 Dziewięćdziesiąt dwa (19)
90 Dziewięćdziesiąt (16)	72 Siedemdziesiąt dwa (17)	54 Pięćdziesiąt Cztery (18)
52 Pięćdziesiąt dwa (15)	94 Dziewięćdziesiąt cztery (22)	70 Siedemdziesiąt (14)

In this Polish version of the *Lee Sam* (magic sum of 216) the number of Roman-alphabet letters to spell the Polish numbers are 20, 12, 19/ 16, 17, 18/ 15, 22, 14. These logorithms add to 51 on any row, column or main diagonal. The author believes that this "bialphabetic" translation of the Russian Cyrillic *Lee Sam* found earlier, **is the first Polish third-order alphamagic square known.**

In his original work, Lee Sallows discussed the possibility of finding higher-order alphamagic squares, that is, 4 X 4, or 5 X 5, or higher. He wrote: "With the transition from order 3 to order 4, and higher, comes a concomitant jump in the perplexities confronting our advance, since hindsight reveals 3 as a special, unusually tractable case." Even-order magic squares are more complex to derive than odd-order ones, and programming a computer to help in the

---

and art. It is only the greater exactitude required by mathematics that precludes us from considering the logarithmic semi-magic squares as evidencing a successful translation. We are abiding by a higher standard here.

task is significantly more difficult. Yet as he discusses these difficulties in his "Alphamagic Squares" article, Ivars Peterson asks: "…are there any instances of four-by-four and five-by-five language-dependent alphamagic squares?" And, surprisingly and without explanation of process, he answers: "A quick search turns up several examples. The following table of numerical values is an example of a four-by-four alphamagic square in English." Peterson's 4 X 4 English alphamagic square, published for the first time, apparently, in 2003, is shown in figure 27.[140]

Figure 27:

26	37	48	59
49	58	27	36
57	46	39	28
38	29	56	47

Now this is a really astonishing array of numbers. It is not a perfect pan-diagonal magic square, but it has a number of amazing symmetries. It is a conventional magic square because all its rows, columns and main diagonals add to a constant sum of 170. But notice that its four corner values add to 170. Its four central values add to 170. If we divide

---

[140] Peterson, Ivars. "Alphamagic Squares" at http://www.sciencenews.org/articles/20030705/mathtrek.asp

the whole square into its four constituent quadrants, then the numbers of each quadrant add to the constant sum of 170. Both sets of 2-2 broken diagonals (i.e. 49, 37, 56, and 28, and also 57, 29, 48, and 46) add to the constant sum of 170. Only the 3-1 diagonals and the central horizontal and central vertical quadrants are divergent to sums of 210 or 130 complementarily. It is only that shy of perfection.

To see that this magic square is alphamagical in English, we need to spell out the English numbers in the Roman alphabet and record the count of letters (i.e. the English logorithms) as in figure 28:

Twenty-six (9)	Thirty-seven (11)	Forty-eight (10)	Fifty-nine (9)
Forty-nine (9)	Fifty-eight (10)	Twenty-seven (11)	Thirty-six (9)
Fifty-seven (10)	Forty-six (8)	Thirty-nine (10)	Twenty-eight (11)
Thirty-eight (11)	Twenty-nine (10)	Fifty-six (8)	Forty-seven (10)

The secondary array here of the numbers of Roman-alphabet letters to spell the English names of the primary numbers does add to a constant sum of 39 in any row, column, or main diagonal. So Peterson's 4 X 4 array does check out to be alphamagical in English.

Another interesting property of Peterson's 4 X 4 array is that it, like the *Lee Sam* 3 X 3, remains a magic square under the "divisional digits" and the "reversed digits" permutations. That is, the digitally reversed 4 X 4 of 62 (from 26), 73 (from 37), 84 (and so on…), 95/ 94, 85, 72, 63/ 75, 64, 93, 82/ 83, 92, 65, 74 adds to a constant sum of 314 on any row, column, or main diagonal. AND, *unlike* the *Lee Sam*, this digitally reversed magic square is proven to be alphamagical in English as well, since its secondary array, formed from the number of Roman-alphabet letters to spell the English number-names in it, (i.e. sixty-two=8, seventy-three=12, …10, 10/ 10, 10, 10, 10/ 11, 9, 11, 9/ 11, 9, 9, 11) adds to 40 on any row, column, or main diagonal (note that the constant sum (40) of the digitally reversed square's secondary square is different than the constant sum (39) of the primary square's secondary square). This is then, to my knowledge, **the first demonstration of an alphamagic square remaining alphamagical with its numbers digitally reversed**.

We now need to ask whether this impressive 4 X 4 array, alphamagical in English, is alphamagical as well in other Roman-alphabet languages. Can we find a translation of it? Let's begin by trying German. In German we can spell the numbers of Peterson's array as shown in Figure 29.

Figure 29:

26 Sechsundzwanzig (15)	37 Siebenunddreissig (17)	48 Achtundvierzig (14)	59 Neunundfünfzig (14)
49 Neunundvierzig (14)	58 Achtundfünfzig (14)	27 Siebenundzwanzig (16)	36 Sechsunddreissig (16)
57 Siebenundfünfzig (16)	46 Sechsundvierzig (15)	39 Neununddreissig (15)	28 Achtundzwanzig (14)
38 Achtunddreissig (15)	29 Neunundzwanzig (14)	56 Sechsundfünfzig (15)	47 Siebenundvierzig (16)

And here we can add the rows, columns, and both main diagonals of the logorithms to 60, a constant sum. This, then, is **the first known fourth-order German alphamagic square**, the translation of Ivars Peterson's 4 X 4 English alphamagic square. In French, this array becomes figure 30.

Figure 30:

26 Vingt-six (8)	37 Trente-sept (10)	48 Quarante-huit (12)	59 Cinquante-neuf (13)
49 Quarante-neuf (12)	58 Cinquante-huit (13)	27 Vingt-sept (9)	36 Trente-six (11)
57 Cinquante-sept (13)	46 Quarante-six (11)	39 Trente-neuf (10)	28 Vingt-huit (9)
38 Trente-huit (10)	29 Vingt-neuf (9)	56 Cinquante-six (12)	47 Quarante-sept (12)

The French logorithms add to 43 in any row, column, or main diagonal, making this **the first known fourth-order French alphamagic square**, a translation of Ivars Peterson's original 4 X 4 English alphamagic square and/or of the German example above. A check of the Italian appears in Figure 31.

Figure 31:

26 Ventisei (8)	37 Trentasette (11)	48 Quarantotto (11)	59 Cinquantanove (13)
49 Quarantanove (12)	58 Cinquantotto (12)	27 Ventisette (10)	36 Trentasei (9)
57 Cinquantasette (14)	46 Quarantasei (11)	39 Trentanove (10)	28 Ventotto (8)
38 Trentotto (9)	29 Ventinove (9)	56 Cinquantasei (12)	47 Quarantasette (13)

The Italian logorithms, like the French, add to a constant sum of 43 on any row, column, or main diagonal, making this **the first known fourth-order Italian alphamagic square.** And another translation can be found for Spanish in figure 32.

Figure 32:

26 Veintiseis (10)	37 Treinte y siete (13)	48 Cuaranta y ocho (13)	59 Cinquanta y nueve (15)
49 Cuaranta y nueve (14)	58 Cincuenta y ocho (14)	27 Veintisiete (11)	36 Treinte y seis (12)
57 Cincuenta y siete (15)	46 Cuaranta y seis (13)	39 Treinta y nueve (13)	28 Veintiocho (10)
38 Treinta y ocho (12)	29 Veintinueve (11)	56 Cincuenta y seis (14)	47 Cuaranta y siete (14)

In the Spanish example of Figure 32 the logorithms add to 51 in any row, column, or main diagonal. So here we also have **the first known fourth-order Spanish alphamagic square**, and another translation. Do there exist any Roman-alphabet translations from languages less closely related to these? Here is the Hungarian array in Figure 33:

26 Huszonhat (9)	37 Harminchet (10)	48 Negyven- nyolc (12)	59 Otven- kilenc (11)
49 Negyven- kilenc (13)	58 Otvennyolc (10)	27 Huszonhet (9)	36 Harminchat (10)
57 Otvenhet (8)	46 Negyvenhat (10)	39 Harminc- kilenc (13)	28 Huszon- nyolc (11)
38 Harminc- nyolc (12)	29 Huszon- kilenc (12)	56 Otvenhat (8)	47 Negyvenhet (10)

Since the logorithms here add to a constant sum of 42 on any row, column, or main diagonal, we also have here **the first fourth-order Hungarian alphamagic square**, and yet another flawless translation. Notice that the constant sums of the logorithms are mostly different for English (39), German (60), French and Italian (43), Spanish (51), and Hungarian (42).

We now have a fourth-order array of numbers with wondrous properties of symmetry that has proven to be magical and alphamagical in English. It has remained magical and alphamagical in English when its every number is digitally reversed. It is alphamagical not only in English, but also in the other Roman-alphabet languages of German, French, Italian, Spanish, and even less closely related Hungarian. By now one might wonder if there are any Roman-alphabet languages in which this array is NOT alphamagical. The author assures the readers that there are many…Hawaiian, for example, Latin and others.

But now we must try to see if there might be a translation of this polylingual alphamagic square into a non-Roman-alphabet language. Here then is the Russian Cyrillic-alphabet version of this fourth-order array in figure 34:

26 Двадцать Шесть (13)	37 Тридцать Семь (12)	48 Сорок Восемь (11)	59 Пятьдесят Девять (15)
49 Сорок Девять (11)	58 Пятьдесят Восемь (15)	27 Двадцать Семь (12)	36 Тридцать Шесть (13)
57 Пятьдесят Семь (13)	46 Сорок Шесть (10)	39 Тридцать Девять (14)	28 Двадцать Восемь (14)
38 Тридцать Восемь (14)	29 Двадцать Девять (14)	56 Пятьдесят Шесть (14)	47 Сорок Семь (9)

And now we can see the discovery of the first non-trivial fourth order (4 X 4) Russian alphamagic square and the first non-Roman-alphabet (i.e. Cyrillic alphabet) fourth-order alphamagic square.[141] The constant sum of

---

[141] Here I remind the reader of the "trivial" fourth-order example (cells with repeated numbers, 0, 1, 5, 7/7, 5, 1, 0/1, 0, 7, 5/ 5, 7, 0, 1 based on the Russian logorithm 4). This

all the rows, columns, and main diagonals of the array of the number of Cyrillic letters in the Russian number names is 51 (identical in secondary or logarithmic sum to the Spanish example in figure 32, though the cells are not the same). And, as unbelievable as it may seem, the digitally reversed version of this array is also alphamagical in Russian Cyrillic, as seen in figure 35:

62　шестьдесят два (13)	73　семьдесят три (12)	84　восемьдесят четыре (17)	95　девяносто пять (13)
94　девяносто четыре (15)	85　восемьдесят пять (15)	72　семьдесят два (12)	63　шестьдесят три (13)
75　семьдесят пять (13)	64　шестьдесят четыре (16)	93　девяносто три (12)	82　восемьдесят два (14)
83　восемьдесят три (14)	92　девяносто два (12)	65　шестьдесят пять (14)	74　семьдесят четыре (15)

Here we see that the constant sum of all rows, columns, and main diagonals is 55 (not the same as in the original's secondary of 51, but evidencing the digitally-reversed array's Russian alphamagicality). And now, in addition to the English version investigated earlier, we have a fourth-order Russian alphamagic square, a true translation of at least English, German, French, Italian, Spanish, and

---

"trivial" predecessor is also published in Croft and Comi (2008), pp. 97.

Hungarian congeners, that remains alphamagical in Russian when its numbers are digitally reversed. The author is reminded of the poet William Blake's wonderment in apprehension of the "Tyger:" "What immortal hand or eye, could frame thy fearful symmetry?"

The wonders, however, do not cease. Further interesting linguistic data was then compiled from the following colleagues of Arizona State University's Critical Languages Institute in the summer of 2008. First, long-time colleague Lupco Spasovski completed an inquiry form given to him by the author that showed that Cyrillic *Macedonian* has neither a translation of the 3 X 3 *Lee Sam* nor of this 4 X 4 array. But then Agnieszka Mielczarek submitted to the author a completed inquiry form for Roman-alphabet *Polish* showing a constant sum of 70 for the logorithmic values of this 4 X 4 array (recall that Polish also provided the only translation of the *Lee Sam* 3 X 3). Linda Meniku submitted an inquiry form for Roman-alphabet *Albanian* showing a constant logorithmic sum of 50. Aygul Fatykhova submitted the form for Kazan *Tatar*, a Turkic language using a version of the Cyrillic alphabet, in which the logorithmic sum was constant at 37. Feruz Akobirov then submitted a form showing the magicality of the logorithmic sums of Indo-Iranian *Tajik* at 33. Siranoush Khandanyan then turned in a form showing a magic sum of 33 for the logorithms of Eastern *Armenian*, which uses its own unique alphabet as shown in figure 36:

26 Քասնվեց (7)	37 Երեսունյոթ (9)	48 Քառասունութ (9)	59 Հիսունինը (8)
49 Քառասունինը (10)	58 Հիսունութ (7)	27 Քսանյոթ (7)	36 Երեսունվեց (9)
57 Հիսունյոթ (8)	46 Քառասունվեց (10)	39 Երեսունինը (9)	28 Քսանութ (6)
38 Երեսունութ (8)	29 Քսանինը (7)	56 Հիսունվեց (8)	47 Քառասունյոթ (10)

Then Aziz Djuraev submitted a form in which BOTH the "Lotin" (i.e. Roman) alphabet variant (at a constant sum of 42) AND the Cyrillic-alphabet logorithms (at a constant sum of 41) showed a double-alphabetic alphamagicality for Turkic *Uzbek*. And finally, Mirzana Pasic completed the form for *Bosnian-Croatian-Serbian* showing alphamagicality in all FOUR versions: 1) latinica (Roman-alphabet) without "i" (constant sum 50); 2) kirilica (Cyrillic-alphabet) without "i" (constant sum 50); 3) latinica with "i" (constant sum 54); and 4) kirilica with "i" (constant sum 54). **In all these cases, the author believes that the language-specific versions of this marvelous fourth-order array are linguistic firsts—i.e. they are not only true translations of the first fourth-order Cyrillic Russian alphamagic square, they are also the *first fourth-order alphamagic squares* in (respectively and alphabetically) Albanian, Armenian, Bosnian-Croatian-Serbian, Polish, Tajik, Tatar, and Uzbek.**

Indeed this fourth-order array turns out to be a multiply magical wonder both numerically and linguistically. It is alphamagical in at least FOURTEEN languages and in at least THREE alphabets. It is digit-reversibly alphamagical in both Roman-alphabet English and in Cyrillic-alphabet Russian.

In what other languages and other alphabets might this fourth-order magic square prove to be alphamagical? *To which other worlds of words and magicality might these numbers provide a bridge?*

Acknowledgements:

For their specific help in the creation of this article, I would like to acknowledge and thank my mother, Mrs. Norma Croft of Cut Bank, Montana, for her patience with me as I was engrossed in alphamagic squares during last New Year's home visit, Mr. Andrew John Conovaloff of Sun City, Arizona, for his editing, posting, and wise counsel, Samuel Comi, my own math "wizard" and co-discoverer of the *Lee Sam*, Dr. Lesley Hoyt Croft, my always supportive wife, son Hayden Lee Croft, and ASU School of International Letters and Cultures (SILC) colleagues Don Livingston, Tatyana Dhaliwal, Danko Sipka, Saule Moldabekova, Rolfs Ekmanis, Sandy Couch, and Peter Horwath, constant inspirations to me. I have dedicated my discovery of the first *German* fourth order alphamagic square to Prof. Peter Horwath of ASU SILC's Faculty of German, Romanian, and Slavic, which I now head, the first *Italian* fourth order alphamagic square to Prof. Pier R. Baldini, Senior Professor of Italian and Head of ASU SILC's Faculty of French and Italian, the first *Spanish* fourth order alphamagic square to Regents Prof. David W. Foster of ASU SILC's Faculty of Spanish and Portuguese, and the first *French* fourth order alphamagic square to Prof.

Deborah Losse, Dean of Humanities in ASU's College of Liberal Arts and Sciences and SILC's Faculty of French and Italian, giving these long-time (35-year) colleagues all signed copies. In addition I acknowledge the aid and encouragement of the staff and faculty of ASU's Melikian Center for Russian, Eurasian, and East European Studies and of its wonderful Critical Languages Institute—specifically Stephen K. Batalden, David Brokaw, Susan Edgington, Kathleen Evans-Romaine, Ariann Stern-Gottschalk (CLI Director), Kyle Cowden, Filip Erdeljac, and all the 2008 CLI faculty: Feruz Akobirov, Aziz Djuraev, Aygul Fatykhova, Gohar Harutyunyan, Siranoush Khandanyan, Julie Kolgjini, Linda Meniku, Agnieszka Mielczarek, Mirzana Pasic, Lubco Spasovski, and Martin Zekic.

SOURCES:

Бонч-Осмаловская, Татьяна. (2006) <u>Курс лекций по комбинаторной литературе</u>. At www.ashtray.ru/main/texts/bonch_course/14AA and at www.ashtray.ru/main/texts/bonch_course/114A.htm. These are two of fourteen lectures put online in October of 2006.

Croft, Lee B. (2005) "People in Threes Going Up in Smoke and Other Triplicities in Russian Literature and Culture," in <u>Rocky Mountain Review,</u> Vol. 59, No. 2, pp. 29-49 and also online at www.threes.com/articles/LeeBCroft.pdf.

Croft, Lee B. and Comi, Samuel. (2008) "Russian Alphamagic Squares" in <u>Word Ways: The Journal of Recreational Linguistics,</u> Vol. 41, No. 2 (May 2008), pp. 95-100.

Croft, Lee B. and Comi, Samuel. "A Fourth-Order, Digitally-Reversible, Polylingual, Bialphabetic Alphamagic Square." <u>Journal of Recreational Mathematics.</u> Vol 34, No. 4 (2007-2008), pp. 247-257.

Holt, Michael. (1978) <u>Math Puzzles and Games.</u> Barnes and Noble Books, New York, (ISBN 0-88029-948-7).

Gardner, Martin. (2001) <u>A Gardner's Workout: Training the Mind and Entertaining the Spirit</u>. A. K. Peters. Natick, MA (63 South Ave) 01760, (ISBN 1-56881-120-9), especially chapter 23 entitled "Some New Discoveries About 3 X 3 Magic Squares," pp. 167-73. See mention of Martin Gardner, and his letter to me from 1975, in this book's first article about my glossolalia hoax by Eric D. Strachan.

Grogono Magic Squares. "A Mini-History of Magic Squares" at <u>http://www.grogono.com/magic/history.php</u>, and "Magic Squares Glossary" at <u>http://www.grogono.com/magic/glossary.php</u>.

Guy, Richard K. and Robert E. Woodrow's (eds.) (1994) <u>The Lighter Side of Mathematics: Proceedings of the Eugene Strens Memorial Conference on Recreational Mathematics and its History,</u> MAA Spectrum (The Mathematical Association of America), pp. 305-339 (ISBN 0-88385-516-X). The articles of Lee C. F. Sallows on the "Alphamagic Squares" are reprinted here.

Heinz, Harvey. "More Magic Squares," at

<u>http://www.geocities.com/CapeCanaveral/Launchpad/4057/moremsqrs.html</u>.

"Magic Square" at <u>http://en.wikipedia.org/wiki/Magic_Square</u>.

"Магический квадрат" in Russian at

<u>http://krugosvet.ru/articles/15/1543/print.html</u>.

"Melencolia I" by Albrecht Dürer (1471-1528) at http://en.wikipedia.org/wiki/Melencolia_I.

Peterson, Ivars. (2003) "MathMUSEments: Magic Squares," from Muse, November/December 2003, pp. 32-33, posted online at http://www.sciencenewsforkids.org/pages/puzzlezone/muse/muse1103.asp.

Peterson, Ivars. "Alphamagic Squares." At http://www.sciencenews.org/articles/20030705/mathtrek.asp. This is the work in which Peterson gives the 4 X 4 array that is key to much of this article.

Pickover, Clifford. (2002) The Zen of Magic Squares, Circles, and Stars. Princeton University Press, Princeton and Oxford, ISBN 0-691-11597-4. See "Alphamagic Squares," pp. 133-. This book is a mind-boggling masterpiece.

Robinson, Andrew. (2002) Lost Languages: The Enigma of the World's Undeciphered Scripts. A Peter N. Nevraumont Book of the Tess Press, New York (ISBN 978-1-60376-003-4).

Runes: See—

http://en.wikipedia.org/wiki/Runic_alphabet

http://www.sunnyway.com/runes

http://englishheathenism.homestead.com/timeline.html.

Sallows, Lee C. F. (1986) "Alphamagic Squares: Adventures with Turtle Shell and Yew Between the Mountains of Mathematics and the Lowlands of Logology," reprinted from Abacus Vol. 4, No. 1 (Fall 1986), pp. 28-45 and also "Alphamagic Squares, Part II: More Adventures with Abacus and Alphabet, Extending Explorations into the Untrodden Realms of Computational Logology," reprinted from Abacus Vol. 4, No. 2 (Winter 1987), pp. 20-29, both in: Richard K. Guy and Robert E. Woodrow's (eds.) The Lighter Side of Mathematics: Proceedings of the Eugene Strens Memorial Conference on Recreational Mathematics and its History, MAA Spectrum (The Mathematical Association of America), 1994, pp. 305-339 (ISBN 0-88385-516-X). This is the seminal work to everything here.

Stewart, Ian. (1997) "Alphamagic Squares" in the "Mathematical Recreations" section of Scientific American, January 1997, pp. 106-109.

Takasugi, Shinji. "Number Systems 1-100 in 69 Languages of the World." At http://www.sf.airnet.ne.jp/~ts/language/number.html. Here is where to find the numbers from many of the world's languages.

Trump, Walter. "How Many Magic Squares Are There?--Results of Historical and Computer Enumeration." At http://www.trump.de/magic-squares/howmany.html.

Weisstein, Eric W. "Magic Square." From Mathworld—A Wolfram Web Resource. http://mathworld.wolfram.com/MagicSquare.html.

APPENDIX:

A Javascript Program to Find 3 X 3 Russian Alphamagic Squares
By:
Samuel Comi
Arizona State University

The editors of the two professional journals (<u>Journal of Recreational Linguistics</u> and <u>Journal of Recreational Mathematics</u>) where Samuel Comi and Lee B. Croft have co-authored works on alphamagic squares have not wanted, for reasons of space, to publish the Javascript program that Samuel Comi wrote to find third-order Russian alphamagic squares. But the obvious significance of this wonderful program to the efforts here make its publication imperative, so here it is, enlarged and in **bold**:

```
//Samuel Comi
//14 Feb 2008
//This program will find 3x3 Alphamagic squares within
//the chosen limit, (up to 1000) for the Russian language and may be adapted to find other alphabetic languages' alphamagic squares by
using different languages' Sallows' "logorithms" (see text).

import java.util.*;
public class Logorithm
{
public static void main (String[] args)
{
//Russian
```

```
int[] zero = new int[10];
zero[0] = 0;
zero[1] = 4;
zero[2] = 3; //These establish the values
zero[3] = 3; //for number length less than
zero[4] = 6; //10
zero[5] = 4;
zero[6] = 5;
zero[7] = 4;
zero[8] = 6;
zero[9] = 6;
int[] ten = new int[10];
ten[0] = 6;
ten[1] = 11;
ten[2] = 10;
ten[3] = 10; //These establish the values
ten[4] = 12; //for numbers from 10 through 19
ten[5] = 10;
ten[6] = 11;
ten[7] = 10;
ten[8] = 12;
ten[9] = 12;
int[] sto = new int[100];
for (int i = 0; i < 100; i ++)
{ //This loop establishes the values
if (i < 10) //for numbers up to 100
sto[i] = zero[i];
else{ if ( i < 20)
sto[i] = ten[i % 10];
else{ if (i < 40)
sto[i] = zero[i % 10] + 8;
else{ if (i < 50)
sto[i] = zero[i % 10] + 5;
else{ if (i > 59 && i < 70)
```

```
               sto[i] = zero[i % 10] + 10;
               else{ if (i > 79 && i < 90)
               sto[i] = zero[i % 10] + 11;
               else sto[i] = zero[i % 10] + 9;
               } } } } } }
               int[] thousand = new int[1000];
               for (int i = 0; i < 1000; i ++)
               { //This loop establishes the values
               if (i < 100) //for numbers up to 1000
               thousand[i] = sto[i];
               else{ if (i < 200)
               thousand[i] = sto[i % 100] + 3;
               else{ if (i < 400)
               thousand[i] = sto[i % 100] + 6;
               else{ if ((i > 499 && i < 600) || (i > 699
               && i < 800))
               thousand[i] = sto[i % 100] + 7;
               else{ if (i > 599 && i < 700)
               thousand[i] = sto[i % 100] + 8;
               else thousand[i] = sto[i % 100] + 9;
               } } } } }

               //Query user for limiting value
               System.out.print("What is the limiting
               value?");

               //Reads input value
               Scanner input = new Scanner (System.in);
               int max = input.nextInt();

               //Sets limit at 1000 if user put a larger
               value
               if (max > 1000)
               max = 1000;
```

```java
//creates array with all pertinent logorithm values
int[] log = new int[max];
for (int i = 0; i < max; i++)
log[i] = thousand[i];

//loop examines all possible triples within the
//prescribed perameters capable of defining a
//magic triangle once, then tests the chosen triangle
//for alphamagicity.
for (int i = 3; i < max / 2; i++)
{
for (int j = 1; j < i - 1; j++)
{
for (int k = j + 1; k < i; k++)
{
test(i, j, k, log, max);
test(max - i, j, k, log, max);
}
}
}
}

//Method tests the alphamagicity of the magic square indicated by the
//first three values, based on the array of logorithmic values and
//the limiting value passed to the method.
public static void test(int i, int j, int k, int[] log, int max)
{
```

```
//instantiation of logarithmic values, and definition
//of values in the magic square based on the defining
//values passed to the method
int sum, l, m, n, o, p, q, r, s, t;
int aa = i + j;
int ab = i - j - k;
int ac = i + k;
int ba = i - j + k;
int bb = i;
int bc = i + j - k;
int ca = i - k;
int cb = i + j + k;
int cc = i - j;

//checks to make sure the values of the magic square
//are within prescribed parameters
if (ab < max && ab > 0 &&
ba < max && ba > 0 &&
bc < max && bc > 0 &&
ca < max && ca > 0 &&
cb < max && cb > 0 &&
cc < max && cc > 0 )
{
//definition of logorithmic squares
l = log[aa];
m = log[ab];
n = log[ac];
o = log[ba];
p = log[bb];
q = log[bc];
r = log[ca];
s = log[cb];
```

```
t = log[cc];
sum = l + m + n;

//checks whether the square with logarithmic values is magic
if (l + m + n == sum &&
o + p + q == sum &&
r + s + t == sum &&
l + p + t == sum &&
n + p + r == sum &&
l + o + r == sum &&
m + p + s == sum &&
n + q + t == sum)

//prints out the three defining values of the square that
//has passed all of the tests
System.out.println(i + ", " + j + ", " + k);
}
}
}

/* //English
//alternate creation of the array "thousand" used to establish logarithmic values
int[] zero = new int[10];
zero[0] = 0;
zero[1] = 3;
zero[2] = 3;
zero[3] = 5;
zero[4] = 4;
zero[5] = 4;
zero[6] = 3;
```

```
zero[7] = 5;
zero[8] = 5;
zero[9] = 4;
int[] ten = new int[10];
ten[0] = 3;
ten[1] = 6;
ten[2] = 6;
ten[3] = 8;
ten[4] = 8;
ten[5] = 7;
ten[6] = 7;
ten[7] = 9;
ten[8] = 8;
ten[9] = 8;

int[] hundred = new int[100];
for (int i=0; i < 100; i++)
{
if (i < 10)
hundred[i] = zero[i];
else{if (i < 20)
hundred[i] = ten[i % 10];
else{if (i < 40 || i > 79)
hundred[i] = 6 + zero[i % 10];
else{if (i < 70)
hundred[i] = 5 + zero[i % 10];
else{if (i < 80)
hundred[i] = 7 + zero[i % 10];
} } } } }

int[] thousand = new int[1000];
for (int i=0; i < 1000; i++)
{
if (i < 100)
thousand[i] = hundred[i % 100];
```

```
else{if (i < 300 || (i > 599 && i < 700))
thousand[i] = hundred[i % 100] + 10;
else{if (i < 400 || (i > 699 && i < 900))
thousand[i] = hundred[i % 100] + 12;
else
thousand[i] = hundred[i % 100] + 11;
}
}
}
*/
```

Lee B. Croft
Arizona State University
Tempe, AZ 85287-0202

Lee.Croft@ASU.EDU

This is how the *"Lee Sam"* 3 X 3 Russian Alphamagic Square (74, 50, 92/90, 72, 54/ 52, 94, 70) would look *if written in the runes of the Elder Futhark* (ca. 4-7th century). It is Prof. Croft's contention that pre-Christian and preliterate Slavs used runic inscriptions of their numbers as "magic." The tradition of magic for "alphamagic squares" is that carrying this set of runes will grant a person 36 years of additional rewarding (protected) life.

PROLOGUE
"What have we learned?"

Working on these articles—engaging in research, both Gutenberg textual and online digital, to find them in the scholarly places where they were published, copying them, giving most of them a new digital reality by bialphabetic (Roman-Cyrillic) word-processing into a uniform mandated WORD template, inserting charts, diagrams, tables, grids, illustrations and several "filler" photographs, and editing through the successive drafts was a lot of WORK. We definitely learned that producing published scholarship is WORK, or as Albert Einstein is reputed to have remarked, more "perspiration" than "inspiration." Since we may be in future need of knowledge about how to publish our own individual creations, we found this work very instructive and valuable. Also we had to produce the contextual "presentations" of each article, requiring personal interviews or various other personal communications with Prof. Croft and with certain others of his professional colleagues. This also was instructive, giving us increased understanding of these professionals' careers in higher education.

We were privy to the process of requesting permission to republish the works given here. Some of the journals or publishing agencies granted this permission without charge, but others charged a "reprint fee." One journal gave Prof. Croft a discount for this (halfing the usual fee from $300 to $150) based on the fact that he is the author of the article he asked for permission to reprint. This process was new to us, and it seemed strange, but it caused us to consider seriously issues of intellectual property and regard for the work of those "who have gone before." We also learned something about the value of a copyright to the financial success of a scholarly journal.

Prof. Croft has told us on occasion that "great careers always start in the simplest ways—the publication of a poem in a student almanac, a news analysis in a student newspaper, a letter to an editor of a popular magazine, writing online reviews of books or films—all are first steps to literary and/or scholarly prominence and renown." We noticed that two of these articles were once term papers that Prof. Croft wrote when he was as a student himself. And we learned that getting these articles published was not easy. One of his articles, the one presented here by Megan Plachecki on the decipherment of a puzzling Igor Chinnov poem, was rejected THREE times before gaining the acceptance of a major refereed scholarly journal (<u>Slavic and East European Journal</u>). Each of these rejections only caused Prof. Croft to re-write the work and send it to another place. But such persistence paid off. He tells us that he has never had a moment in his thirty-five years at ASU that he did not have at least one written work under the consideration of some editor to be published. No wonder he was destined "Not to Perish" here.

We increased, in the process of this project, our mastery of the Russian language, and that is important to us. Only one article, the biography of Irving Langmuir presented by Patrick J. Heuer, had to be translated entirely from Russian into English. And another, on the "Neurolinguistics of Rote Memorization" presented by Jeremy Ecton, needed to be separated from a Russian facing-column version of formidable grammatical difficulty and sophisticated terminology…with even a Russian diagram of specific loci in the human brain. But there are Russian terms, words, and phrases, ordinary and "winged" (**Крылатые слова и фразы**) used in all the others. One article, the one on "modality" presented by Kyle M. Kucharski, included philosophically "deep" discussion of Russian semantics and syntax, so that the difficult concept of modality in grammar is now clearer to us.

And we learned what glossolalia is, who Igor Chinnov was, what an interlingual homograph is, what grammatical modality is, how Charlie Chaplin's films influenced Soviet literature, how the mind recalls linguistic information, how translation of poetry has to preserve the form, why we should memorize things, who Mikhail Armalinsky is and who he isn't, who Irving Langmuir was, why there are so many THREES in Russian language, literature, and culture, and what is an alphamagic square and how might a computer be used to find one. Who knows when we might need to know some or all of this in the future…but, it's like Prof. Croft always says: "Don't ask 'Why do I have to know this?'." We want to KNOW EVERYTHING.

КОНЕЦ

Shamella Tribble at the Kremlin Gate, Moscow

www.ingramcontent.com/pod-product-compliance
Lightning Source LLC
Chambersburg PA
CBHW082110230426
43671CB00015B/2662